Praise for *World Out of Balance*

World Out of Balance is a wake-up call to today's chief executives, who must work hard to seize the opportunities—and manage the risks—that an increasingly complex global environment offers.

John Quelch, Senior Associate Dean for International Development and Lincoln Filene Professor of Business Administration, Harvard Business School

Stock movements, talent wars, competitors, regulatory requirements and brand battles distract us from engaging the more fundamental forces that shape our world. *World Out of Balance* provides a framework for holding conflicting perspectives together and beginning to engage the world again.

Sandra Dawson, Director, Judge Institute of Management, KPMG Professor of Management Studies, and Master, Sidney Sussex College, Cambridge University

Paul Laudicina persuasively argues that in the current era of uncertainty, corporations should have a bold vision, and that now, more than ever, strategic planning is of the essence. His book is must reading for CEOs, political leaders, and others interested in our future!

Sebastian Edwards, Henry Ford II Chair in International Management, and Professor, Business Economics, Anderson School of Management, University of California, Los Angeles

Globalization was an intellectual bubble that burst on 9-11... strategic planning was a wasteful fad of the 1980s... CEOs should leave public policy debates to politicians and academics. Paul Laudicina dispels these and other myths, drawing from his deep experience in both corporate strategy and public policy.

Moises Naim, Editor, Foreign Policy Magazine

Real leaders live by the maxim "Value builders take charge of their own destinies." But they must know the forces that shape a world out of balance. This book's discussion of the drivers of global business in the twenty-first century is indispensable preparation for the topsy-turvy world ahead.

Josef Joffe, Die Zeit

Once again the turn of the century marks incredible change. Governments and enterprises alike are wrestling with the challenges of adapting their policies and strategies to emerging realities. This book will help to guide us through the uncertainties. Building on his extensive experience and constant learning in global developments, Paul Laudicina presents an approach to strategic planning that will appeal to many.

Jan Oosterveld, Philips Electronics

Humans by their nature prefer balance, but it is imbalance that triggers the search for better methods and new ventures. Paul Laudicina takes a fresh look at turbulence in a complex world, encouraging us to think beyond its random nature to the business opportunities it can present.

Carlos Represas, Chairman, Nestlé Mexico, and former Executive Vice President, Nestlé S.A., Switzerland

Business can make the world a better place if it tackles challenges like inclusion and sustainability. But it's a long and perilous road to this sort of stability. This book will help smooth the journey.

Kevin Roberts, Saatchi & Saatchi Worldwide

Capitalism is tough, as Paul Laudicina reminds us in this sobering and challenging description of the world as it is. He concludes that today's perils and uncertainties are not just a temporary turbulence, and that hunkering down and cutting costs are poor short-term substitutes for brains, courage, and preparedness.

Brian Jenkins, Senior Advisor to the President, RAND Corporation

WORLD OUT OF BALANCE

Navigating Global Risks to Seize Competitive Advantage

PAUL A. LAUDICINA

McGraw-Hill

New York   Chicago   San Francisco
Lisbon   London   Madrid   Mexico City
Milan   New Delhi   San Juan   Seoul
Singapore   Sydney   Toronto

The **McGraw·Hill** Companies

1 2 3 4 5 6 7 8 9 0   DOC/DOC   0 9 8 7 6 5 4

ISBN 0-07-143918-8

McGraw-Hill books are available at special discounts to use as premiums and sales promotions, or for use in corporate training programs. For more information, please write to the Director of Special Sales, McGraw-Hill Professional, Two Penn Plaza, New York, NY 10121-2298. Or contact your local bookstore.

This book is printed on recycled, acid-free paper containing a minimum of 50% recycled, de-inked fiber.

Dedicated to Ivo John Lederer, a dear friend and colleague, whose inspiration in helping found the Global Business Policy Council continues to guide its direction.

Contents

Foreword

If you're reacting to change, you're too late. You must anticipate change. You must understand change as an opportunity and make it happen. Clearly, the future is full of variables, and the realm of possibility is impossibly wide, but leaders in business, government, and other spheres cannot wait patiently to see how world events will play out.

I wish it were otherwise, but the business environment does not offer the prospect of a leisurely stroll under a sunny economic sky. Economic and political developments are becoming increasingly difficult to predict. Incalculable events, from the SARS crisis to the war in Iraq to terrorist attacks and the volatility of crude oil markets, can have a massive impact on today's closely networked global economy. As a consequence of these factors, organizations need to increase their resilience, reaction speed, and flexibility.

So much change, turbulence, and information flow can lead even highly competent executives to the point of reflex action, or even paralysis. Successful companies encourage people to reach for the future and shape it actively and responsibly. Successful companies are bold companies that invest in the markets of the future. And above all, successful companies do not dwell on *anxieties*—rather they seize *opportunities*.

At BASF, we're strongly attuned to the urgency of preparing for tomorrow's realities. We have asked ourselves: How can we—how *must* we—position ourselves so that we will still be the world's leading chemical company in 2015?

My colleagues and I looked hard at where we wanted to be in the future and made a detailed review of our strategy to date. This meant undertaking an intensive effort of precisely the kind that Paul Laudicina describes and urges in *World Out of Balance*. We modeled, tested, and digested the key drivers of the future business environment and their implications at both macro and micro levels. We knew we needed to understand better how our markets, our customers, and our own company were likely to be transformed by these powerful drivers of change.

As we looked to the more distant future, we began working to prepare ourselves for the increasingly challenging conditions that lie ahead. Our markets are changing because the biggest growth in the numbers of new consumers is in the emerging economies, in particular in China. There, improvements in the standard of living mean that the number of consumers is expected to rise nearly tenfold by 2015. By understanding the implications of this trend, we can position ourselves to make the most of it.

Fortunately, we retained our strategic planning capabilities over the decade, through both prosperous and lean times. There is no doubt we have benefited from better foresight as a result. And although we remain faithful to our core strategies, we will continue to build on them and adapt or extend them, as circumstances require. Commitment to sustainable development in a volatile world is a must.

Whether you are in a corporate, government, or nonprofit environment, this book will help guide your endeavors. As you work to shape your future, you will need to explore how major trends could combine and converge to change our world. Globalization, demographics, emerging consumer preferences, scarce resources, the rise of activism, and a reinvigorated regulatory environment will play key roles in determining tomorrow's challenges and opportunities. *World Out of Balance* explores each of these important drivers that shape the global economic environment, as well as their implications.

An organization that pursues the right strategy and acts decisively can succeed—even in a difficult business environment. The prerequisite is being prepared for a wide range of possible outcomes, from the disastrous to the wildly positive.

I am pleased to commend this book to those who are anxious to seize the opportunities and manage the risks on the horizon. *World Out of Balance* delivers an important message: Now is the time to act. Take stock today, and you will be able to face tomorrow successfully with focus, confidence, determination, and, perhaps, serenity.

Dr. Jürgen Hambrecht
Chairman, Board of Executive Directors, BASF Aktiengesellschaft

Acknowledgments

Readers will note the use of the personal pronoun "we" as the voice of this book. The reason is simple enough. This volume results from the collective efforts of a number of very talented professionals whom I have had the great privilege to work with over the course of the last 15 years since the founding of the Global Business Policy Council of A.T. Kearney. Our mission is to help the CEO members of the Council better understand and seize new world opportunities while monitoring and managing the risks. In so doing, the Council has provided an extraordinary vantage point from which to derive insights that are central to successful corporate practice and performance in the twenty-first century, many of them contained in this book.

This analysis has also benefited from the 100 or so extraordinary thought leaders from every corner of the earth across a broad swath of disciplines who comprise the "faculty" of the Global Business Policy Council. Academics, journalists, policy figures, scientists, and corporate practitioners have all contributed generously to the regular roundtable, off-the-record Council deliberations with some of the world's most accomplished and globally aware chief executive officers, who represent virtually all business sectors in some two dozen countries and bring a rich diversity of perspectives to our gatherings.

While the individuals who have helped enrich this book with their insights are too numerous to cite, clearly the direct and dedicated support of a handful of my colleagues deserves special mention. My Council co-conspirator over the years, Stephen Klimczuk, not only has contributed his intellect and analytical rigor, but he also has been a constant provocateur, encouraging me to get this book done. Nor would this book have been possible without the considerable substantive and editorial direction which Jay Scheerer has brought to the successful completion of this project. This book also reflects the very distinctive and talented editorial workmanship of Mark Strauss, who took leave from his position as managing editor of *Foreign Policy* magazine to shape the development of this manuscript. Wynne Rumpeltin, Janet Pau, David Attis, and Aaron Harms also made important contributions to the book, as did my long-suffering and very able executive assistant, Patty Fabian. I also must note the important support from A.T. Kearney's Marketing and Communications team, particularly Nancy Bishop and Beth Crawford. Nancy helped expertly and successfully guide me through the publishing process from day one. And this book's narrative has benefited from Nancy and Beth's editorial finesse. To all these people and my A.T. Kearney colleagues past and present, I say "thank you." I also want to extend warm thanks to Mary Glenn, our editorial director at McGraw-Hill, for her energy and careful management of *World Out of Balance*. She was an enthusiastic champion from our very first discussion.

Finally, those who know the peripatetic life of today's global management consultant know that behind every successful career is a spouse and family often left to fend for themselves for long periods of time while the consultant is working across the miles, usually in very intellectually rewarding endeavors. To my wife and best friend Louise, and to my four wonderful children—Chris, Lee, Carla, and Nicole—I say "thank you" for putting up with me (and my absence) over the years and, in so doing, allowing me the time and providing the support critical to the work of this book. My immodest hope is that today's "world out of balance" which my children and theirs inherit might benefit in some small way from the insights contained herein. Our aspiration for them is that they may live in a more balanced world.

Preface

As British troops surrendered their arms to George Washington in 1781, they reportedly marched to a popular tune of the day, "The World Turned Upside Down." For these red-coated professional soldiers the world had, indeed, been turned on its head. The mighty army of Cornwallis had been defeated by a group of ragtag colonials.

And so it is throughout history; dramatic events have often prompted a fundamental rethinking of the world and one's place in it. But this book will argue that today's earth-shattering events are fundamentally different from those of previous eras of history, as technologies are collapsing distance and spawning unprecedented global interdependence.

The oil shock, stagflation, fall of the Shah of Iran, and escalating Cold War tensions in the 1970s all helped shape the defensive strategic mindset of the corporate executive of that era, much as the explosion of information and communication technologies, the rise of the Internet, and the demise of the Soviet bloc shaped the exuberant strategic worldview of the executive at the turn of the millennium. These developments brought radical changes in their wake and had a profound effect on corporate decisions of the time—and more importantly, on *how* those decisions were made.

Multinational corporate strategic planning in the 1970s was very much a headquarters-directed exercise that relied on varying degrees of disciplined decision analysis methodologies and data on business environment variables and performance targets. But over time, business variables began to shift more rapidly than such tightly choreographed planning systems could handle, and demand for lean cost structures grew. As a result, this kind of centrally directed planning fell out of vogue. In fact, it was often abruptly suspended.

With the dawn of the heady 1990s, the pace of globalization accelerated along with the enhanced global economic performance it facilitated. Both the time horizons and the locus of corporate decision-making shifted radically. Just-in-time manufacturing, global sourcing, supplier consolidation, and outsourcing and offshoring all relied upon open and porous borders central to the rapid movement of people, goods, capital, services, and ideas. Networks empowered individuals within corporations much in the same way they were empowered throughout societies. Strategy was often reduced to the "let's make a deal" mentality of the day. The rapid increase in volumes of foreign direct investment, the crush of major merger and acquisition deals, and the management innovations that piggybacked on integrated markets all demanded quick, local decision-making. Senior executives and boards of directors subjected these developments to little scrutiny, lest deals be lost to the competition. Corporate behavior became increasingly risk tolerant as larger returns were sought and delivered. The corporation was perhaps as guilty of Alan Greenspan's charge of "irrational exuberance" as were U.S. consumers and the bulls of Wall Street.

Then the world was transformed again. The start of the twenty-first century has been marked by a heightened sense of the risks that interdependence poses to business continuity. These include macroeconomic contagion in the form of transnational financial crises and microbial contagion in the form of AIDS, SARS, and other rapidly moving diseases, not to mention sophisticated terrorist networks that have grown more powerful as the world grows more integrated. This new perception of vulnerability, compounded by a litany of corporate scandals, pushed the strategy/oversight pendulum to the opposite end of the continuum from where it had been just a few years earlier. Corporate strategists who had audaciously confronted the marketplace now seemed overcome with timidity, isolation, and inaction.

Only now do we see executives emerging from their foxholes, still listening for the shouts of "Incoming!" from every direction. They are looking for guidance, approval, and a degree of certainty not likely to come from a casual, undisciplined, or one-dimensional assessment of today's global dynamics. If they don't engage the world and recover from the shellshock of the early twenty-first century, their inaction will put the modern corporation more at risk than any exogenous factor will.

This book, then, is a call to restart and reinvigorate the strategic planning process. A disciplined strategy will, as it should, embolden corporate management to engage the world and seize the many opportunities it presents. It will also help business executives manage the risks that inevitably accompany such engagement. Since a planning protocol must be specific to the character, culture, and needs of a given sector and individual company, this book is not about *how* to plan for the new world realities. It's about *why* it's crucial to develop a structured, dynamic way to accurately read the signs of change in a complex and often perplexing world.

A Call to Action

If what you have done yesterday still looks big to you, you have not done much today.

—Mikhail Gorbachev

LOOK AT THE WORLD "as it is," not as you might "wish it to be." Jack Welch's admonition is sound advice in these times of chronic global volatility. Whether the CEO of a Fortune 100 company or the head of a small business, a private investor or a pension fund manager, a lobbyist or a politician, today's leaders will be sorely disappointed if they expect clarity and stability to emerge anytime soon.

The post–Cold War world is not the "New World Order" that President George H. W. Bush thought he had helped usher into existence at the fall of the Berlin Wall on November 9, 1989. Rather, the world has made a perverse trade: the post–World War II stability of a superpower nuclear standoff for a much more elusive search for global security. "I've often said that it's as if we were fighting with a dragon for some 45 years and slew the dragon and then found ourselves in a jungle full of a number of poisonous snakes," observes former CIA director James Woolsey. "And in many ways, the snakes are a lot harder to keep track of than the dragon ever was."[1] Those "snakes" include threats as diverse as terrorism, computer hackers, rogue states armed with weapons of mass destruction, and failed states that are zones of anarchy and civil strife. Each has an impact on politics and societies, as well as the global business environment.

Today's yearning for global stability and a new equilibrium follows years of dramatic progress in global economic integration, wealth generation, and expanded life expectancy. These incredible advances have been spawned by the policy liberalizations of the last 50 years and turbocharged by breakthrough technologies that have accelerated the movement of people, goods, services, capital, and ideas. But these same forces of globalization and integration are also subject to Newton's Third Law of Motion, which promises an equal and opposite reaction for every force in nature. A "kinder, gentler" globalization has given way to the flip side of the coin. Interdependent risks and insecurities have emerged, along with heightened possibilities that porous borders will bring new vulnerabilities and pushback from at-risk populations.

It's easy to hide behind the notion that volatility is so fundamental and so difficult to manage that the best we can do is bury our heads in the sand and hope for the best. This trend toward inaction and excuse is particularly pronounced in the private sector. In their 2002-2003 annual reports, 43 percent of Fortune 100 companies blamed external events—terrorism, war in Iraq, foreign exchange crises, and the Latin American financial crisis—for their failure to meet earnings expectations (*see Figure I.1*). An outside observer might say that's perfectly understandable, given the highly unusual confluence of unexpected events in recent years. But this "don't blame us" mindset began well before the September 11th terrorist attacks in the United States. An A.T. Kearney study of corporate growth conducted between 1998 and 2000 found that underperforming companies routinely claimed to be victims of forces beyond their control. They attributed their problems to macroeconomic imbalances, the Asian financial crisis, and the unexpected tactics of their competitors. Insurance firms and utility companies even blamed Mother Nature, attributing declines in short-term performance to unexpected shifts in the weather.[2]

The Masters of Destiny

However, a very different picture emerged when we examined the attitudes among what might be defined as *value-building firms*. These companies aggressively pursue long-term revenue growth even as they balance the need for short-term profitability. Value builders take charge of their own destinies. They understand that, although the external landscape is important, it has a marginal long-term impact on how robustly

Figure I.1   The Blame Game

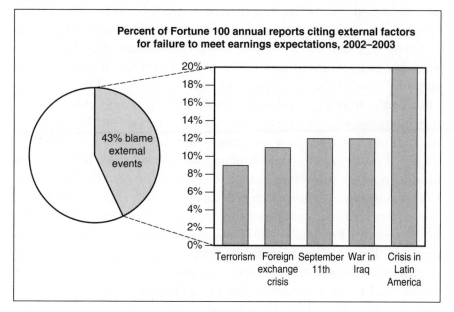

Sources: *A.T. Kearney analysis and company annual reports*

they grow. Value-building companies believe that only 13 percent of their total performance is determined by external factors beyond their control. They acknowledge that the remaining factors, for better or worse, are their own responsibility. By contrast, companies that are not value builders attribute 44 percent of their performance to external factors. As A.T. Kearney colleagues noted in their recent books, *The Value Growers* (McGraw-Hill, 2000) and *Stretch: How Great Companies Grow in Good Times and Bad* (Wiley, 2004), a non-value-building company might bemoan unanticipated events by saying, "Our market is changing," but a value builder confidently declares, "We're changing our market."[3] Unlike their counterparts, value-building firms depend heavily on geographic expansion for growth, rather than sticking to familiar markets.[4]

These diverging mindsets are reflected in how companies respond when the topography suddenly shifts beneath their feet. A non-value-building company stresses efficiency, which it achieves through extensive cost cutting and repeated restructuring. It scales back resource commitments and squeezes all it can from what remains. Eventually, it may find itself with a highly productive, lean organization that operates on a shoestring. Equity analysts and investors may respond well to these cost reduction efforts, leading to a short-term boost in share prices. However, over the long term, this value proves to be ephemeral. The company that has scaled back so much risks finding that there is no place left to go. Current earning streams account for, at most, 20 percent of a firm's value (as defined by equity markets).[5] The rest of its value comes from expected profit growth, which is most closely linked to revenue growth. Share prices rise with the expectation of future profits, regardless of whether a company is showing profits here and now. Expected profit growth could emerge from cutting costs, but there is a limit to how far those cuts can go. Consider, for example, the Coca-Cola Company, which announced in early 2000 that it planned to expand its profits with a restructuring that would cut its staff worldwide by 20 percent. Predictably, these necessary actions won the praise of investors. But imagine the outcome if the company were to repeatedly implement such a strategy. With every passing year, a shrinking staff would need to work harder to run the global corporation, with ever-declining resources. The stress would eventually take its toll, and the company would lose the ability to compete and grow.

In other words, a non-value-building company seeks to become lean, but risks ending up anorexic. By contrast, a value builder puts on muscle even as it trims the fat. The objective is to become both strong and lean. This approach is far more conducive to revenue growth. If good ideas can be transformed into sales, profits will follow. Value builders don't adhere to boundaries; they break them. They focus on various modes of growth by offering innovative products or product extensions, with the inherently risky investment they warrant. They build upon their existing business rather than building up an entirely new business. They avoid cutting back on research and development during difficult times, and they have capitalized upon the opportunities globalization has offered during the past decade. International sales accounted for one-third of their overall growth, and their average annual international sales were more than four times higher than firms with below-average revenue growth. Put simply, they are the

> *A value builder puts on muscle even as it trims the fat.*

better global companies. Value builders also realize that there is a big difference between a company that actively takes risks and a company that—whether it knows it or not—is passively at risk.

Taking on a World of Risk

Any company that seeks to expand its operations and markets abroad takes on a host of new risks. Political and social upheaval. Natural disasters. Terrorist attacks. Labor unrest. Rising demands of accountability from activists. Intensified government oversight. But are companies prepared to anticipate and deal with the risks that come from true global operations? In a 2002 survey of corporate strategists, two-thirds of them admitted they were surprised by three or more high-impact events during the previous five years.[6] In addition, 97 percent of the corporate executives who were interviewed indicated that they had no significant early warning system in place to help them discern new threats or opportunities.[7] What's more, there is an astonishing divide between how companies perceive risks and how they address them. The 2003 A.T. Kearney Foreign Direct Investment Confidence Index® revealed that external factors—notably, government regulation, country financial risk, currency risk, and political and social disturbances—have a considerable impact on the cross-border investment decisions of global corporations. Yet these very same corporations focus most of their resources on developing and strengthening internal controls rather than external risk management (*see Figures I.2 and I.3*).

In effect, companies are peering at the world through a microscope, focusing on their own businesses. Once in a while, they need to pick up a telescope, look around, and develop a better sense of the strategic context within which they operate. Too often, corporations focus on raw data about market size and growth when venturing into new markets, while ignoring the bottom-line impact of external risks. Or they rely on broad country risk measures or conventional wisdom that does not reflect risks specific to their industries or their particular regions of operation. At other times, they downplay the possibility of damaging international scenarios and work under overly optimistic assumptions. Worse yet, some companies simply stay close to home, believing that only the biggest corporations can manage the risks of going global.

Figure I.2 Greatest Risks Affecting FDI Decisions, as Reported by Global Companies

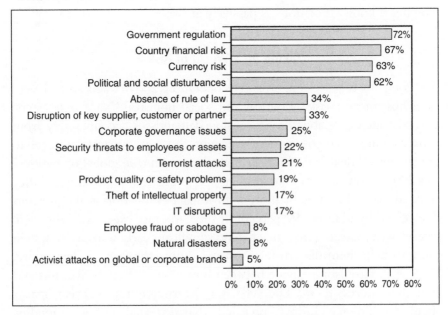

Source: A.T. Kearney Foreign Direct Investment Confidence Index®, 2003

But the inexorable demographic tide and the incredible tug of technology will continue to compel all value-building companies—large and small, multinational and domestically focused—to look beyond their borders. The question is not "whether" a successful company will need to operate transnationally; it is "how" a company must behave transnationally in order to grasp opportunity and succeed.

The complexity of the twenty-first century is no reason for companies to shy away from deeper engagement with the outside world. In fact, rapid external changes often punish indecision or inaction severely, knocking successful companies from their pedestals and handing victory to rivals. Of the 100 biggest U.S. companies at the beginning of the twentieth century, only 16 are still around today. One-third of the companies in the Fortune 500 in 1970 had ceased to exist by the early 1980s, and during the 1980s a total of 230 companies, 46 percent, vanished from the same Fortune 500 list. Neither size nor reputation proved enough to guarantee their success or survival.

Figure I.3 Global Corporations Focus Most on Internal Risk Management

	Action taken	Action planned	No action
Develop or strengthen internal risk management	82%	13%	6%
Invest in back-up IT or physical infrastructures	63%	11%	25%
Implement scenario and contingency planning	63%	15%	23%
Implement new corporate ethics policies	63%	12%	25%
Coordinate risk across supply chain	55%	16%	28%
Revise board and executive committee	53%	15%	32%
Increase coordination with stakeholders	46%	13%	41%
Increase coordination with public and private entities on governance issues	42%	16%	42%
Develop new corporate social responsibility strategies	38%	23%	39%
Develop new branding strategies in response to anti-corporate public sentiment	25%	17%	58%

Source: A.T. Kearney Foreign Direct Investment Confidence Index®, 2003

Plotting a New Course

Not so long ago, most leading companies had possessed strong in-house capabilities for monitoring changes in the external environment. Companies like Royal Dutch/Shell pioneered increasingly sophisticated risk management and strategic planning functions to balance the considerable opportunities they saw overseas with the enhanced vulnerability to social and political unrest, economic upheaval, and natural disasters to which global expansion exposed them. Rounds of cost cutting and corporate restructuring took their toll on strategic planning departments in the 1980s, and a decade of "benign globalization" in the 1990s shaped an exuberant world view among a new generation of business leaders. Many believed that careful planning against external exigencies was largely unnecessary for success in global markets—and might even impede their ability to seize opportunities as rapidly as they became available. As a result, the vast majority of companies today lack the means to identify and manage external risks and find themselves without bearings in this increasingly complex world. Instead of risking a devastating shipwreck, many captains of industry keep their corporate ships stubbornly docked at shore.

Yet business leaders need not be paralyzed. Executives and companies can—and should—undertake expansion strategies even when external uncertainties and shocks can have as much impact as traditional industry dynamics. With the most promising opportunities located outside home markets and far from familiar territory, hiding from risks is simply not an option. Instead, companies must use that telescope, scan distant horizons, and try to make sense of the complicated world. They must bring insights about the external environment into the planning process in order to spot and act on new opportunities and avoid emerging threats.

This book is a call to action to the corporate community to do just that—to understand the external world in order to engage it. It provides the rationale for why companies should develop their own structured, dynamic processes for reading the signs of change in a complex and often perplexing world, with at least one eye firmly directed toward the future. The objective is not to predict tomorrow before it arrives, but to sort false signals from meaningful developments. That way, leaders can anticipate and prepare for changes with the greatest potential impact on business operations down the road. Since specific planning protocols must be built around the character, culture, and needs of each individual company, there is no "how to" rulebook for playing the global game. But this book does provide a practical framework for making sense of changes in the external environment and offers straightforward scenarios of how the future global business environment might evolve.

The key to this approach is plotting the five drivers that are most likely to shape the global business environment. These drivers—including the globalization of markets, demographic developments, changes in consumer attitudes and tastes, natural resource trends, and growing regulation and activism—are interdependent but not always mutually reinforcing, as succeeding chapters will show.

The Gas Pedal: Technology

Global integration today mirrors but far surpasses the activity of the nineteenth century, when a growing number of companies leapt at the opportunity to operate beyond their national borders, thanks to industrial age innovations such as steamships, locomotives, and the telegraph. But what makes this era of globalization truly unique is how inexpensive and powerful technology has become. As then-president Bill Clinton once observed, "The blocks, the barriers, the borders that defined the world for our parents and grandparents are giving way, with the help of a new generation of extraordinary technology. Every day millions of people use laptops, modems, CD-ROMs and satellites to send ideas, products and money all across the planet in seconds."[8] The digitization of data and the advent of low-cost communication have allowed individuals and companies to leap across boundaries with unprecedented speed at unfathomably low cost.

The same technology that destroys geographic boundaries and enables just-in-time delivery networks also empowers activists. The anti-globalization movement, for example, relies on e-mail and websites to spread information and mobilize activists to participate in international protests, such as the 1999 "Battle of Seattle" that shut down the annual meeting of the World Trade Organization (WTO).

Technology is also helping fuel the dramatic demographic shifts that will reshape societies and alter consumer preferences. Advances in medical technology—from vaccines to sophisticated diagnostic equipment such as CAT scans—have boosted the average life expectancies to new highs and

> *What makes this era of globalization truly unique is how inexpensive and powerful technology has become.*

(especially in advanced economies) contributed to a widespread aging crisis. Meanwhile the Internet has opened the doorway of nearly unlimited choice to shoppers, increasing the demand for customized products and making it harder for global brands to maintain differential pricing schemes.

It is technology that has enabled humanity to keep one step ahead of Malthusian predictions that the supply of natural resources would not keep pace with population growth. For instance, while conventional drilling techniques can leave up to 70 percent of oil in the ground, better drilling techniques and four-dimensional seismic imaging is helping lower this "leave rate" to below 30 percent, significantly expanding the global oil supply.[9] In addition, genetically modified plants are enabling farmers to grow more disease-resistant, productive crops that make do with less land, less water, and less pesticides.

At the same time, technology is creating new challenges in the regulatory sector. The United States, Asia, and the European Union have widely divergent views on the safety and ethics of genetically engineered crops and human cloning. Countries cannot come to terms over universal standards for encryption technology, as governments seek to strike a delicate balance between an individual's right to privacy and the need to enable law enforcement agencies to crack coded messages over the telephone and Internet. New technologies create new opportunities, but if governments continue to fail to implement universal standards, corporations might find themselves confronted with an increasingly complex patchwork quilt of regional and national regulations. This complexity will curtail organizations' ability to expand their markets and their operations abroad and limit the opportunities these technologies offer to presently underserved populations.

The First Driver: Globalization

By any measure, the world today is more integrated and wealthier than at any other time in human history. Advances in macroeconomic performance—fueled by policy liberalizations and technology—account for the ever more rapid movement of people, goods, services, money, and ideas. Trade flows have grown 300 percent larger over the last 20 years alone. In 1970, $10 billion was traded on foreign exchange markets in a day; in 2002, the same amount was traded in one second. The average global per capita gross domestic product (GDP), largely static for centuries, nearly tripled between 1950 and 2000, and is likely to grow another 60 percent to more than $10,000 per person by 2025, in constant 1990 dollars.

Yet one-third of the world has not participated in this process of wealth-creating integration. The word's 225 richest individuals control as much wealth as the 2.5 billion poorest—nearly half the total global population. Thanks to pervasive modern communications technology, these tremendous and growing inequities are fully transparent. We should not be surprised by simmering resentments and violence throughout the Middle East, one of the least globalized regions of the world and one of the biggest losers in the globalization process. Since

1980, the Middle East's share of global trade and investment has collapsed, falling 75 percent even as the region's population has almost doubled.[10] At the turn of the century the Arab League's 22 member states had 278 million people—but a combined economic output significantly less than that of Spain, a country with one-seventh the population.

Even more surprising is the challenge to the "integration-globalization" proposition in industrialized nations. The globalization of corporate operations has created new wealth, but it has also triggered a heightened sense of personal insecurity, as individuals grow increasingly aware of their vulnerability to ricocheting global economic developments. Greater mobility of people brings not only opportunity, but also the prospect of migrating microbes. Open economies and borders allow not only people and products to move with greater ease, but also terrorists and security threats to infiltrate once-safe societies. "E-business" gives consumers and producers options beyond the wildest expectations of the previous generation, while also making major systemwide infrastructures vulnerable to interruption or even sabotage.

The paradox of this era of globalization is this: The same forces that ushered in unprecedented opportunity have also given rise to unprecedented vulnerabilities and insecurities. That doesn't mean globalization will now inexorably slip into reverse, any more than it will inevitably move forward without interruption. Rather, it means that how much benefit global integration brings will depend on how the principal proponents and beneficiaries of globalization interact with the governments that safeguard the process and answer to their constituents. The multinational corporate sector also has the capacity to influence, for good or ill, the critical public policy decisions of the next decade or so. Can globalization's beneficiaries effectively build the institutional framework required to protect and enfranchise those made vulnerable by integration? The answer will likely determine globalization's future course.

The Second Driver: Demographics

A great demographic tide is ebbing and flowing within and between continents. Instead of a population boom, industrialized countries are experiencing a "baby bust" owing to declining fertility rates. Europe is depopulating more quickly than at any time since the Black Death.[11] Industrialized nations, which account for three-quarters of global economic output, are also confronting older, atrophying populations. In a matter of years, several nations will house a greater proportion of elderly than the U.S. state of Florida, where pensioners and retirees account for one in five residents. The costs of caring for these retirees, coupled with the dramatic decline in the working-age population, pose one of the most critical challenges for governments and the private sector alike in the coming century. Absent serious reforms, developed countries will have to spend up to 16 percent more of GDP simply to meet their old-age benefit promises.[12] The "pay-as-you-go" social security system that served advanced economies so well in the previous century will soon be unsustainable, since there will not be enough young people earning enough money to support their elders.

At the same time, much of the developing world is confronting a "youth bulge" as the 15- to 29-year-old crowd accounts for a rising percentage of the population. New international tensions are brewing over immigration, as migrants from the poor south seek entry to the rich north, which in turn seeks to balance its need for labor against its desire to protect cultural and social cohesiveness.

In developing countries, young people will continue to migrate from the countryside to cities in search of higher wages and a better standard of living. Within a decade, for the first time, the majority of the world population will live in cities, and nearly half of the people living in developing countries will be urban dwellers. The number of megacities, with populations greater than 5 million, will jump from 40 to 58, and the majority will be in the developing world.[13] Some of these urban areas—such as Seoul and possibly Kuala Lumpur—will emerge as bustling centers of commerce and culture. They are already heavily investing in new infrastructure and are likely to grow enough to keep their new arrivals productively employed. But other megacities—Dhaka, Karachi, Lagos, Manila, and Jakarta—threaten to emerge as ungovernable zones of crime, poverty, disease, and environmental degradation. Unemployed youth, frustrated at their inability to emigrate abroad or find jobs at home, may become fodder for radical movements and terrorist groups.

> *A deeper understanding of demographics will help corporations maintain their bearings and emerge intact.*

Companies navigating through an aging population on one side and a youth bulge on the other might feel caught between Scylla and Charybdis. But a deeper understanding of demographics will help corporations maintain their bearings and emerge intact. Industrialized world population declines will yield worker shortages, which can only be addressed by importing labor or exporting jobs. Although some countries might be reluctant to open their borders to foreign workers, companies can take advantage of demographic trends to outsource increasingly sophisticated business functions to the swelling ranks of skilled information technology (IT) workers in key emerging markets such as India, Malaysia, and Chile. Also, by monitoring demographic trends in the developing world, companies can acquire a sixth sense for which countries will likely remain stable and which are at risk of dissolving into zones of political and social instability. As governments in advanced economies increasingly burden the private sector with pension and healthcare costs, companies will be able to strategically target their foreign investments by monitoring which countries offer the most favorable labor costs relative to productivity for specific kinds of work.

The Third Driver: The New Consumer

The sweet spot of tomorrow's consumer markets will prove harder than ever to find. If there was ever a golden age of homogenous markets, predictable consumer behavior, and mass marketing, it is long gone. Consumers have grown empowered, fragmented, less predictable, and more demanding. They want products and services that fulfill their own personal needs and simplify their harried daily lives.

The sweeping demographic changes reshaping the world offer a glimpse of how age and lifestyle will shift future spending patterns. Within a decade, middle-class consumers in the advanced economies will graduate into upper consumer groups with increased spending power above and beyond basic middle-class needs and concerns. For the first time in history, nearly two-thirds of middle-class consumers will live in key emerging markets.[14] Management scholar John Quelch suggests that, among these new middle-income entrants, the defining mantra of consumption will be *more stuff*: status-oriented merchandise, electronics, consumer durables, new vehicles, and housing. By contrast, consumers living in advanced markets will seek *more experiences*: high-end luxury goods, custom features and add-ons, individualized leisure activities and entertainment options, travel and tourism, and vacation homes.[15] This divergence between advanced economies and emerging markets will be further accentuated by aging patterns. Already, kids and older spenders are challenging traditional middle-age dominance. From China's pampered children (the so-called Little Emperors) to the graying masses in North America and Europe, these consumers are wielding their clout. Young people will seek out clothing, consumer durables, and first homes. Older consumers will spend their savings on healthcare and pharmaceuticals, expensive home furnishings, and dream vacations.

As the consumer market becomes more and more fragmented, one-size-fits-all global marketing strategies are doomed to failure. Companies may respond with strategies built around psychographics, a social science that allows marketing messages to tap into deeply shared "cultural codes" in an effort to maximize appeal. But they will also have to understand and serve the intrinsic needs of their increasingly diverse constituents. Young people, for instance, will respond to products and services that promise empowerment and individual choice, while overworked upscale consumers in advanced economies will likely continue to desire new luxury products that meet their emotional needs by soothing the body and soul and rewarding them for hard work. Even poor consumers, accounting for some 65 percent of the world's population, will look for consumer durables and services that better their lives in the here and now. Corporations must develop tactics that make the most of their marketing dollars in reaching these fragmented consumers. Fortunately, tools such as viral marketing and Internet-based advertising campaigns are enabling corporations to rekindle the bond with the consumer while making their brands less intrusive and less culturally threatening.

The Fourth Driver: Natural Resources and the Environment

Attention has long been focused on the strains in global energy markets. Although most analysts believe that oil reserves will be sufficient to meet worldwide consumption over the next several decades, proven oil reserves (barring major geopolitical upheaval) are highly concentrated in the Middle East and Central Asia, where ongoing political instability raises concerns about future costs and availability. Industrialized countries and key emerging markets are turning toward alternative resources that lessen their dependency on oil, but these alternatives also carry many hidden costs. Surging economic growth in China and India will drive two-thirds of the global demand for coal by 2030—but burning all this coal may significantly erode air quality and public health in these countries. China, with one-twentieth the per capita oil consumption of the United States, already ranks as the world's second largest importer of oil. The country accounts for 26 percent of the world's coal consumption and has announced plans to build at least 100 additional power plants by 2020, most of them powered by coal.[16] The United States and Europe have begun consuming so much natural gas that domestic reserves are already overstretched and utility prices are rising. Ample supplies of natural gas can be found elsewhere, but energy companies will have to invest billions of dollars to develop the infrastructure to extract and deliver it.

Challenges also loom in another resource that is at least as critical, if not so often discussed. By 2050, as much as half the world population may suffer from insufficient access to water—a condition that will not only undermine human development but could also touch off competition among countries and within communities for access to water resources.[17] Some of the world's toughest "hot spots" involve competition for water, and the number is likely to grow. Moreover, dwindling supplies of freshwater may lead to a crucial shortage of locally produced food in developing countries, since agriculture accounts for 70 percent of global water use. This could increase dependency on foreign aid among the poorest countries and raise prices as countries compete for imported food.

Adding to the list of global challenges are such slow-moving trends as climate change. Even one-time skeptics of global warming now grudgingly acknowledge that the accumulation of greenhouse gases in the atmosphere is steadily increasing the temperature of the planet. The United Nations Environment Programme warns that economic losses due to catastrophic natural disasters are doubling every decade and may cost $150 billion per year by 2010 if current trends continue. Climate change alone could stress banks and insurers to the point of impaired viability or even insolvency.[18] Countries could limit greenhouse emissions by relying more on cleaner, alternative sources of energy such as wind, the sun, and hydrogen. But there is little market incentive to develop these technologies given the comparative abundance of fossil fuels.

As governments and consumers become increasingly concerned about the costs of environmental degradation, forward-thinking global companies such as Coca-Cola and BP are working to minimize water pollution and greenhouse gas emissions. Value-building companies are pouring more resources into the research and development of new technologies that will satisfy the world's insatiable demand for clean, renewable, natural resources.

The Fifth Driver: Regulation and Activism

A regulatory perfect storm is sweeping through the private sector. Nervous electorates in many countries have reacted to security concerns, botched attempts at privatization and deregulation, and a rash of corporate scandals with growing dependence on their governments. The public no longer trusts corporations to watch over themselves, and governments have responded with stringent legislation covering everything from new auditing standards to corporate boardroom practices. These new measures could translate into billions of dollars worth of compliance costs. Governments are also spending more money and intervening more frequently in the marketplace, creating both opportunities and perils for firms.

Even as this regulatory storm gathers force, however, government policymakers are increasingly missing in action. The public sector is experiencing a critical brain drain as more public servants retire and fewer talented university graduates opt for careers in government. The timing couldn't be worse, given the growing demand for government services an aging population will generate and the host of increasingly complex regulatory issues just over the horizon. For instance, biotechnology pits food and nutrition against concerns for minimum safety and standards. Stem cell research and human cloning challenge ethical beliefs but promise

> *The public no longer trusts corporations to watch over themselves.*

huge health advantages. The proliferation of e-commerce and digital technology raises key questions about privacy, intellectual property rights, and tax liabilities. Without a coherent global consensus on the regulation of these new technologies, corporations face an obstacle course of contradictory local and regional legislation that can thwart efforts to expand their operations and markets across international borders.

Moreover, against a backdrop of continuing pressures on the environment—climate change, water scarcity, deforestation, soil degradation, and pollution—companies find they must also confront activists from within and without. Shareholders are increasingly focusing on the activities of companies that operate in developing nations, demanding a commitment to sustainable development and new transparent corporate governance procedures. Nongovernmental organizations seek to blame and shame companies into adopting policies more friendly toward the environment, labor, human rights, and other social issues. Using strategies ranging from Internet information campaigns to protests to boycotts, activists have proven increasingly adept at getting their message out. They sometimes even co-opt brands and use them against their corporate creators.

To maintain a steady course through this regulatory storm, corporations must be prepared to engage in combat with activists and develop savvy media strategies that defend their reputations. They must also be open to the idea of forming strategic alliances with activists and implementing codes of conduct that could reshape their global operations.

Scenarios and Wild Cards

These drivers sketch a picture of an increasingly complex world in which change is endemic. But they also serve as a framework for understanding and making sense of the changes that matter most. We gather insights on all five drivers and assemble them into a bigger picture for a glimpse of how the future business environment may evolve.

Each driver chapter will conclude with three subscenarios—a range of potential outcomes based on possible future directions and impacts of the given driver. These subscenarios, in turn, feed into a broader series of scenarios illustrating a spectrum of conditions for the future global business environment, ranging from the possible to the probable over a given planning horizon (*see Figure I.4*).

Based on our current assessment of the five drivers, we will outline the scenario most likely to prevail in 2015. This scenario, which we call "Open Borders, Lingering Fears," projects a bipolar world dominated by the United States and China, which will have carved out often complementary economic and geopolitical spheres of influence, contributing to a reasonably stable new world order. This scenario assumes that a substantially

Figure I.4 Scenario Road Map

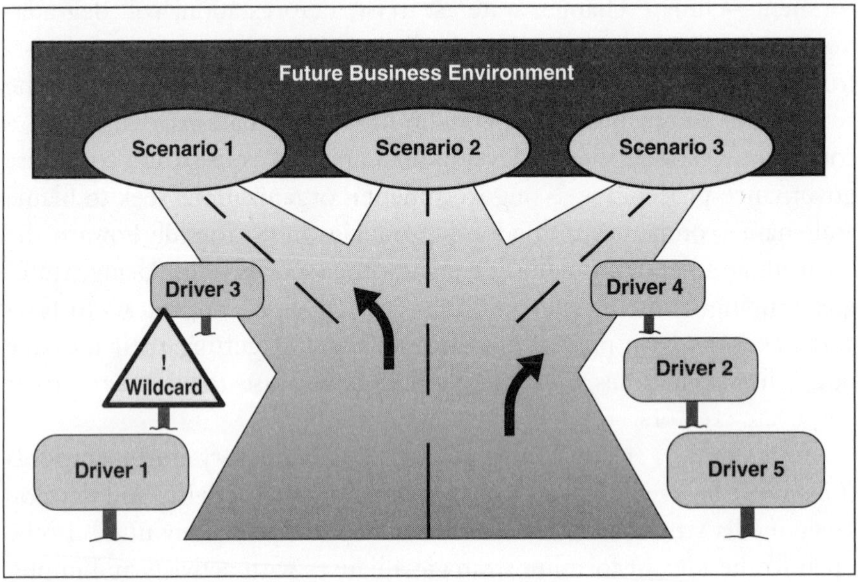

Source: A.T. Kearney

open and integrated global environment prevails for business, although not without some divergence and disruption in certain markets often complicated by an uneasy alliance between government and industry.

It should be stressed here that the likely prevalence of a given scenario is neither intrinsically good nor bad for all companies. Defense-related businesses, for example, are more likely to derive some benefit from periods of geopolitical tension and unrest than are travel and tourism companies. But plotting the global business conditions most likely to prevail in the future makes it easier to reckon with and manage the present.

The point, of course, is not to predict the future, but to be better prepared than rivals for a range of potential developments, and in so doing, also protect against some other more common business risks. For example, mobile telephone maker Ericsson learned the hard way about the consequences of not being prepared after lightning struck a critical supplier's plant in New Mexico, starting a small fire. The Swedish company did not learn about disruptions in its supply chain for weeks, but major competitor Nokia, which also depended on the same supplier, had contingency plans in place within days. By the end of the year, Nokia had improved its market share, while Ericsson posted a $1.7 billion loss and outsourced its handset manufacturing to another firm.[19]

Change is too rapid and endemic to make predictions with any confidence, and predictions risk creating a static "plot it and forget it" mentality that ignores new information and emerging developments. These future visions are by no means assured. Exogenous forces with extremely low probability but very high impact can disrupt even the most carefully constructed scenarios, as they have throughout history. These "wild cards" often have a sharply negative impact on emerging developments, as evident from those most easily imagined—from new global disease epidemics and catastrophic computer virus attacks to major wars and the disintegration of key countries such as China or Indonesia. However, positive shocks are also possible, as we have seen in the past from new inventions. We might experience additional quantum leaps in the coming years that combine, for example, advances in information technologies, the life sciences, and nanotechnology.

Managing Risks in an Interdependent World

Monitoring the external environment and preparing for future developments is only part of the equation of intelligent—and ultimately successful—corporate practice. A rigorous and realistic assessment of the risks these global drivers unleash is equally important. Smart, value-building companies realize that every opportunity requires some risk. Understanding vulnerabilities, surveying global risks, and implementing safeguards and contingency plans are not just about avoiding the costs of disaster. By integrating risk management into strategic planning, companies can transform smart risk-taking into a competitive advantage.

Risk management and operational resilience allow companies to respond quickly to a rapidly changing global business environment. Business leaders will need agility to navigate their companies through the cycles of calm and storm that are inevitable for years to come. The final chapter of this book explains how better risk management can mesh with better monitoring to prepare companies for the journey ahead.

Throughout this whole process of trying to understand and manage the future, our precept is that the journey is more important than the destination. Simply put, enlisting headquarters and field organizations in an all-hands process of being sensitive to the future is likely to reveal both a rich range of new opportunities and a wide spectrum of risks. This process of managing the future will be central to the success of any twenty-first century enterprise operating in a world otherwise "out of balance."

CHAPTER

Globalization

Two Steps Forward, One Step Back

Globalization is a fact of life. But I believe we have underestimated its fragility.

—United Nations General Secretary Kofi Annan

The 1990s marked one of the greatest expansions of global economic integration and wealth creation in human history. Liberalization of trade and investment policies—acting in concert with technological advances that super-charged the movement of goods, services, capital, ideas, and people—helped spawn incredible advances. But where some see opportunity, others see growing inequality and insecurity that feed a growing backlash against globalization. Jobs are moving, strange new diseases are spreading, and security threats are crossing national borders. Global integration is contributing to a heightened perception that jobs, privacy, security, and identity are under siege by outside forces beyond the control of existing governments and institutions. We can't take continued progress toward a more deeply integrated and prosperous world for granted unless we can all find a way to bring larger shares of the world population into the process and distribute the benefits more broadly.

A (Very) Brief History

The notion that the world is growing smaller is not exactly new. In fact, our sense of time and distance has been shrinking for hundreds of years, since innovations in navigation and shipbuilding launched the great age of discovery and brought Europeans into contact with populations around the world. As naval exploration ushered in an era of trade and conquest, European powers built imperial footholds that brought far-flung lands into increasingly tight political and economic orbits. By 1774, the world appeared so closely intertwined that German philosopher Johann Gottfried von Herder asked, quite reasonably, "When has the entire earth ever been so closely joined together, by so few threads? Who has ever had more power and more machines, such that with a single impulse, with a single movement of a finger, entire nations are shaken?"[1]

Industrialization Unleashed

Of course, empires were only the beginning of a more integrated world order. Throughout the nineteenth century, new technologies unleashed the power of industrialization, ratcheting up levels of commercial exchange and communication that mutually reinforced one another. Machinery opened up new frontiers. Textile machines transformed economies in the early part of the century; steamships, railways, and telegraphs dominated the latter years. Marveling at the power of steamships to make "distances disappear," French diplomat François René de Chateaubriand saw as early as 1841 that, "it will not only be commodities which travel, but also ideas which will have wings."[2]

The race began in earnest. Workers, companies, and capital leapt at the opportunity to operate beyond national borders. Up to 60 million people left Europe for new opportunities in the Americas, Australia, and elsewhere, helping fill the cities and plains of the United States. Largely unfettered by customs, tariffs and other restrictions, trade flourished. Exports from such countries as Germany, Great Britain, and the United States reached levels not seen again until the end of the next century. At the same time, accumulated savings in wealthy European countries financed massive investments elsewhere in the world. Foreign capital bankrolled one-third of domestic investment in Canada and New Zealand and one-quarter of domestic investment in Sweden. Great Britain alone invested 40 percent of its savings abroad, a larger share than at any other time in its history. Even in the United States, historians suggest that investors might well have had a larger share of their stock portfolios invested abroad than they do today.[3]

The first modern multinational companies were born in this era. The Singer Manufacturing Company expanded the production of its sewing machine abroad in the 1860s. In 1863, a Singer sewing machine was presented as a gift to the King of Siam, whose acceptance helped establish the brand locally and provided the company with a successful model of celebrity endorsement and mass-marketing that it would replicate across the globe. Before long, the company had a substantial presence in both Europe and Czarist Russia, and ultimately established a global market share of some 80 percent, with annual worldwide sales of 1.35 million machines in 1903.[4]

Singer set an early model for multinational expansion, and companies involved in the production of mass consumer goods or advanced new technologies quickly set up shop across the globe. Banking scion Carl Meyer Rothschild noted that for companies of the time, there was only one economic unit that made sense: the world. British synthetic fiber company Courtaulds, which had made its early fortune weaving black silk for mourning crepe, purchased process rights for the new synthetic fiber rayon. The firm soon had six factories in the United States, one factory each in Canada and France, and joint ventures in Germany and Italy.[5] General Motors began its international expansion in 1911 with the creation of the GM Export Company, and soon had sufficient demand to establish factories in Belgium, Denmark, Australia, and the United Kingdom.[6] Similarly, commodities companies like United Fruit linked Latin American producers to markets in the United States and around the world. By the eve of the first Great War, some 3000 multinational firms were in operation.[7]

For the most part, these early multinationals remained companies with dispersed production and decentralized management. Long-distance shipping was difficult and communication was costly, so local managers enjoyed considerable autonomy in manufacturing and marketing products.

Modern Globalization

By contrast, contemporary globalization is a very different breed. Rapid transport, sophisticated logistics, and instantaneous communication have allowed for increasingly complex, dense forms of interaction. Executives can easily meet face-to-face. They can send sales and production data anywhere and anytime. Companies are able to disaggregate their production around the world, relying on just-in-time deliveries to keep manufacturing facilities running.

By the end of the twentieth century, nearly 63,000 multinational corporations were operating worldwide. Boeing, for example, assembles its 777 aircraft from over 130,000 parts made around the world. The company's suppliers are hand picked for their individual comparative advantage and Boeing integrates them into an agile and responsive global supply chain.

It's a Small World—and Getting Smaller

The forces behind corporate globalization are also at work in the rest of society. The sheer volume and complexity of interactions at every level have made the countries of the world increasingly interdependent, whether it is governments bound by treaties, travelers vacationing abroad, or migrants crossing borders en masse to find jobs. Suddenly, the "few threads" that bound the world together in von Herder's day have become more numerous, more dense, and more tightly woven than ever before.

The speed of new technologies helps drive this process, but dramatically declining costs and accessibility are even more important. When the first telegraph cable was laid across the Atlantic in 1866, messages between New York and London cost $1 (U.S.) per letter, payable only in gold.[8] Even when the telephone offered an alternative, it was a pricey one—well into the 1930s three minutes cost as much as $300 (U.S.) in today's money.[9] That call today costs a few cents, and anyone with a computer and a modem can send and receive e-mail anywhere in the world for next to nothing. At the same time, the number of people with access to information has grown exponentially. We've progressed from 50,000 computers in 1975 to 160 million (and counting) and more than one billion mobile phone users.[10] As the *Economist* magazine notes, "Together, globalization and IT crush time and space."[11]

Globalization is no longer simply an economic phenomenon. It drives cultural trends, influences domestic politics, challenges traditional notions of state sovereignty, and reshapes societies everywhere. The complexity of modern-day globalization explains why it is such a popular topic of discussion, even as it defies easy definition. *The A.T. Kearney/ Foreign Policy Globalization Index,*™ developed by A.T. Kearney in conjunction with *Foreign Policy* magazine, is the first attempt to define and measure globalization so as to gain a more nuanced understanding of its consequences. The Index reverse-engineers globalization into four component parts: economic integration, political engagement, technological connectivity, and personal contact. These components provide the basis for measuring the depth of global integration in 62 countries representing 84 percent of the global population and 96 percent of the world's economic output. The Index also gauges the impact of globalization on key indicators of well being, from levels of political freedom and corruption to social spending and health. Its results can also be used to graphically depict how globalization has grown since 1990 (*see Figure 1.1*).

Economic Integration

Economic globalization is perhaps the easiest to grasp and define. Consider the expansion of global trade in particular. Seasonal fruit grown in Chile and fresh flowers from Colombia are shipped to North

Figure 1.1 Growth in Globalization

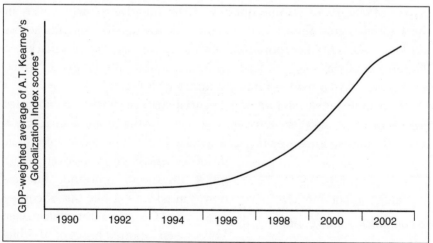

Based on compilation of separate indicators measuring economic integration, personal contact, political engagement, and technological connectivity.

Source: *A.T. Kearney/Foreign Policy Magazine Globalization Index*™

American markets. Japanese and European firms assemble sophisticated electronics in South Korea and Malaysia. According to the World Trade Organization (WTO), global merchandise trade grew by about half during the 1980s, then surged from $3.45 trillion to $6.45 trillion (U.S.) in the 1990s. Trade in services underwent an equally rapid evolution during the same period, doubling during the 1980s and again during the 1990s to reach $1.48 trillion (U.S.) by the turn of the century. At the same time, levels of foreign direct investment (FDI) exploded as countries rushed to join the expanding global economy. China transformed itself from a quiet backwater country that held little attraction for global investors in 1990 to the world's largest recipient of FDI by 2003. And despite the Asian financial crisis and other emerging market volatilities, capital markets continue moving funds around the world more rapidly than ever, now to the tune of some $1.8 billion (U.S.) every day.

An even more fundamental issue than where firms choose to deploy their capital is how they raise it in the first place. The global economy is witnessing a migration toward equity markets as the key allocators of capital. As such, a new global equity culture is emerging in which share ownership ties the fortunes of individuals to the fortunes of global corporations, weaving yet another connective thread into the transnational tapestry. In Western Europe, share ownership nearly doubled over the course of the 1990s to one-quarter of the population, with levels in the United States almost twice as high. As ownership spreads across borders, oversight of corporations becomes a top priority. A remarkable 90 percent of the shareholders in Finnish mobile phone giant Nokia, for instance, live outside its home country of Finland.[12]

Deepening integration among financial markets further complicates how companies act on the international stage. As the Asian financial crisis revealed, malaise in one market can quickly evolve into a contagion that infects others. Even in relatively stable times, unexpected currency fluctuations can take a big bite out of corporate profits. German automobile maker Volkswagen reported losses of $1.5 billion (U.S.) as a result of the volatile dollar-euro exchange rate in 2003 alone. Porsche took a major hit on its auto

> *Malaise in one market can quickly evolve into a contagion that infects others.*

exports during an early period of currency turbulence. Now the automaker hedges its exposure to the dollar four or five years out—a costly maneuver to stabilize earnings against one of globalization's many risks.[13]

Not surprisingly, the explosion of economic globalization has bene-fited the advanced economies, along with Asia's handful of emerging markets, more than it has the rest of the world. Developing countries did see a modest rise in foreign investment inflows, in response to economic liberalization programs. Yet, most missed out on the late-1990s wave of mergers, acquisitions, and the attainment of dynamic new technologies. As a result, the share of foreign investments to developing countries grew only marginally from 15.3 percent to 19.6 percent between 1980 and 2000.[14] With the movement of goods and services inside multina-tional firms a driving force behind international trade, developing nations also lost out in the quickening race to expand trade. Latin America accounted for just over 5 percent of the surge in global trade over the past two decades, while Africa and the Middle East together accounted for less than 2 percent.[15]

Political Globalization

Global or regional trade initiatives—or the lack thereof—often affect corporate decisions. The multinational's bottom line is inexorably tied to the viability of global political institutions like the WTO, which work to lower trade barriers and facilitate foreign investment. Virtually all major trading nations have joined the organization, but a host of vexing issues remain on the agenda. Among them are the regulation of genetically modified organisms, access to cheaper generic drugs, rules governing intellectual property rights, antitrust enforcement, corporate gover-nance and accounting standards, and agricultural subsidies in the United States and Europe. The growing trend to bypass the WTO altogether in favor of bilateral or regional agreements on free trade is also a cause of concern. Recent bilateral initiatives by the United States, Japan, China, and India suggest that these countries are jockeying to gain posi-tion in the global trading system. If not managed properly, this trend could pose problems for future progress on free trade.

On a larger scale, political globalization involves a body of institutions designed to minimize conflict and keep the global system operating smoothly, from the Customs Cooperation Council and the International

Civil Aviation Organization to the even more obscure International Organization for Standardization. Many of these organizations are showing their age. They are struggling to maintain effectiveness in a world where corporations and nongovernmental organizations are joining nation states as influential global actors.

Chief among them is the United Nations, a sprawling organization that has its hand in issues ranging from humanitarian relief and human rights to atomic energy and global security. The UN, explains senior Singaporean diplomat Kishore Mahbubani, "is a crucible of complexity . . . It is both a sunrise organization, providing the only village council for our shrinking global village, and a sunset organization, based on the strange principle that nation-states pursuing national interests will somehow take care of our global commons."[16] The UN's ability to live up to the hopes placed in it will have considerable impact on how the world community evolves.

The Role of the Individual

Globalization is not only driven by governments, multilateral organizations, and corporations. Indeed, as the Globalization Index shows, economic integration has had its ups and downs, and political engagement has remained more or less constant in recent years. Yet the role of individuals in shrinking the world has only intensified. The rapid rise in travel, inexpensive communication, and the Internet empowers activists to coordinate social and environmental movements around the world and allow far-flung families to stay in close touch.

In 2002 alone, more than 130 million new Internet users came online, driven by exponential growth in large developing countries such as China, India, and Brazil. International telephone traffic grew by 15 billion minutes to average more than 21 minutes per person. Developing countries such as Botswana, Hungary, Indonesia, and South Africa became better connected than ever before, as the rapid build-up of wireless networks allowed customers to leapfrog over poorly developed fixed-line infrastructure directly into mobile telephone service. Even international travel saw a rebound as the number of people crossing national borders surpassed 700 million for the first time.[17] Despite dire predictions that the September 11, 2001, terrorist attacks would put an end to globalization, the world was more integrated in 2002 than ever before.

Living in a Globalized World

Globalization is a complex phenomenon, with all its component parts working together in tandem. Consider the case of remittances, the money earned by migrant workers and sent to family and friends back home. Remittances to developing countries have surged from $17.7 billion (U.S.) in 1980 to $60 billion (U.S.) in 1998 to more than $80 billion (U.S.) in 2002. The most obvious driver of this phenomenon is the increasing movement of people across national borders. According to the United Nations, some 175 million people lived and worked outside their own countries in 2000, up from 154 million the decade before.[18] But other forces are also at work, including the political considerations behind H1-B visas that the United States issues to foreign high-tech workers who fill the ranks of Silicon Valley, or the training program that Pakistan developed to export nurses in the hope of getting a return on its investment when they send their earnings back home.

Technology also underlies the worldwide flow of remittances. Harvard University's Devesh Kapur and Queens School of Business's John McHale point to the global expansion of Western Union as the most visible expression of the burgeoning infrastructure that allows migrants to quickly and safely wire money back home. Between 1996 and 2002, the number of agent locations outside of North America jumped from 10,000 to 95,000, and it dominates the market in regions such as Latin America. The company's share of the global market is just above 10 percent, and this high-margin business is swiftly attracting new competitors, such as Internet giant Yahoo!

These financial spillover effects also reshape how migrants interact with one another and with their governments back home. For instance, Mexican immigrants in the United States began forming "hometown clubs" during the 1960s to more effectively pool their resources and send money south of the border. During the last 20 years, these clubs have banded together to form larger coalitions representing individual Mexican states, funding projects that sometimes receive matching funds from the Mexican government. As remittances to Mexico have grown— between $12 billion (U.S.) and $14.5 billion (U.S.) in 2003 alone—so too has the political clout of the Mexican diasporas.[19] In 2004, a delegation of Mexican governors met with a coalition of migrant groups in

Los Angeles for the first time ever. Jose Guadelupe Gomez, president of the state of Zacatecas federation of Southern California, recalls how in the 1970s the Mexican government had nothing but scorn for those who left the country. Today, he says, "remittances have revolutionized the way our government looks at us."[20]

Looking Deeper

In some cases, migrants offer their home countries more than foreign earnings. The Indian government, for example, has launched a major initiative to encourage its 22 million expatriates working abroad—in particular, the estimated 150,000 Indian millionaires outside the country—to channel their savings into investment projects at home. Silicon Valley's large population of Indian programmers and computer scientists has responded, making substantial contributions to building and funding successful software firms in Bangalore and elsewhere. In April 2004, one of India's top software service firms, Infosys, announced that it would begin expanding overseas through its first wholly owned subsidiary in the United States, with two prominent nonresident Indians among its founding members.

By the same token, linguistic and cultural affinities between countries create opportunities for businesses to expand globally. In a business that turns on personal relationships, Spanish banks BBVA and Banco Santander have built a distinct competitive advantage by looking to Latin America for growth opportunities at a time when key competitors were preoccupied with consolidation in Europe.

The complex interplay of globalizing forces is rapidly transforming our world. Contrary to the claims of some critics, the results hold promise for a better tomorrow. The most open and globalized countries in both the developed and developing world generally have the lowest levels of government corruption and the highest levels of political freedom and civil liberties. Led by Western European countries, they show the most fair and equal distribution of income. Governments in the most globalized countries typically spend more on education, health, and

> *Because the benefits of globalization are not distributed evenly, it suffers from a profound image problem.*

social welfare programs, and their citizens, on average, have longer and healthier lives. Measures of women's education and financial well being are better in the most globalized countries, and environmental protection is more robust. For these reasons, global integration is on par a positive force for change. However, because the benefits of globalization are not distributed evenly, it suffers from a profound image problem.

Paradoxically, the same forces behind interconnectivity and integration can work at cross-purposes with globalization. In parts of the world that have yet to reap benefits from global integration, many people resent the growing inequality between North and South and perceive globalization as a modern-day reincarnation of economic imperialism. Even people living in societies that have, on measure, benefited from globalization are experiencing a rising sense of anxiety and insecurity. Forces beyond their control seem to threaten their jobs, their privacy, their security, and even their national cultures. Around the world, people feel disenfranchised and powerless against these emerging trends. Whom do they hold accountable? The most visible beneficiaries and drivers of global integration: corporations. Global businesses must adjust to these constantly moving targets and threats.

Offshoring Revisited

One contradiction of contemporary globalization is that *offshoring*—the outsourcing of jobs to lower-cost locations overseas—is becoming a victim of its own success. The increasing number of jobs outsourced to other countries is generating a backlash among the media and domestic politicians in countries such as the United States, the United Kingdom, and Germany. The source of this discontent is white-collar workers, who worry that developing countries are stealing jobs from computer programmers, engineers, researchers, and other professionals, just as blue-collar workers fret about the impact of free trade agreements on manufacturing jobs. The irony of this backlash has not been lost overseas. As an editorial in Singapore's *Business Times* newspaper notes, "India has become a major outsourcing center for American companies as a result of, among other things, strong pressure by the [United States] to liberalize its economy and open it to foreign trade."[21]

In the United States, unemployed programmers are beginning to flex their political muscles through lobbying organizations such as the

Information Technology Professionals Association of America (ITPAA). The organization was founded by an IT worker after a large investment bank asked him to train the Indian worker who ultimately replaced him.[22] It's clear that politicians are getting the message. Even if Congress does not legislate new restrictions on contracts with firms that use offshore labor, local governments have proven more than willing to pick up the slack. Indiana's state government cancelled a $15 million (U.S.) contract with Tata Consultancy Services, an Indian consulting firm, even though it was lower than competing bids from two U.S. firms. The debate is spreading throughout industrialized countries. Germany's manufacturing powerhouse is increasingly feeling the presence of Poland, the Czech Republic, and other Central European countries right at its doorstep, particularly as national champions such as Volkswagen drift toward the eastern frontiers of the EU. British labor unions have protested companies like the BT Group, which offshored several hundred jobs to India, and have teamed up with other European unions to put pressure on the European Parliament to take action. Governments are reluctant to impose restrictions that might undermine the long-term competitiveness of their domestic companies.

Economic Nationalism and Picking Favorites

For lack of other options, some governments have tried to resist the winds of change, sometimes substituting appeals to economic nationalism for a more pragmatic policy approach. German Chancellor Gerhard Schröder, generally a proponent of market liberalization, called British mobile phone operator Vodafone's buyout of the German firm Mannesmann a threat to Germany's well being.

In response to this trend, Gerard Kleisterlee, CEO of Royal Philips Electronics, has complained that, "In a rapidly and radically changing world, Western Europe seems to be more preoccupied with maintaining the existing economic order than building another future."[23]

Yet resistance to no-holds-barred globalization is not a purely European vice. When partly German-government owned Deutsche Telekom began its purchase of VoiceStream Wireless, U.S. Senator Fritz Hollings went to the Senate floor to declare, "We didn't deregulate telecommunications from under U.S. government control to put it under German government control."[24]

Korea, once known as the "Hermit Kingdom" because of its staunch resistance to imports, has reverted to some old protectionist habits after years of market liberalization. The Korean government, responding to domestic concerns that foreign companies control nearly 40 percent of the banking sector, excluded overseas bidders from the auction of LG Card, the nation's largest issuer of credit cards.[25]

These strokes against the current of globalization will continue to complicate the lives of global executives. It's hard to overcome a preference for "national champions" (a term many thought was retired) and the perceived national interest in supporting "domestic" companies (however defined)—even when the nondomestic alternative is demonstrably superior. When political and cultural interests clash with economic ones, the outcome is far from clear.

Companies cannot discount public sentiment—or even sentimentality. After all, as *Time* magazine pointed out in the late 1990s, the citizens of former East Berlin—who for years envied the material culture of the West—now "crowd bars every evening to drink second-rate GDR champagne called *Rotkäppchen* and fill the air with a haze of acrid smoke from *Cabinet* cigarettes as they sit in booths made from the back seats of old *Trabant* automobiles and speakers blast vintage recordings by defunct East German rock bands."

More recently, the phenomenon of *Ostalgie*, or nostalgia for the east, has become part of the German cultural dynamic.[26] There are even websites that sell chic merchandise such as t-shirts, mugs, and clocks bearing icons of the defunct communist state. As we'll discuss in more detail in Chapter 3 (The New Consumer), companies that face cultural resistance to foreign brands must employ psychographics to decipher archetypes that have universal or local emotional appeal and that break the cultural codes of markets.

The Invisible Hand

Cultural identity, nationalist sentiment, political posturing—these are among the macro forces propelling the globalization backlash. Yet global integration takes place on numerous levels, some less visible than foreign brands, cross-border mergers, or job losses. Foremost among these unseen threats to globalization is disease, which spreads as goods and people move. The Black Death of the fourteenth century made its way from Central Asia to Europe via the Silk Road trading route. Open borders and rapid transportation exponentially increase the potential for spreading disease. In 1990, 457 million people traveled internationally. By 1998, approximately 650 million did so, and by 2010, the number is expected to grow to over one billion.

The volume of international travel is only part of the equation. So too is travel to new destinations. Germs once confined to small, remote villages are now global. The U.S. Public Health Service reported 124 suspected cases of the potentially fatal dengue fever in 1988, carried by travelers returning from other countries.[27] Experts are still not sure how the West Nile Virus found its way to the United States. One scientific report suggested that "infected frogs flown into the States were bitten by exotic Asian mosquitoes that had hitchhiked from Asia to New York in a shipload of tires. The mosquitoes then went on to bite animals and people . . ."

> In part, these outbreaks are the consequence of the collision between urbanization and agriculture.

The West Nile Virus is just one of many emerging zoonotic diseases that human beings can contract either by consuming infected meat (such as Mad Cow disease), through direct transmission (such as being bitten by a tick infected with Lyme disease), or through carriers (such as prairie dogs in the United States who were infected with monkey pox after being bitten by a Gambian giant rat imported from West Africa). Globalization is helping to break down the barriers between species: an estimated two-thirds to three-quarters of the infections identified in the last 30 years are zoonotic in origin.[28]

In part, these outbreaks are the consequence of the collision between urbanization and agriculture, as humans and animals increasingly encroach on one another's environments. The globalization of the food supply has also made humans more susceptible: The meat for hamburgers bought at fast-food chains and the shredded lettuce in salad bars are pooled from hundreds of animals or plants, potentially imported from several countries. Asian food markets are way stations for innumerable exotic species—including turtles, birds, and snakes—that can be incubators for contagion.

Interestingly, advances in global health have partially contributed to the problem. Hospitals in the developing world can be "hot zones" for incubating new viruses. (A hospital in Zaire that lacked proper sterilization procedures served as the venue for spreading the Ebola virus in 1995.) And our medical miracles—antibiotics—are faltering. Multi-drug-resistant tuberculosis (TB), for example, kills half of those infected. And the bacterium that causes TB is just one of many that is waging a brutal counter-offensive against modern medicine. Resistance to antibiotics is a global crisis. One study revealed that in Korea, an astonishing 98 percent of the staph bacteria are resistant to penicillin and that in the United States, 32 percent of the same bacteria are resistant to methicillin. Worldwide, studies suggest that an astonishing 95 percent of staph bacteria are already resistant to penicillin, and resistance among the pneumonia-causing pneumococcus bacteria has risen above 60 percent in countries such as Korea, Hungary, and Mexico.[29] In the United States alone, 14,000 people die each year as the result of drug-resistant bacteria picked up in hospitals, and the number of multiple drug-resistant strains appears to be on the rise.

Devastating Effects

Infectious diseases can have a devastating impact on national economies. They perniciously erode globalization through public health quarantines that close off borders to travel and trade, while further widening the gap between rich and poor nations by dampening socioeconomic development. African countries ravaged by malaria see their GDP growth hindered by 1.3 percent every year as the disease grinds down the foundations of their economies. Laborers are too sick to come to work, children miss school, and corporations are reluctant to invest because they are fearful for the safety of their foreign managers.[30] (Taiwan's economic boom didn't take off until the country completely eliminated malaria in the 1950s.) Similarly, the Asian Development Bank estimates that the SARS epidemic cost developing countries in the region $18 billion (U.S.), or as much as $60 billion (U.S.) if the loss in demand and business costs are included. The Canadian economy lost $3 billion (Canada) in one year due to a near-simultaneous occurrence of SARS and Mad Cow disease. More than 30 countries immediately banned the import of Canadian beef after the reported May 2003 Mad Cow outbreak, costing beef producers about $11 million (Canada) a day in exports, plus an additional $7 million (Canada) from depressed beef prices at home.[31] In Toronto, media images of masked city workers broadcast around the world led to millions of dollars worth of canceled hotel reservations. The problem grew worse after the World Health Organization (WHO) issued a travel advisory and numerous companies restricted employee travel to Toronto.

There's something important that's not captured in these numbers. It is the anxiety people feel in their everyday lives when they are stopped at airport customs, when they are told they can no longer donate blood, or when they see trucks spraying chemicals into the night air because a virus born in a distant jungle is growing in their hometown. Developing countries, already resentful in their belief that globalization is a zero-sum game that predominately benefits industrialized nations, see these kinds of actions as further evidence.

Adverse developments, and the responses to them, have undermined public trust in global institutions such as the WHO. For example, Canada, generally a strong supporter of the United Nations, expressed outrage at the organization for issuing travel advisories that many Canadians believed were disproportionate to the threat of the SARS outbreak.

Contagion at the Speed of Light

Another form of infection, one that is unique to our globalized era, is the computer virus. As corporations increasingly rely on networked systems to manage information, they have opened a million little doors for computer viruses to infect and damage those systems. Electronic Data Systems Corporation (EDS) alone intercepts an average of 20,000 viruses a month in the messaging services it monitors and runs for clients, and the time for viruses to spread has become nearly instantaneous, and the damages they cause have gone through the roof (*see Figure 1.2*). The Jerusalem Virus, first unleashed on an unsuspecting world in 1987 and designed to delete infected files on Friday the 13th, took three years to propagate through global computer networks and ultimately caused $50 million (U.S.) in damage.

Fast-forward to January 2003, when a computer worm dubbed SQL Slammer (aka Sapphire) slowed Internet service around the world by

Figure 1.2 Worldwide Economic Damages Caused by Computer Viruses at Peak Distribution

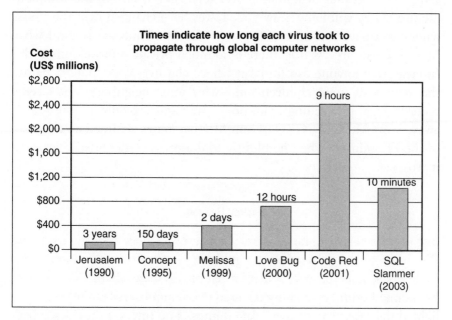

Sources: Richard Powers, Tangled Web, *and Reuters*

exploiting a vulnerability in computers running Microsoft's SQL Server. In just 10 minutes it spread to hundreds of thousands of computers, creating so much volume that at the height of the attack, half of all Internet signals could not reach their destination. Although the worm was not designed to destroy data, it caused nearly $1 billion (U.S.) in lost productivity. Bank of America's ATM system shut down. Telephone systems from Korea to Finland were disrupted. Continental Airlines was forced to delay flights. Microsoft released a patch to fix the problem six months earlier; however, many IT administrators hadn't fully installed it by the time the virus hit. Ironically, even a number of servers at Microsoft headquarters were affected.

As with biological contagion, computer viruses make people everywhere feel less secure. The perception that technology is wrenching more private information away from individuals and casting it into the public arena only heightens that anxiety. Cookies systematically gather data about people's web-surfing habits. Corporate databases have vast amounts of personal information.

And this is only the beginning. Today, firms know what websites you visit. After decades of watching you surf, they will have the complete picture. They will know how your tastes have changed over the years, where you have moved to, who your family members are, and what their interests are. As it is, there is so much private information on the Internet that anyone can find out where you live, your spouse's name, the names of your children, and who your neighbors are. Credit records, legal proceedings, and police warrants are only a mouse-click away. Scott McNealy, CEO of Sun Microsystems, summed up the view of the IT industry when he bluntly told a press conference, "Get over it. You have no privacy . . ."

Hacker Heaven

Just as collecting data raises privacy concerns, so does ensuring its safety. Poorly protected databases are a goldmine for hackers and snoops. The hack attack into the personal information database of the 2002 World Economic Forum, containing the credit card numbers of attendees, highlighted the insecurity of these data dumps. The Internet provides cybercriminals with plenty of places to hide, and they can hit just about anyone. Take for example an attack launched by a young Argentinean hacker in 1995. After getting onto the Internet, Julio Cesar Ardita (aka "griton," which is Spanish for "screamer") logged into a telephone company in Argentina. From there he broke into Harvard computers, and then struck sites throughout North America, South America, and Asia. Ardita's attack shows that distance no longer offers protection to victims. Cyber criminals take elaborate measures to conceal their identities—and finding them is not enough. Many national laws have not yet adapted to this global problem. Authorities were only able to charge Ardita with "improper use of telecommunication equipment," rather than computer espionage. International efforts to crack down on computer crime are progressing, but frequently trip over privacy concerns. The FBI's Carnivore e-mail surveillance software has people worrying as much about the cops as about the robbers.

Hackers are emblematic of what Pulitzer-prize winning journalist Thomas Friedman has dubbed the "super-empowered angry men." These individuals, or small groups, can wreak havoc on a scale that was once thought limited to the capabilities of nation-states. As Friedman notes, global integration is a two-edged sword. It provokes outrage

among individuals who see globalization as corporate-led, U.S.-domi-
nated imperialism; yet at the same
time globalization "shrinks both time
and distance."[32] Put another way,
globalization can facilitate networks
of terror as well as investment, trade,
and travel. The sheer destructive

> *Globalization can facilitate networks of terror as well as investment, trade, and travel.*

power of such super-empowered angry men became apparent on
September 11, 2001, when synchronized terrorist attacks in
Washington, D.C., and New York City murdered nearly 3000 people.
Although security experts had worried for years about a catastrophic
terrorist attack on American soil, none could have predicted the vast
economic impact that would follow. It's sobering to consider that
hijackers armed with nothing more than inexpensive box cutters triggered a costly chain of events. In the aftermath of the attack, the U.S.
government spent hundreds of billions of dollars to invade and occupy
Afghanistan and Iraq—not to mention the $32.8 billion (U.S.) in lost
productivity that the private sector is likely to incur annually as a result
of increased security (an amount that is nearly equal to the U.S. federal government's homeland defense budget).[33]

Globalization: Three Possible Scenarios

The tensions embedded within von Herder's tightly interwoven tapestry
leave the future path of globalization uncertain. On the one hand, countries may decide that the threats are too great and retreat to a more iso-
lated position. On the other hand, globalization has proven itself time
and again to be an adaptive phenomenon that takes more steps forward
than back. Below are three scenarios that sketch different possibilities of
how globalization may evolve between now and 2015 (*see Figure 1.3*).

The Rise of Localization

In the first scenario, *the rise of localization*, mounting security threats and
economic uncertainty start to unravel the threads of globalization.
Protectionism and nationalism proliferate. New security regulations
restrict the cross-border movements of potentially harmful cargo,

Figure 1.3 Globalization: Three Possible Scenarios

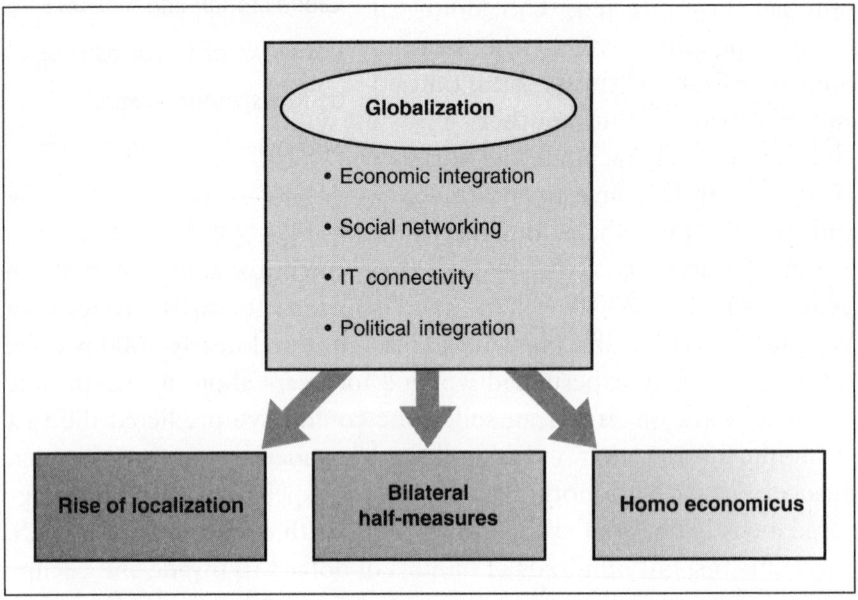

Source: A.T. Kearney

people, and money. Consequently, international trade and investment slows substantially. Income inequality both between and among nations rises sharply. Caught in a cycle of worsening economic conditions, even traditionally free-market governments respond to intense public pressure to safeguard jobs. Exporting nations in Asia seek restitution through the World Trade Organization (WTO), but the multilateral institution is unable to enforce free trade rules without the consensus of the advanced economies. Countries dependent on export-led growth, such as China, suffer serious economic setbacks. As international organizations lose their power to enforce global rules, they become little more than debating societies. Global problems, such as international terrorism, infectious disease, and environmental degradation, lack the institutions to develop workable global solutions. Countries instead opt for limited bilateral and regional arrangements.

Many protectionist regulations are implemented to bolster "national champions"—businesses that reflect each country's comparative advantage or its strategic interests in certain crucial industrial sectors. These companies are granted limited monopolistic power at home in the hopes that they will become more competitive on the global market. Multinational companies scale back their international operations, generally limiting their scope to specific regions or small groups of affiliated countries, where the perceived risks are low or where local trade agreements have minimized regional tariffs and taxes.

On a psychological level, individuals are increasingly disdainful of global culture, global brands, and global norms, and seek refuge in the sanctuary of national identity. The anti-globalization movement, once the domain of nongovernmental organizations and street activists, finds growing resonance in the white-collar suburbs. Unfettered global integration is believed to cause more harm than good. Confronted with these fears, the representative democracies of the industrialized world increasingly favor stability over efficiency.

Bilateral Half-Measures

In the second scenario, *bilateral half-measures*, countries take incremental and modest steps toward globalization, but the pace is far slower and more cautious than during the heady 1990s. As countries seek to maintain their competitive advantage in the global marketplace, it becomes increasingly tricky to paper over differences such as levels of agricultural subsidies and the scope of intellectual property laws. Consequently, multilateral trade and investment agreements are supplanted by regional treaties among nations whose interests most closely converge. The world becomes a collage of contrasting international, regional, and national norms.

With no coherent global standards on issues such as the environment and biotechnology, companies that seek to expand globally must navigate a complex regulatory obstacle course. As a result, all but the largest corporations limit their expansion to a specific region, opting to dominate in one local standard while competing in other parts of the world on a more limited basis.

The agendas of world regions have become more divergent, owing in part to the absence of strong international leadership. Although the United States maintains a dominant position in the global economy, it has limited its commitments to multilateral institutions in favor of a more unilateralist stance. And the U.S. government no longer can claim the moral high ground on free trade, having embraced mild protectionist measures to enhance its own economic and military security. The expanded European Union still lacks the mechanisms to implement a common political and foreign policy. A select group of poor, developing countries that possess valuable natural resources and other industrial inputs fare rather well, but most are still trying to find their economic niche. Some of these countries fall back on protectionist policies; others remain engaged in the global economy and see modest improvements in overall standards of living.

Homo Economicus

In the final scenario, *homo economicus*, the world returns to the path of ever-deepening global integration that began in the 1990s. Global trade is on a rebound. Offshoring and other capital flows continue, and their powerful developmental impact on Asia generates positive returns for Europe and the United States in the form of increased purchasing power abroad. All major economies are members of the WTO, which has eliminated the most onerous barriers to international trade. Still, in some specific areas, free trade negotiations have reached an impasse, as governments find it difficult to reach consensus on several thorny issues. Trade in services is booming, and secure digital connections allow far-flung, truly global production and distribution networks to emerge.

The countries that benefit the most are those, such as the United States, China, and India, that are the most open to economic integration. Advanced economies have relocated the bulk of their manufacturing capacity to emerging markets. China remains the world's manufacturing powerhouse and more and more back-office and service functions head to India. Developed and developing nations start to bridge the income inequality gap. This increased globalization does not benefit everyone, however, and the losers voice their dissatisfaction. Responding to the public outcry over lost blue-collar jobs, governments divert more federal spending toward social safety nets and retraining programs, which helps mollify some of the opposition. Anti-globalization activists remain a small, but influential, group and focus their efforts on helping the least developed countries.

More often than not, transnational problems such as infectious diseases, computer crimes, terrorism, and financial instability foster international cooperation among governments and institutions, since no country can reasonably hope to completely isolate itself from such threats. Finally, although "global culture" remains a popular buzzword, it's countered by the increased exposure to an ever more diverse set of people—and all the creativity, ideas, and perspectives they bring to the table. This return to benign globalization does not offer limitless opportunities—but they are vast, and they penetrate many levels of society.

Demographics

An Age of Extremes

Demography is destiny.
—Auguste Comte, Nineteenth Century French Philosopher[1]

A great demographic tide is ebbing and flowing. The developed world is aging, and health, retirement, and social security programs are feeling the resulting squeeze. Meanwhile, in the developing world, the number of ambitious young people is outpacing prospects for jobs and economic growth. Managed properly, these powerful global demographic trends could benefit all sides. Migrants from the developing world could help offset acute labor shortages in industrialized countries; increased emigration could ease explosive social conditions in the developing world. The political challenges remain substantial, and in the end, it may be easier simply to "export" jobs instead of "import" workers. Either way, companies will need a truly global view to accurately assess the risks and opportunities. They will have to cooperate closely with governments and citizens as they move through the tidal eddies.

A World Gone Gray

Prophets of doom dominated the bestseller lists in the late 1960s and early 1970s. Declaring that "the battle to feed all humanity is over," Paul Ehrlich warned in *The Population Bomb* that 65 million Americans would die of starvation between 1980 and 1989.[2] Several years later, the Club of Rome argued in its seminal report, *Limits to Growth*, that global economic decline would be inevitable in a world of expanding population and limited resources.[3] Even the U.S. government sponsored a nationwide exhibit for schoolchildren in the mid-1970s called "Population: The Problem Is Us," which declared that, "There are too many people in the world. We are running out of space. We are running out of energy. We are running out of food. And, although too few people seem to realize it, we are running out of time."[4]

Three decades later we are indeed running out of time, but not in the way that Ehrlich, and others, had imagined. We may have averted catastrophe because new technologies have made it possible to use resources more efficiently and the "Green Revolution" has fostered more productive forms of agriculture throughout the developing world. Yet the global community stands on the brink of new demographic challenges that come from the rapid aging of the world population. For most of human history, only 2 to 3 percent of the global population lived long enough to become senior citizens. The World Bank now predicts that 16 percent of the global population—more than one billion people—will be over 60 years old by 2030.[5]

> The global population in 2050 could range from 7.4 billion to 10.6 billion.

As a result, the future of many countries may well resemble the U.S. state of Florida, where pensioners and retirees represent nearly one-fifth of the population. The "Floridaization" of the world will be most acute in wealthy, industrialized countries, which will pass this same demographic benchmark in a matter of years: Germany in 2006, France and Britain in 2016, the United States in 2021, and Canada in 2023.[6]

But the phenomenon will certainly not be limited to Western countries. East Asia is experiencing the most rapid aging in the world; by 2025, it will be considerably more "gray" than Europe or North America is today. The most extreme case is Japan, where one in three people will be older than 65 and one in nine older than 80. Taiwan and South Korea will also see median age levels leap substantially, up 11 and 12 years, respectively. (This compares with a change of only two years in the median age in the United States, where it will move from 35.6 in 2000 to 37.6 in 2025.) But China might have the most difficult transition. The median age there is expected to grow from 30 to 39, making it older—but considerably less affluent—than the United States only decades from now.[7]

What explains this phenomenon of global aging, which crept up and took so many of us by surprise? The first and most obvious factor is rising longevity, thanks to improvements in healthcare and better standards of living. Since World War II, average world life expectancy at birth has jumped from 45 years to 65 years—a higher gain in the last half century than in the previous 5000 years.[8] By 2030, the average global citizen can expect to live to 72. (Japan has already become the first country in history to achieve a life expectancy beyond 80 years, due in part to the nation's fish- and vegetable-rich diet.)

The Baby Bust

The second, less-discussed cause of global aging is declining birthrates. Instead of a population boom, there is actually a "baby bust" in countries and territories that today account for 44 percent of the world's population. Birthrates around the world have declined steadily since the early 1950s, when each woman had an average of five children. Today, the global fertility rate is 2.7. In developed countries, the average number of births per woman has fallen to just 1.7—far below the rate of 2.1 children per woman that maintains stable population size.[9]

The shortage of babies is most severe in Europe and Japan, where demographers predict populations could decline by 50 percent before the end of this century.[10] Europe will likely experience the greatest period of depopulation since the Black Death, shrinking to a mere 7 percent of the world's population by 2050 (from nearly 25 percent just after World War II).[11] The working-age population (aged 15 to 64) is already shrinking in countries like Italy and Japan. Most other industrialized nations, including the United States, Britain, and Canada, can expect the same in the 2020s.

This baby bust is the consequence of several economic, political, and even cultural drivers. The growing availability of birth control and the widening social acceptance of abortion since the 1950s represents part of the equation. Likewise, as population control emerged as a dominant mantra of economic development, family planning programs sponsored by international agencies and national governments began to have a lasting impact. Also, higher standards of living meant that families didn't have to raise so many children to enter the workforce as potential breadwinners. Similarly, government pension plans and old-age benefit programs reduced the need to have multiple children as a form of insurance to support parents as they entered their older years. Families have also shrunk as more and more women have entered the workforce.

Japan's population implosion, in particular, is the product of a clash between modern emancipation and outdated social mores. Ayako Doi, the editor of *The Japan Digest*, notes that even after Japanese women began taking professional jobs in the 1970s, the rules at home didn't change. She bemoans a national culture that condemns "married women to 100 percent of the household chores so that husbands can devote 100 percent of their time and energy to their employers." Many Japanese career women simply choose not to get married and raise a family at all. Despite this crisis, it is clear that change will come slowly. One former prime minister, Yoshiro Mori, argues that financial sanctions are the best way to motivate higher fertility: "It is wrong for women who haven't had a single child to ask for taxpayer money when they get old, after having enjoyed their freedom and had fun."[12]

The extent to which birthrates decline will have a major impact on future demographic trends. A recent report from the United Nations Population Division demonstrates how sensitive world population levels may be to even small changes in fertility rates, or the number of children per woman. With a difference of no more than half a child per woman, on average, the report estimates that the global population in 2050 could range from 7.4 billion to 10.6 billion. But even more dramatic is the look forward to the year 2100: The difference could be a global population shrinking to 5.5 billion or a world crowded with 14 billion people.[13]

Such discrepancies could be further exacerbated by medical advancements that improve our ability to treat the world's most pervasive, deadly diseases. AIDS is barely under control in much of Africa, but without strong intervention it could also spread unchecked throughout much of Eurasia. If so, warns demographer Nicholas Eberstadt, the total number of AIDS deaths between 2000 and 2025 could reach as high as 12 million people in Russia, 58 million in China, and 85 million in India.[14]

Brave Old World: The Impact of Global Aging

No country will be unaffected by this brave old world. Aging countries are likely to feel the demographic pinch first and most intensely through labor forces, which will contract as older workers head into retirement without large groups of young workers to replace them. In the United States alone, more than 70 million baby boomers are expected to exit the workforce by 2020, while only 40 million new workers enter.[15] Similar trends are likely throughout Europe. Germany, for instance, started the century with the same working-age population as a much younger Mexico. However, Germany will have only 43.1 million workers by 2030—little more than half the 80.5 million workers Mexico will have by that time.[16]

The shrinking pool of labor will make jobs in the developed world increasingly difficult to fill. Already, the trend has created serious problems for leading petrochemical firms, among others. By some estimates, 10 to 20 percent of senior scientists in the chemical industry have already retired, and 50 percent of employees overall may be eligible to retire over the next decade.[17] Though many will be available as external consultants, their demands for flexible working arrangements are upending established human resource practices. Competition for younger workers is increasingly intense, so many companies find themselves hiring experienced senior engineers, technicians, and research professionals from competitors, often at higher cost and with lower expectations of company loyalty.[18]

On a broad level, the All India Management Association estimates the gap of talented workers will reach 32 to 39 million by 2020—with 17 million jobs unfilled in the United States, 9 million in Japan, and 2 million each in France, Germany, and the United Kingdom.[19] Very few companies are preparing for the loss of older workers and the institutional knowledge they represent. One study in the United States found that two-thirds of firms had no plans or programs to keep older workers or capitalize on their experiences, and few company executives knew anything about their state of preparedness for the coming wave of retirement.[20] This lack of foresight could become a significant drag on overall economic growth and competitiveness. According to the Organization for Economic Cooperation and Development (OECD) projections, the scarcity of working-age citizens will decrease economic growth rates in Europe to 0.5 percent, in Japan to 0.6 percent, and in the United States to 1.5 percent between the years 2025 and 2050.[21]

Aging populations will also affect consumer spending, which accounts for as much as 60 to 70 percent of GDP in industrialized countries. To be sure, financial planning will continue to grow in importance, as older people prepare themselves for retirement. Within the decade, some three-quarters of all investible assets in the United States will be owned by people over 55 years of age, and the institutional retirement and pension funds that represent them will become even more powerful players in financial markets.

But questions remain about what exactly will happen when these retirees begin spending their accumulated savings. As their total spending exceeds the savings generated by current workers, retirees in OECD countries could depress savings rates by some 8 percent of GDP by the year 2020. Savers in industrialized countries seeking out higher rates of return might be increasingly inclined to invest their money in fast-growing emerging markets. This could weaken currencies and increase capital outflows among industrialized countries, as well as heighten financial risk as the life savings of pensioners becomes more dependent on the economic well being of China or India. On the other hand, spending on certain items will soar, as retirees who are well off direct their hard-earned savings toward improving their healthcare, going on extended vacations, and filling their homes with expensive furnishings.

Meanwhile, at the opposite end of the age spectrum, key economic sectors such as housing construction and durable goods might take a hit, since it is young professionals who are most inclined to buy new homes and appliances as they settle down and start a family. The United Nations estimates that the European Union and Japan will see respectively a 13 percent and 20 percent decline in this age bracket by the end of the decade.[22] But as smaller families lavish their resources on fewer children, younger consumers in industrialized countries and key emerging markets (such as China) will also likely have more disposable income than ever before. In the United States alone, kids are already spending nearly as much annually as the total economic output of Turkey.

Social Insecurity

Without question, the greatest challenges confronting countries with graying populations are the escalating costs of funding pensions and providing affordable healthcare. Most social security systems throughout the developed world operate on a pay-as-you-go basis—a system of transfers whereby workers support retirees by paying out a percentage of their earnings in the form of payroll taxes. The system was perfectly suited to the demographic patterns of the previous century, when growing populations, large families, and comparatively short life spans worked in tandem to keep the system solvent.

Today, declining fertility rates, longer longevity, and the forthcoming retirement of the baby boomers are turning this pyramid upside down. When the U.S. government first instituted Social Security, the average lifespan was 63 years, although eligibility didn't kick in until people turned 65. At present, the average lifespan in the United States is 77, yet eligibility has shifted only slightly to 67.

Before too long, there will simply not be enough young people earning enough money to support the growing burden their parents and grandparents will place on social systems. According to projections published by the Center for Strategic and International Studies (CSIS), the average cost of public pensions in the developed world will grow by 7 percent of GDP between now and the middle of the century.[23]

The bill will grow even larger among countries that have generous pension plans and are experiencing even more rapid aging. For continental Europe, the additional cost will be 8 percent of GDP, and in Japan, a staggering 10 percent.[24] But the number of workers available to keep those systems afloat is shrinking. Already, the ratio of working taxpayers to nonworking pensioners in industrialized countries is barely 3 to 1. If current trends continue, that ratio will fall to 1.5 to 1 by 2030. In some countries, such as Japan and Germany, it will drop all the way down to 1 to 1 or lower. In the United States, the retirement of baby boomers will lower the ratio from 4 to 1 to 2 to 1 over the same period.

Now factor in rising healthcare costs among older populations—not just medication and visits to the doctor, but nursing care facilities and assisted-living services. Again, CSIS projections offer a startling assessment. Within the next 50 years, public health spending on the elderly could well increase by 5 to 6 percent of GDP in developed countries.[25]

In the United States, the General Accounting Office predicts that two-thirds of the entire federal budget could go to medical care by 2050. The combined costs could well ruin the financial situation of many countries that now enjoy fiscal health—and global investors have taken notice. Standard & Poor's recently warned that country credit ratings could come under intense pressure within the next decade, and that without changes, half of the world's most advanced economies could slip to BBB ratings (or lower) by the late 2020s.[26]

Business Takes a Hit

The private sector is also facing sticker shock. Based on the Kaiser Family Foundation Health Benefits Survey, average monthly employer contribution to health insurance premiums in the United States increased 240.7 percent from 1998 to 2003. General Motors, the largest private purchaser of healthcare in the United States, spends $5 billion per year on healthcare, more than it spends on steel, two-thirds of which is for its 450,000 retirees.[27] The price of an average GM vehicle now includes over $1000 in costs related only to the company's healthcare burden.[28]

Worldwide, employers are confronted by growing pension shortfalls. Between 2001 and 2003, the combined assets of U.S. corporate pension plans plunged by more than $500 billion. The Confederation of British Industry estimates that the total shortfalls of British firms reached £160 billion (US$298 billion), excluding the cost of a proposed law forcing financially healthy firms to pay up any deficits in their pension schemes before closing them. Including the costs of these and other factors, the black hole in Britain's company pensions would go as high as £300 billion, or $559 billion (U.S.).[29]

In the United States, the growing burden of pension and healthcare costs is one reason LTV Steel and Bethlehem Steel were compelled to file bankruptcy under Chapter 11. The Pension Benefit Guaranty Corporation (PBGC)—the federal agency that insures the pensions of millions of American workers—is facing an $11.2 billion deficit as it has been forced to pick up the retirement benefits for more and more businesses. (PBGC is not funded by taxpayer money; it underwrites pensions using premiums paid by viable companies.) Steven A. Kandarian, the head of PBGC until February 2004, wrote in his resignation letter:

"Workers and retirees have lost promised benefits, PBGC has suffered multibillion-dollar losses, and responsible companies have been placed at risk. If we do not take action soon, these consequences will repeat themselves."[30]

Investors are become increasingly skittish about companies with large pension liabilities. Responding to pressure from ratings agencies, German conglomerate Siemens announced a major change in its pension program to cope with rising life expectancy among its workers. The ratio of active employees to pension recipients had slipped from 4.5 to 1 in 1975 to only 1.2 to 1 at the end of 2002.[31] A growing pension shortfall expense cost Siemens €2.601 billion, or $3.1 billion (U.S.), in 2002 alone and eventually forced the company to switch from a defined benefit system to individually managed retirement accounts.

Paying the Bill and Passing the Buck

In the developed world, unfunded liabilities for pensions, plus projected healthcare costs, amount to a staggering $70 trillion (U.S.)—six times the size of official public debts.[32] How will developed countries pay the bill? One possible solution is to increase already heavy tax burdens, as is happening in countries like Japan. However, in many countries, higher taxes may not be sufficient to cover the spiraling costs of providing for the elderly, and these days there is not much room for tax increases. In Germany, France, and Italy, payroll taxes already exceed 40 percent of total payments to workers. (The average total tax burden for the European Union is 46 percent.) Paying for promised benefits through increased taxation is simply not feasible, since doing so would raise the total tax burden by an unthinkable 25 to 40 percent of every worker's taxable wages.

Financing the costs of these benefits by borrowing would be just as disastrous. Governments would run unprecedented deficits that would quickly consume the savings of the developed world, driving up interest rates and increasing the cost of debt among highly indebted nations. Most European countries wouldn't even be able to pursue this option unless they decided to ignore the Economic and Monetary Union's imposed ceilings on budget deficits, which amounts to 3 percent of GDP.

Frits Bolkestein, the European Union's Internal Market Commissioner, openly worries that divergent fiscal policies among EU members could set in motion a chain of events that would unravel the continent's economy. "Pension payments could easily turn into a vicious circle. If pension spending were not reformed, but led to higher deficits, some countries would not respect their obligations under the growth and stability pact; which in turn could lead to inflationary pressures; which in turn would result in the ECB [European Central Bank] having to set higher interest rates with negative impact not only on investment, but also on growth and employment, which are the basis of sustainable pension systems . . . 'Pay more, work longer, get less,' is not an easy message to sell."[33]

No Good Options

If governments can't increase revenue through borrowing or higher taxes, then what about cutting other public spending? Unfortunately, this may not be a viable option. The projected growth in retirement spending is so large that "some governments could eliminate all general purpose spending—from defense and infrastructure to police and schools—and still find themselves running deficits twenty-five years from now," according to CSIS.[34]

It is also unlikely that developed governments will cut back spending on public pensions. To stabilize spending as a share of GDP, those cuts would have to be between 30 percent and 60 percent. This rollback would be the fiscal equivalent of a shock-and-awe campaign against retirees in the developed world, whose income is highly dependent on their antici-pated benefits. For the average retiree in the United States, Social Security accounts for 60 percent of total income. In Sweden, Germany, and France, public pensions account for an average 80 percent.

> *In OECD countries, senior citizens are becoming a formidable special-interest group.*

Faced with fiscal options that vary from bad to worse, governments in Europe and North America are also shifting the burden to employers and workers. The United Kingdom's new accounting rule, FRS 17, which will be fully enforced from 2005 onward, will compel British firms to account for their pension funds' assets at market value (as opposed to smoothing out the effects of stock market volatility). In practical terms, British firms will be forced to double their pension contributions, compared with those they made in 2000, to £43 billion, $80 billion (U.S.). The future trajectory of these pension schemes promises to have a profound effect on the competitiveness of developed economies. FRS 17 could leave British firms with much less money to invest, which may lead to lower economic growth for the nation's economy for years to come. Since pension contributions are tax-deductible, the government will suffer a direct loss of up to £2 billion, or $3.7 billion (U.S.), a year in tax revenues.[35]

As employers raise their contributions to social security in Belgium, France, Sweden, and Spain, it becomes increasingly expensive to invest in these countries. By contrast, the low employer social security contribution in Ireland (which still has a sizable younger population) helps to further increase its attractiveness to foreign investors. Similarly, although the United States has wage and salary rates comparable to the Netherlands and Germany, it has much lower costs associated with statutory plans and employee benefits. Yet Canada is likely to get most future automobile plants in North America because direct healthcare costs to companies are so much lower than in the United States. With the highest "fully loaded" labor costs among advanced countries, Germany could be the biggest loser, as firms leave for countries that offer a better trade-off between labor costs and labor productivity.

Japan offers a sobering example of how difficult the reform process is likely to be. Already faced with the largest public debt burden among the advanced economies, Japan's national parliament simply mandated higher contributions from companies and employees in order to cover looming shortfalls in the public pension system, essentially ignoring an economic malaise lasting more than a decade. The new requirement adds a heavy burden to Japan's ailing businesses that Keidanren, the nation's largest business group, estimates will reduce consumer spending and cut corporate profits in half by 2007.[36] Commentators suggest that the additional costs will make Japan even less attractive to foreign investors, particularly in labor-intensive industries such as manufacturing, retail, and logistics.

Forecasts in such "young" countries as Australia suggest that the pension burden will be manageable with only modest changes in taxation and spending levels. But the picture grows more difficult with each year in which additional revenue is not raised. One study in the United States suggested that delayed response could leave the country with an overwhelming $51 trillion (U.S.) deficit in its Social Security program, necessitating a 78 percent increase in corporate and personal income tax rates.[37] To date, New Zealand is one of the few countries to raise taxes now with a concrete plan for generating surpluses and smoothing out the burden.

Rewriting the Social Contract

One thing is already clear: Societies must make the unenviable choice of either renegotiating social contracts or risk becoming less competitive in the global economy. That task is proving especially formidable in Europe. The government of former French Prime Minister Jean-Pierre Raffarin introduced reforms in 2003 that required public sector workers to pay into the state pension scheme for 40 years, instead of 37.5. The government also sought to increase the amount of time French citizens must work before they could qualify for a pension, to 41 years from 2012, and 42 years by 2020.[38] The result of these arguably modest reforms was a massive wave of strikes and protests that reduced that nation's industrial output by 1.4 percent.[39]

Likewise, in February 2003, almost 100,000 people, waving signs with slogans like "Schröder the Thief," participated in a general strike against the German government's Agenda 2010, which introduced modest cuts to the public healthcare system and changes in labor market laws. Next door in Austria, the government's plans for a fundamental reform of the public pension system led 200,000 workers to participate in one of the country's biggest mass protests in 50 years.

To complicate matters further, the growing ranks of the elderly are flexing their political muscles. In OECD countries, senior citizens are becoming a formidable special-interest group. They vote consistently and have more money to contribute to political campaigns because they are richer than the young people who are paying the taxes to support social security systems.

With more than 30 million members, the AARP in the United States is the largest advocacy organization on behalf of the elderly in the world and one of the most influential in American politics. (In fact, the business newsweekly *Modern Healthcare* cites John Rother, the Washington, D.C.-based policy director of the AARP, as one of the 100 most powerful people in healthcare.)[40]

Pensioners and retirees in other countries are forming their own political parties, as is the case of Russia's Party of Pensioners, which, since it was founded in 1997, has seen its membership surge to over 200,000 in 46 regions of the Russian Federation.[41] The stronger the political power of pensioners and older workers, the greater the pressure is on governments when they consider cutting pension and healthcare benefits. This, in turn, limits changes to the pension systems and maintains the political power of retirees.

Healthcare companies are also a political power to reckon with, having spent more than any other industry to lobby the U.S. government in 2002. The industry hired 625 different lobbyists to press lawmakers on such issues as pending legislation that would curb rising drug prices. According to Public Citizen, a health and safety nonprofit organization in the United States, U.S. pharmaceutical companies spent $262 million (U.S.) during the 1999-2000 election cycle.

High on pharmaceutical companies' priority list is preserving differential pricing schemes. Medication costs are higher in the United States: For instance, a month's supply of the antidepressant Zoloft costs $82 in the United States, $42 (U.S.) in Canada, and $29 (U.S.) in France. Prices are lower in Europe and Canada because their governments regulate the prices of drugs and use their immense bargaining power to dictate hefty discounts. As such, pharmaceutical companies are compelled to charge more to U.S. consumers to recoup their massive research-and-development expenses. (The pharmaceutical industry is also coping with declining revenues as top-selling drugs go off patent, opening the door to competition from cheaper generics.) Lobbyists for the pharmaceutical industry argue the best solution is not lowering drug prices, but helping patients pay for drugs through expanded, government-subsidized Medicare benefits.

On the one side, governments are struggling to keep a lid on fiscal spending and out-of-pocket expenses for patients; on the other, the healthcare and pharmaceutical industries are seeking to maintain their bottom lines. Caught somewhere in between are physicians, who are increasingly discontented with cost pressures, excessive bureaucracy, and declining compensation. Growing frustration with the system is prompting an exodus from the medical profession. Applications to U.S. medical schools, following a 1996 peak, have since declined by 25.9 percent.[42] More than 126,000 nursing positions currently remain unfilled, a shortage that has become so severe it is endangering the lives of patients. Foreign nationals already account for 11.5 percent of the registered nurses, 17 percent of the medical aides, and 25.2 percent of the physicians working in the United States.[43]

Other countries are experiencing similar problems. Canada is currently losing an average of 250 doctors each year, primarily to the United States. The shortage couldn't come at a worse time, with the baby boomers nearing retirement. The demand for skilled surgical specialists will be especially high for those entering old age. Patients in need of eye procedures, such as cataract surgery, will jump 15 percent by 2010 and 47 percent by 2020. The demand for heart surgery is projected to rise 42 percent by 2020, and 70 percent of a heart surgeon's workload is among patients over the age of 65.[44] Yet there will likely be a shortage of 85,000 physicians in the United States by 2020.[45]

The New Import: Purchasing Power

Confronted with escalating pension and healthcare costs, countries and consumers are experimenting with innovations. Some governments are seeking to import pensioners and the purchasing power they bring with them. More and more Japanese retirees, in search of more hospitable climates and lower costs of living, are choosing to live in Southeast Asian countries to further stretch their savings and pensions. Malaysia, Thailand, and the Philippines are all competing for a stake in this market.

The Malaysian government, for instance, has sought to attract 20,000 foreign retirees through its aptly named "Silver Hair Program," which allows those over the age of 50 to reside in the country through an annual renewal of their entry visas. (The Malaysian tourism minister even traveled to Japan to personally assure residents: "Malaysia has all that you need for your retirement plans—from the climate to safety, medical facilities, low living cost, natural attractions, and accommodation facilities.")[46]

Likewise, medical tourism promises "First World Treatment" at "Third World Prices." Developing countries—notably Thailand, Jordan, India, Malaysia, South Africa, and Cuba—are jockeying for a share of the OECD countries' healthcare market (worth $4 trillion [U.S.] by 2005) by offering services such as cosmetic surgery, cardiac care, organ transplants, fertility treatments, and joint replacements. South Africa boasts a travel package (referred to by some as the "beauty and the beast tour") that offers foreigners facelifts at a fraction of the cost in Europe and the United States, and then allows them to recuperate while on safari.[47]

Dr. Prathap C. Reddy, the head of India's largest chain of private hospitals, believes his country could earn more than $1 billion (U.S.) annually and create 40 million new jobs by subcontracting work from the British National Health Service (NHS). Medical treatment is free in the United Kingdom, but the waiting times for surgery such as hip replacement and coronary bypass are so long that many patients opt instead for expensive private medical care. Consequently, the proposed plan would simultaneously reduce pressure on Britain's NHS while offering subcontracted healthcare at vastly lower rates. "There is no reason why we should not become the healthcare destination of the world," says Reddy.[48]

Focusing on the Family

Governments need to begin thinking outside the demographic box if they are to cope with the aging crisis. One solution advocated by Peter Peterson, chairman of the Blackstone Group and the Council on Foreign Relations, is for Western countries to "stress filial obligation" and encourage the younger generation to play a more active role in caring for their parents. "Societies in which the extended family is weak, elder poverty is high, and long-term care costs are rising rapidly have much to learn from Confucian societies such as Japan, where most elders still live with their adult children."[49]

Also, developed nations could strive to reverse the baby bust by implementing pro-natal policies. The French government, for instance, classifies a couple with three or more children as a "famille nombreuse." This designation makes the family eligible for a variety of special benefits including income-tax breaks, state-subsidized rent reduction, and even reduced train fares for commuting to work.[50] Such policies offer a dual prize for politicians, allowing them to appear pro-family to voters while fostering a new generation of productive taxpayers.

They may also have some benefit for companies, which for better or worse are finding that family matters have a powerful impact on employee productivity. A 1999 study by insurance giant MetLife found that one-third of U.S. employees had reduced their work hours and 13 percent chose to leave their jobs entirely in order to care for aging parents. Such responses were required, in part, because only one in 20 companies offered any benefits to help employees care for aging relatives.[51]

At the other end of the age spectrum, companies like Ford Motor Company have found positive returns from its strong support of parents. The company claims higher retention, lower absenteeism, and higher levels of creativity and innovation as a result of its generous parental leave program and its efforts to create a family friendly environment—complete with special classes for mothers returning to work, on-site childcare, flexible hours, and work-from-home opportunities. The program also helps to manage prenatal healthcare costs, among the most costly items on corporate health insurance bills.

Planning Early, Retiring Late

One of the most promising approaches in coping with the pension crisis is to encourage or require people to save or invest more of their earnings before they retire. CSIS identified multiple benefits to this strategy, since it "decouples retirement security from the ups and downs of demographics—and, to the extent that foreign investment is allowed, from the ups and downs of national economic performance as well. The funding strategy will allow workers and retirees in the aging developed world to benefit from the growth opportunities of a still younger developing world."[52]

Several countries, including Sweden, Chile, Poland, and Australia are already tinkering with private funding mechanisms. Chile stands out as a success story. In 1981, the country began phasing out its government social security program and instead set up a private funding plan wherein employers automatically deduct 10 percent of each worker's earnings into a pension savings account. Employees were also permitted to deduct another 10 percent of their salaries tax-free. This money was then invested in any of the 12 (later 21) licensed companies the government authorized to act as pension fund managers or "Administradora de Fondos de Pensiones" (AFPs). The government only intervened to the extent that the AFPs were monitored to avert potential fraud and to ensure they remained competitive. Employees make their own investment decisions, reflecting their own tolerance for risk and desired retirement income. By 1997, the new system was providing the Chilean workforce with as much as 70 percent of their final salary upon retirement.[53]

Other options include reducing employment barriers for the elderly and increasing retirement ages. Many countries in Europe and Asia still maintain outdated mandatory retirement rules. In South Korea, 57 is the average retirement age in firms with more than 300 employees, despite public opinion polls that reveal Koreans in their 50s and 60s desire to work until an average age of 67.8.[54] Recently, as part of its "National Strategy for a Low-Birth Rate and Aging Society," the Korean government announced that it would raise the retirement age for workers in both the private and public sectors to 60 by 2008, and to 65 by 2033.[55]

The German government has spearheaded an information and recruitment program called *Campaign 50 Plus: Die Können Es* ("Over 50: They Can Do It!"). Nevertheless, gradual increases in retirement age alone will not solve the problem. Demographers at the CIA estimate that "to hold dependency ratios steady and therefore benefits and tax rates constant, by 2030 retirement would have to begin at 78 in Japan, 74 in France, 73 in Italy, and 72 in the United States. By 2050, retirement ages in these countries would need to rise to 81, 78, 79, and 75, respectively."[56]

Evidence suggests that attitudes among aging workers are beginning to change. In the United States, for instance, most workers no longer expect to stop working and have unlimited leisure time during their retirement years, and they do not necessarily expect their companies or the government to provide financial security. In a 2003 survey by employment consulting firm Towers Perrin, more than three-quarters of the respondents indicated that they expect to continue working in some capacity during retirement. By and large, employees expected lower coverage from their employee benefit programs, and they understood why companies needed to trim retirement plan costs. Within these constraints, however, employees expect their companies to continue providing benefit plans that are well designed to meet their changing needs.

The Youth Bulge: A Ticking Time Bomb?

One of the great ironies of our unbalanced world is that as many developed nations (and a few emerging markets, such as China) cope with depopulation and advanced aging, much of the developing world is confronting an unprecedented "youth bulge." Even where populations are not growing rapidly, the number of young people between the ages of 15 and 29 is on the rise, as is their share of total population. India's working-age population, for instance, is projected to grow by 335 million people by 2030—almost as many as the entire working-age population of Europe and the United States today. As a result, poor countries throughout Latin America, the Middle East, and sub-Saharan Africa are struggling to deal with an abundance of workers, while advanced economies contemplate a future of jobs without the labor force to fill them (*see Figure 2.1*).

Of course, jobs are a powerful motivator, and their abundance in advanced economies will attract young workers from the developing world. Today, legal and illegal immigrants account for more than 15 percent of the population in more than 50 countries. That number will only continue to grow, as citizens in the developing world flock to industrialized countries in search of employment and higher wages. If developed countries hope to maintain a fiscally sustainable ratio of workers to pensioners, they would have to accept a vast number of migrants: for each of the years between 2010 and 2015, more than nine million in the European Union and nearly eight million in Japan.

Figure 2.1 Age Profile by Region, 2001

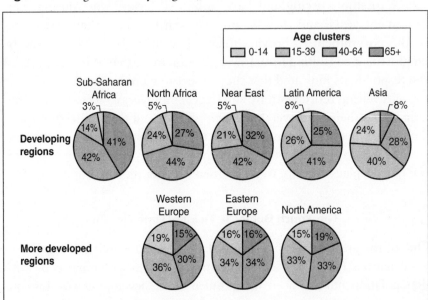

Sources: U.S. Census Bureau and A.T. Kearney analysis

Managing these immigration flows will put a tremendous strain on governments in the decades ahead and may spark friction between nations. An estimated four million would-be migrants living in the eastern and southern periphery of the EU are poised to emigrate (mostly illegally) into the region.[57] Already, Italy is known as the "soft underbelly" of EU immigration barriers; it is home to 1.5 million legal immigrants and probably 500,000 illegal immigrants.[58] The Italian government has had frequent diplomatic spats with Libya, which it accuses of being a funnel for illegal immigrants from all over Africa. Similarly, Mexico and Central America will remain a substantial source of illegal immigrants into the United States, while illegal immigration in the Russian Far East will be a point of contention between Russia and China.

Massive migration also promises increased friction within societies as new arrivals reshape national cultures. Canada, with a population of only 30 million, receives over 130,000 new Asian immigrants every year. More than one-third of Vancouver's population is of Asian descent, and over 60 percent of the city's primary school students speak English only as a second language. France's five million Muslims constitute 8 percent of the population and now outnumber Jews and Protestants combined. In Germany, foreigners will make up 30 percent of the population by 2030, and over half the population of major cities like Munich and Frankfurt.[59] The United States, the largest recipient of immigrants in the world, will undergo a profound demographic change. Hispanics have just replaced African-Americans as the largest minority group in the country, and their demographic importance will continue to grow rapidly. By 2025, Hispanics will likely be the major ethnic group in Arizona, New Mexico, California, and Texas. By 2050, whites may constitute less than half the population in the United States. As we'll discuss in the next chapter, these trends are already changing the rules of consumer behavior and creating new opportunities for forward-looking companies.

Societies characterized by centuries of cultural homogeneity might be reluctant to accept immigrants—even though such a policy could prove vital in replenishing their dwindling labor forces. In Japan, where national identity remains predicated on the concept of *minzoku* (race), fewer foreigners are naturalized each year than in tiny Switzerland, whose population is only 5.8 percent the size.[60] In Europe, sluggish economic growth coupled with latent xenophobia has fostered the rise of far-right politicians, such as Jean-Marie Le

Pen in France and Jörg Haider in Austria, who campaigned on anti-immigration platforms.

Migrant workers are the very embodiment of the anxieties fostered by globalization—the fear that outsiders are threatening jobs and cultural cohesion. Even the European left has lashed back, with some warning that Muslim immigrants and their allegedly backward traditions threaten free speech, gay rights, and women's emancipation. Internationally renowned Italian journalist Oriana Fallaci gave voice to the latent fears of Europeans when she published "The Anger and the Pride" in the Italian newspaper *Corriera della Sera*, declaring that, "Giving space to the immigrants is equivalent to throwing out Dante Alighieri, Leonardo Da Vinci, Michelangelo, Raffaello, the Renaissance, the Risorgimento, the Liberty we have conquered, our Fatherland . . . If in certain places the women are so stupid as to accept the *chador* or rather the thickly-embroidered veil through which they see the world, too bad for them . . . But if they presume to impose the same things on me, in my home . . ."[61]

Denying access to migrants could create other problems. Immigration offers a pressure valve for developing countries lacking the economic and political infrastructure to integrate their youth into society. Ominously, the largest youth bulges are among the world's poorest and most politically unstable countries, including Pakistan, Afghanistan, Saudi Arabia, Yemen, and Iraq.

The CIA warns that "the failure to adequately integrate large youth populations in the Middle East and Sub-Saharan Africa is likely to perpetuate the cycle of political instability, ethnic wars, revolutions and anti-regime activities that already affect many of these countries. Unemployed youth provide exceptional fodder for radical movements and terrorist movements, particularly in the Middle East." (The U.S. government has even developed a demographics formula to predict political volatility: A country's probability of instability increases when the cohort of 15- to 29-year-olds surpasses the 30- to 54-year-old group by a ratio of 1.27 or more.)

The youth bulge is said to have been one of the underlying causes of the revolution that toppled the Shah in Iran, where, by the mid-1970s, 50 percent of the population was under 16 and two-thirds was under 30.[62] (Interestingly, the conservative Islamic regime in Iran now boasts the most effective fertility-control program in the world. Contraceptives are distributed for free, and engaged couples are required to take family-planning classes before they can qualify for a marriage license. Fertility rates have dropped from 5.2 in 1986 to 1.9 in 2002.)[63]

Developing nations that have not effectively curbed fertility rates are besieged with social crises. In Zimbabwe, where half the population is under the age of 18, young people are bearing the brunt of escalating unemployment and a deteriorating economy. Inflation there is expected to reach up to 700 percent, and as many as five million people are undernourished.

The Rise of the Megacity

Rapid urbanization compounds the problem. By 2007, for the first time in human history, the majority of people will live in cities. The subset of developing countries will follow quickly, crossing this threshold in 2020.[64] Driving this trend is the surge of rural workers who migrate to these cities in search of higher wages and better living conditions. Since the early 1980s, 130 million farmers have relocated to urban areas, where their earnings in just one month can be equivalent to their yearly income on a farm. Asian cities alone are home to 1.4 billion people—more than the urban centers of Europe, North America, Australasia, and Latin America combined. Megacities with populations of greater than five million will increase in number from 40 to 58 by 2015.[65] The most explosive growth of megacities will be in the developing world, where by 2015 the populations of many cities will exceed that of Los Angeles (*see Figure 2.2*).

> *By 2007, for the first time in human history, the majority of people will live in cities.*

According to the World Bank, 80 percent of future economic growth will occur in urban areas. Yet these vast metropolises will also create massive needs for infrastructure development. The Asian Development Bank estimates annual costs between $20 to $40 billion (U.S.) for the region.[66] Some of these megacities—such as Seoul and possibly Kuala Lumpur—are poised to be bustling

Figure 2.2 Growth in Megacities

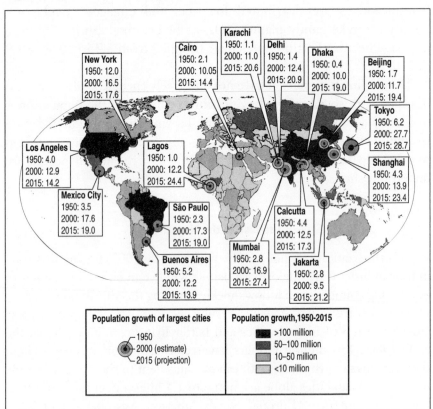

New York
1950: 12.0
2000: 16.5
2015: 17.6

Cairo
1950: 2.1
2000: 10.05
2015: 14.4

Karachi
1950: 1.1
2000: 11.0
2015: 20.6

Delhi
1950: 1.4
2000: 12.4
2015: 20.9

Dhaka
1950: 0.4
2000: 10.0
2015: 19.0

Beijing
1950: 1.7
2000: 11.7
2015: 19.4

Tokyo
1950: 6.2
2000: 27.7
2015: 28.7

Los Angeles
1950: 4.0
2000: 12.9
2015: 14.2

Lagos
1950: 1.0
2000: 12.2
2015: 24.4

Shanghai
1950: 4.3
2000: 13.9
2015: 23.4

Mexico City
1950: 3.5
2000: 17.6
2015: 19.0

São Paulo
1950: 2.3
2000: 17.3
2015: 19.0

Calcutta
1950: 4.4
2000: 12.5
2015: 17.3

Buenos Aires
1950: 5.2
2000: 12.2
2015: 13.9

Mumbai
1950: 2.8
2000: 16.9
2015: 27.4

Jakarta
1950: 2.8
2000: 9.5
2015: 21.2

Population growth of largest cities
- 1950
- 2000 (estimate)
- 2015 (projection)

Population growth, 1950-2015
- >100 million
- 50–100 million
- 10–50 million
- <10 million

Sources: United Nations and the National Geographic Society

centers of commerce and culture. They are already heavily investing in new infrastructure and are likely to maintain sufficient economic growth to keep their new arrivals productively employed. But other megacities threaten to emerge as ungovernable zones of crime, poverty, disease, and environmental degradation. Mumbai, Dhaka, Karachi, Lagos, Manila, and Jakarta face grave problems because economic growth and infrastructure investment have not kept pace with the urban boom. In Karachi, there are now fewer than three telephones for every 100 people.[67] Only half of Jakarta's residents have running water, while 80 percent of the surrounding country lacks access to piped water.[68]

Lagos, in particular, may be ground zero for the world's worst urban crisis in the coming decades. The Nigerian city already is struggling to accommodate a population of some 13 million. The combined influx of citizens—people seeking refuge from the country's civil conflicts, foreign refugees, and rural migrants—has driven annual population growth rates up to 8 percent.[69] The city is also a microcosm of the nation's feuding 250 ethnic and religious groups, among them Christians, Shi'ite Muslims, Sunni Muslims, Yoruba, Hausa, and Ibo. Add inadequate sanitation, water, and housing to this already volatile mix, and the explosive results are all too predictable.

Yet, the developing world is not just home to teeming, restless masses. Many countries also boast growing numbers of skilled workers that constitute a huge untapped pool of talent for global corporations. China produced 739,000 university graduates in 2000, equivalent to 13 percent of the total in advanced OECD economies.[70] Universities in India graduated some 167,000 students with science and engineering degrees, nearly two-thirds more than the United States.[71] Together, China and India now produce one-fifth of all doctoral students in science and engineering fields.[72] Numbers alone make them attractive locations for companies struggling to find skilled employees. But with substantially lower labor costs than Europe, North America, or Japan, these and other emerging markets also offer huge savings to corporations with production, research, and development facilities there. Already, China has the second highest number of researchers in the world, behind the United States but well ahead of rival Japan.[73]

Assessing the Implications

Corporations can take action to minimize the adverse affects of these demographic changes and maximize the bottom line. As labor markets tighten in aging societies, companies must tap into underutilized labor pools. Japanese corporations, for instance, might encourage more women to enter the workforce. Chikako Usui, an associate professor of sociology at the University of Missouri at St. Louis, urges Japanese companies to "engage in more mid-career and contractual hiring, snapping up talent for short-term projects to supplement a small number of core workers."[74]

Some companies are already embracing family-friendly policies that intend to encourage longer, more productive careers among female employees. The Japanese beauty products company Shiseido has 25,600 employees, 70 percent of whom are female. Shiseido has recognized that a declining birthrate means more female employees will be working and parenting at the same time. Since 1990, the company has implemented maternity leave and flex-time childcare systems. In 2003, the company opened its first on-site childcare facility named "Kangaroom" to provide a conducive employment environment for women and advance the company's ideal of promoting women's participation in the workforce. Similarly, Shinsei Bank provides childcare services for its employees, including free laundry services. The number of women leaving the company to raise children was high enough, in the eyes of Shinsei's human resources manager, to justify the operating costs of providing free childcare, about $94,250 (U.S.) per year.[75]

Searching More Shores

In tight labor markets where companies do not find critical talent at home, companies might lobby governments for more liberal immigration policies to attract foreign talent. Such open door policies are an easier sell in the United States, Canada, and Australia—countries created from scratch by immigrants—than in more culturally homogenous societies, such as Europe and Japan. That's not to say European companies aren't trying to change the status quo. They've begun lobbying governments for more foreign workers, despite the rising political backlash against migrants. "We have full employment here [in the Netherlands], and companies can't find workers," complains venture capitalist Roel Pieper, a former executive at Royal Philips Electronics and Compaq Computer Corp. "Yet politicians want to close the door."[76]

If companies have little luck bringing qualified labor to their home markets, the alternative is to outsource functions to key emerging markets. A.T. Kearney's *Offshore Location Attractiveness Index* demonstrates that countries such as India, Malaysia, the Czech Republic, Brazil, and the Philippines offer a combination of low costs, qualified labor, and solid business environments that makes offshoring particularly appealing. The world's top 100 financial institutions alone could save nearly $140 billion (U.S.) per year through 2008 by moving various operations abroad.[77] Offshore workers can provide such diverse services as back office support, call centers, help desks, and research and development. Outsourcing also helps promote economic growth in emerging countries, which in turn become expanding markets for Western goods and services.

Thanks to improved infrastructure, advancing Internet technologies, and increasing vendor sophistication, companies ranging from small physician groups to Fortune 100 companies like Aetna and UnitedHealth Group are already taking advantage of "brain arbitrage" and exploiting the cost differences between skilled professionals in countries around the world. In the United States alone, healthcare administration costs such as medical transcription, medical coding, and billing are estimated to be as high as $350 billion (U.S.).[78] Moving IT and business processes offshore to countries such as India has saved an average 30 to 40 percent.[79] Wipro Technologies in India is even offering clinical process outsourcing, whereby Indian radiologists analyze medical scans conducted in overseas hospitals and report back with their diagnoses.

The strategic advantages of offshoring, coupled with the demographic changes affecting the domestic labor supply, suggest that the current trend of corporate outsourcing may just be the beginning. In the future, offshoring may become even more prevalent in advanced economies as the aging workforce retires, middle managers move up, and younger workers are lacking. Some corporations may recruit a majority of their employees from an abundant pool of young, skilled men and women overseas.

A New Look at Older Workers

Alternatively, companies in the coming decades might find themselves embracing initiatives such as flexible, part-time employment with benefits to attract pensioners and retirees back to work, in contrast to the 1990s, when many corporations offered early retirement as a way to downsize.

A study by the National Council on the Aging found that the experiences of employers who deal with older workers often fly in the face of popular myths regarding older employees in the workplace. Companies report that they found older employees "had low turnover rates, were flexible and open to change, possessed up-to-date skills, were interested in learning new tasks, did not experience transportation problems, were willing to take on challenging tasks, had low absentee rates, [and] had few on-the-job accidents."[80]

Indeed, Peter Drucker (who's past 90 himself) estimates that the appropriate age for retirement today should be 79, rather than 65, since a 79-year-old now has the same physical and mental health as a 65-year-old did half a century ago. Daniel Yankelovich, the co-founder and chairman of Public Agenda, believes that companies may soon innovate programs that would use elder employees "for staff work assistance in relation to childcare, worker training, and judgment based on experience, especially for knowledge workers."[81]

Controlling the Healthcare Cost Spiral

Corporations can also minimize healthcare expenses in countries where they typically bear the cost burden. One option is to expand consumer choice and create more cost transparency by having employees purchase health services with specially designated funds instead of an annual deductible. For instance, medical technology company Medtronic pays up to $2000 (U.S.) a year per worker into a personal care account, while some 3000 Xerox employees have opted for a limited personal healthcare budget in return for complete control over how the money is spent.[82,83] General Motors is reducing healthcare expenses by compelling its more than 100 HMOs to share best practices with one another. The automaker ranks each healthcare provider on a number of critical services. "Health plans that do a better job on quality will get a greater market share from us," says Bruce Bradley, director of health plan strategy and public policy at General Motors.[84] The company is also reducing drug costs by encouraging its in-house pharmacists to optimize dosages and by encouraging the use of less expensive generics.

An estimated 81 percent of corporations do not have their own disease management programs, but they could potentially save millions by finding ways to motivate employees to better deal with chronic health problems such as diabetes and high cholesterol.[85] General Motors' asthma program in Indiana is reducing emergency room visits by 40 percent and hospital admissions by 15 percent. A pilot program on diabetes management at Ford gives bonuses to doctors who achieve treatment goals and rewards employees who agree to monitor blood glucose levels. The March of Dimes has even urged companies to implement prenatal education programs, since expenses related to pregnancy are the single largest component of healthcare costs for numerous corporations.

Finally, if corporations are to maintain their bearings, they must keep a careful eye on demographic trends. By doing so, they can acquire a sense of which countries will remain stable and which ones will dissolve into zones of political and social instability. As governments in advanced economies increasingly shift pension and healthcare costs to the private sector, companies will be able to strategically target their foreign investments by monitoring which countries have comparatively lower overall cost burdens relative to productivity levels.

Demographics: Three Possible Scenarios

Economic uncertainties, breakthroughs in agricultural and medical sciences, and government decisions on social insurance programs, healthcare issues, and immigration policies will all affect global population growth and migration patterns. As these variables interact, the outcomes are truly uncertain. Below are three possible scenarios that could play out between now and 2015 (*see Figure 2.3*).

Figure 2.3 Demographics: Three Possible Scenarios

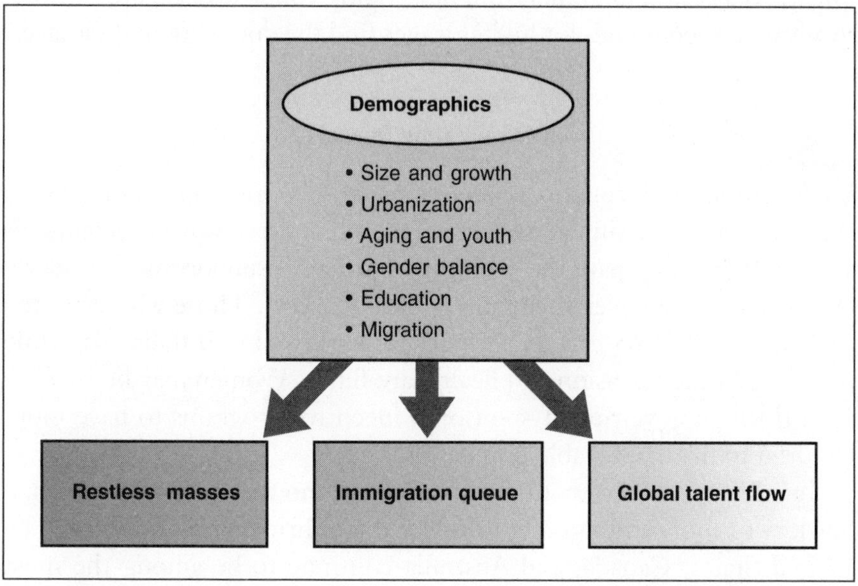

Source: *A.T. Kearney*

Restless Masses

Under the first scenario, *restless masses*, the global population surges, mostly in developing countries. Government promises on improved social insurance programs fail to fully materialize. Fertility rates climb as families insure themselves against economic uncertainties by relying on additional children to bring in extra income and to care for parents and grandparents in their old age. Millions of young people migrate from the countryside to the cities in pursuit of a better standard of living. Yet, in the poorest countries, there are not enough jobs to meet this surging demand, and urban centers become a breeding ground for widespread discontent, especially among restless young men. Africa, the Middle East, and Central Asia occasionally witness localized explosions of social and political unrest.

In developed countries, pension and healthcare programs are under serious strain: Older workers exit the workforce en masse as the costs of social programs skyrocket and retirement funds underperform. Yet, governments of Western countries decide to implement highly restrictive immigration policies, as other pressures such as the threat of terrorism and discontent with job losses to foreign workers in preceding years linger. As a result, migrants from developing countries who are flocking to advanced economies for higher wages find the door shut in their faces.

Immigration Queue

Under the second scenario, *immigration queue*, world population growth continues along a similar trajectory as today. In advanced economies such as Italy and Japan, the economic burden of supporting the elderly falls heavily on an ever-shrinking pool of workers. Those who expected to retire at 60 or 65 can now expect to work well into their 70s, while receiving limited pension and healthcare funds. Women may be encouraged through government-sponsored incentive programs to have more children to maintain stable population sizes.

In addition, governments of advanced economies may open national borders to more immigrants to offset their shrinking workforces. The United States, Canada, and Australia continue to be among the most popular destinations, since they are countries with a long history of immigration and offer more accommodating cultures. Immigration programs focus on attracting individuals with important skills and advanced education, permitting only a small number of immigrants with unique technical expertise to relocate to advanced economies. Other jobs will be outsourced to skilled workers abroad.

Corporations in advanced countries engage in a war for global talent as they fight for the limited pool of high-skilled, high-wage workers. At the same time, higher wages in advanced economies draw unskilled, low-wage workers from developing countries. The inflow of immigrants helps moderate wage pressures at the lower end of the income scale. Large numbers of poor, young, unskilled populations throughout Africa, Latin America, and developing Asia seek menial labor in North America, Europe, Australasia, and Northeast Asia.

Global Talent Flow

In the third scenario, *global talent flow*, population growth slows globally. As economic conditions improve and family planning programs become more widespread, fertility rates decline rapidly in developing countries. Among the advanced economies and China, dropping fertility rates and rising life expectancies have swelled the ranks of senior citizens. Some countries experience declines in their total workforce, which add to the fiscal burdens associated with supporting their aging societies. As seniors gain political clout through lobbying groups and pensioners' parties, most governments are compelled to expand their already generous medical coverage for retirees. Pension funds dominate equity markets, and up the pressure on traded companies to emphasize immediate dividends over long-term investment, which in turn impedes innovation and growth.

As the ratio of workers to retirees continues to shrink, countries increasingly utilize previously untapped demographic groups—such as women and younger people—to enter the workforce. Moreover, to make up for the labor shortage, industrialized countries have no choice but to open their doors to substantial levels of immigration from all regions of the world. Immigration programs expand for all categories of labor, placing special emphasis on recruiting workers with advanced degrees and rare skills. With open labor markets, skilled professionals migrate to major emerging markets such as China, Korea, and Malaysia, where new metropolitan areas expand to accommodate economic growth and absorb the new skilled migrants.

At the same time, higher wages in advanced economies draw unskilled, low-wage workers from developing countries, since industrialized countries view immigration as a force for moderating wage pressures at the lower end of the income scale. The billions of dollars of wages that migrants send back to their families at home provides a crucial lifeline for developing countries that have not yet found their place in the global economy.

Another Paradox

Demography is destiny—yet that destiny is still very much a work in progress. Which scenario will win out? It depends on multiple, intertwining dynamics, whose timing and likelihood may elude even the most skilled demographers. Demography reveals yet another paradox in our "world out of balance"—namely, that the drivers of the global business environment are not inherently good or bad. It's all a matter of perspective.

For instance, nobody would dispute that the advances in medical technology during the last half-century have been a positive development. Yet the longer lifespans that have resulted from those medical breakthroughs have yielded a negative impact through the global aging crisis.

Similarly, as the next chapter will reveal, changing demographic trends offer unique opportunities to businesses that can anticipate these developments. For example, lower fertility rates and smaller families translate into more disposable income for women. While rapid urbanization will challenge developing countries, sprawling megacities offer a prepackaged infrastructure for marketing and selling products and services to those living at the bottom of the income pyramid.

Successful corporations will understand that they operate in a world shaped by these trends, and that they have a critical stake in the outcomes. Those that recognize the impact of external trends may be less vulnerable to strategic surprises. More than that, corporations that capitalize on the ebb and flow of the demographic tide will find themselves ahead of the game as they compete for human capital and consumers worldwide.

The New Consumer

Forging Bonds in a Fragmented World

I know half the money I spend on advertising is wasted, I just don't know which half.

— John Wanamaker, department store pioneer, 1886

With demographic transformations taking place in societies worldwide, the lives and lifestyles of the world's consumers are changing dramatically. In emerging markets, low-income consumers are poised to graduate into the middle class, while consumers in advanced markets will become increasingly wealthy and demanding. Companies will need to create emotional bonds with consumers worldwide who have become more empowered, less predictable, and increasingly fragmented. These twenty-first century consumers are pushing companies beyond their traditional roles: Providers of goods and services must now satisfy deeper emotional needs, convey distinctive ideals, or provide unique experiences for users. While companies face unprecedented opportunities to expand consumer markets and deepen consumer loyalty, building enduring relationships with consumers will only grow more difficult. Among other factors, rising consumer activism has prompted corporations to devise strategies to minimize the risk of backlash against their brands.

Consumer Power Shift: The Rise of Emerging Markets

The consumer class has gone through rapid transformations throughout its relatively short history. Modest advances in income were largely diluted by population growth, and the average standard of living remained at a subsistence level. Beginning with the Industrial Revolution, conditions began to change, and per capita income has been rising rapidly ever since. With incomes on the rise, individuals finally escaped the Malthusian trap and mass consumer markets were born.

Until very recently, middle- and upper-income spending power has been concentrated in the advanced economies, with 70 percent of global consumers located in the industrialized countries of North America, Europe, and Japan.[1] These "global consumers" purchase the bulk of the world's consumer products. At the other end of the scale, Africa and the Middle East barely register at all, and the world's most populous nations—such as China, India, and Indonesia—have remained disappointing consumer markets with only a relatively small group of potential customers. Ten years from now, though, the map of consumption power could be quite different. As we saw in the previous chapter, demographic changes and the widespread effects of globalization will likely shift the locus of consumer markets. For the first time in history, nearly 80 percent of middle consumers may be living outside the industrialized world (*see Figures 3.1 and 3.2*).

China alone may boast 595 million middle-income consumers and 82 million upper-middle-income consumers. In India, between 30 and 40 million people are joining the middle class each year.[2] Throughout the developing world, these new middle entrants may tip the scales and shift purchasing power away from North America, Europe, and Japan. They will be able to buy world-class products like cars, refrigerators, and washing machines. The defining mantra of consumption of these consumers will be *more stuff*. These middle-class spenders will concentrate on acquiring goods that improve their quality of life and display their new status. They will have a range of options, including competitive local brands.

Meanwhile, much of today's middle class in the advanced economies will likely graduate into higher-income groups to make up the upper consumer class of tomorrow. These consumers, having just moved up from the comfortable but nonextravagant middle group, will be seeking

Figure 3.1 Global Consumption Patterns

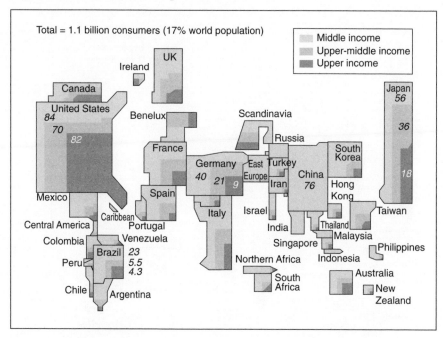

Total = 1.1 billion consumers (17% world population)

Legend:
- Middle income
- Upper-middle income
- Upper income

A block this size represents 10 million consumers; consumer population is in millions
Sources: World Bank, Economist Intelligence Unit, U.S. Census Bureau, and A.T. Kearney analysis

more experiences: high-end luxury goods, custom features and add-ons, individualized leisure activities and entertainment options, travel and tourism, and vacation homes.[3] Changing demographic trends may make them increasingly heterogeneous, as they express new lifestyle choices, spending patterns, and increasingly varied needs.

Traditionally, middle-aged workers in their peak earning years have led consumer spending. But already, spending power of different age groups is changing, with kids and older spenders challenging middle-age dominance. In the United States, 33 million teenagers are spending $175 billion annually—nearly as much as the gross domestic product (GDP) of Turkey.[4] "Tweens" aged 8 through 14 (with the support of their beleaguered parents) spend an additional $164 billion.[5] These young trendsetters spend differently than their parents do, focusing on education, electronics, and entertainment, in addition to influencing

Figure 3.2 2015 Global Consumption Patterns

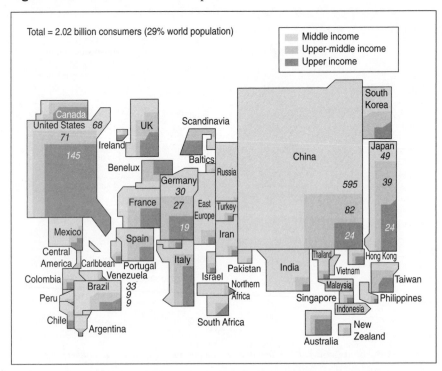

☐ *A block this size represents 10 million consumers; consumer population is in millions*

Sources: World Bank, Economist Intelligence Unit, U.S. Census Bureau, and A.T. Kearney analysis

their parents' spending patterns. And they are the wave of the future in emerging markets, where young consumers may seek out clothing, consumer durables, and first homes.

At the other end of the age spectrum, spending by older consumers has grown the fastest over the past ten years as these shoppers direct their money toward healthcare and pharmaceuticals, expensive home furnishings, and dream vacations. The amazing thing is that these increases are being seen even before the baby boomers retire. When that happens, spending by this older consumer group may soar.

Changing social and cultural trends are also contributing to the diversity and complexity of consumer markets. In industrialized countries, growing female workforce participation, later marriages, and lower fertility rates mean that women have more disposable income for consumer goods that fulfill individual rather than family needs. For instance, young, single Japanese women are some of the most fervent purchasers of expensive luxury goods. In Tokyo 94 percent of women in their twenties own a Louis Vuitton luxury good, and 92 percent own something by Gucci, even though these goods sell for 40 percent more than they do in Europe.[6]

Higher divorce rates also translate into higher personal spending, as newly single men and women seek to boost their self-images and find new life partners. In the United States, the number of two-wage families has been rising for the past three decades, growing from 46 percent to 60 percent.[7] The proportion of working mothers with young children has risen in most Western European countries in the past decade, doubling from 30 to 60 percent in the Netherlands, and from 40 to almost 60 percent in the United Kingdom.[8] These trends contribute to increased demand for products from pre-assembled meals to gifts and other goods that make up for lack of time to spend with children.

In addition, rising exposure to international brands, coupled with higher levels of education and travel, have prompted consumer tastes to become more sophisticated. Today's consumers want much more than products with functional and technical value. They're looking to satisfy emotional needs, convey cultural values, or offer new experiences.

From Minorities to Majorities

The complexity of consumer markets is also influenced by migration across national boundaries. The percentage of foreign-born population in the United Kingdom has increased from 3.4 percent to 4.5 percent from 1995 to 2002, and in the United States, from 8.8 percent to 11.5 percent.[9] Immigration into the United States, Europe, and potentially Japan will not only alter the ethnic composition of these developed nations, it will also reshape their purchasing habits.

In the United States, people of African, Asian, Hispanic, and Native American ancestry already make up a quarter of the population, with minorities actually a majority in the District of Columbia, New Mexico, and Hawaii. By 2025, California and Texas will join the list.

By 2050, the Hispanic population alone is projected to make up a quarter of the country's population.[10] U.S. companies spent years virtually ignoring America's surging Hispanic population, acting under the assumption that Latinos would eventually blend in, assimilate, learn English, and behave like any other U.S. consumer. Companies also assumed that Hispanics were too poor to have any significant purchasing power.

That was a big mistake. The purchasing power of the Latino population may soon triple. There is an emerging Hispanic middle class, with slightly more than 25 percent of the workforce earning $35,000 or more, while 12 percent earn $50,000 or more. This community's disposable income is growing at nearly 9 percent per year, with collective spending power expected to reach more than $900 billion by 2007.[11] Hispanics represent the only segment of the U.S. population with large, growing families, driving demand for diapers, clothes, and toys. Hispanic women spend 0.86 percent of their median household income on apparel, as opposed to the national U.S. average of 0.76 percent.[12]

Hispanic communities are just one of the many ethnic and religious groups that are attracting companies' attention. Muslim communities are another long-neglected consumer demographic. The New York-based Center for American Muslim Research and Information estimates that the purchasing power of the six to eight million Muslims living in the United States is $12 billion annually, equivalent to the GDP of a small country like Panama.[13] France has the largest Muslim population in Europe, with three to six million who represent a large and growing market.

Within the next decade, the number of middle-income consumers will increase dramatically in Islamic countries such as Indonesia, Pakistan, Malaysia, and Iran. Currently, the Muslim population in Indonesia already totals some 200 million, and in India, 130 million. These consumer markets have remained largely untapped by global companies. Moreover, the perception that America's war on terrorism is anti-Muslim, coupled with ongoing resentment of the United States' close relations with Israel, has sparked boycotts of many prominent U.S. brands and franchises operating overseas. U.S. exports to Saudi Arabia alone fell by more than 40 percent in the first three months of 2002.[14]

Enthusiasts of everything from Gaelic football to Polynesian cooking are coming together online.

A more diverse demographic, discomfort with large corporations, and technology have all converged, allowing new identity groups to emerge and express their preferences. Niche consumer groups, which previously had been unable to coalesce, have been drawn closer by the World Wide Web, as enthusiasts of everything from Gaelic football to Polynesian cooking are coming together online and forming virtual communities.

Now that the Internet has opened the doorway of nearly unlimited choice to shoppers and alternative transaction schemes, global brands are finding it harder to retain customers. Privacy concerns are changing the dynamics of Internet commerce. Net-savvy consumers are purchasing cyberscrub software and e-mail encryption to protect their personal information. Advances in cryptography, digital currency, and smart cards may spell the death of hard currency and break open e-commerce markets in the developing world where credit cards are scarce. This makes the Internet's most appealing shoppers—tech-savvy and affluent—more difficult to track and understand. The number of these shoppers may continue rising, as both Internet usage and increases in purchasing power appear to be cutting across age groups, income levels, and cultures. At this rate, the manner in which consumers communicate and spend money may become unrecognizable to us in just a few years.

The Myth of the "Global Consumer"

If there was ever a golden age in which mass marketing was all companies needed to reach homogenous markets and predictable consumers, it is long gone. Traditional brand management systems, pioneered by Procter & Gamble, were very successful in the 1950s and 1960s. Theodore Levitt, emeritus professor at the Harvard Business School, pushed the idea of the virtues of mass marketing to new heights in his famous 1983 article, "The Globalization of Markets." In it, he wrote: "Different cultural preferences, national tastes . . . and business institutions are vestiges of the past . . . Everywhere everything gets more and more like everything else as the world's preference structure is relentlessly homogenized."[15]

But the world has not become what Levitt envisioned. Rather, tastes have become more fragmented. Worldwide, people are increasingly spending their money in ways that reflect their individual values, which, in turn, are embedded in their respective cultures. As such, global strategies based on uniform tastes have not lived up to their early billings.

Instead, companies are "going native" in terms of product expansion. Ford's Mondeo sought to be a "global car." But the car was only successful when adapted—in name and design—for local markets in Europe and North America. MTV relies primarily on local music and local administration for programming in Europe, Asia, and South America. Coca-Cola now has over 230 brands in more than 200 countries, and one of its top sellers in Japan is a canned coffee drink. In China, Volkswagen and General Motors have both introduced small family cars, the VW Santana and the Buick Sail. The Sail even features jumbo-sized cup holders big enough to accommodate the thick jars the Chinese use to hold their tea.[16]

The sweeping changes in consumer demographics, demands, and perceptions of global brands simultaneously present new opportunities and challenges for retailers and suppliers. How have firms responded to these consumer changes? With global branding under siege, firms are exploring new ways to adapt. Corporations are attempting to bring consumers back into focus by identifying the attitudes, needs, and values underlying different age brackets, income levels, and ethnic groups.

For instance, companies are increasingly targeting senior citizens in advanced markets who—after being tied down by jobs and child-rearing—hunger for experiences that were denied them in their youth. Healthier and wealthier than grandparents of generations past, the over-65 crowd seeks to flex both their minds and bodies. As Roger Heeler, professor of marketing at York University observes, it is dawning on the travel industry that not all elderly tourists "want to sit in a coach with 30 other seniors and two 20-year-old guides and be shown the sights they shouldn't miss before they pass from the mortal coil." The Canada-based Eldertreks was one of the first companies to adapt to the senior travel market by offering people 50 years and older small-group adventures—such as camel trips through Mongolia—in more than 50 countries. Elderly travelers are also fuelling a growing field of "study travel," sponsored by professional organizations, zoos, universities, and museums.[17]

Similarly, DeBeers marketed its new line of three-stone jewelry to elderly women in Japan by appealing to a similar desire for personal journey and experience. Marketing research found that, among elderly women, purchases of upscale products were largely driven by desires for self-improvement. The company's campaign emphasized that the three-stone jewelry represented the past, present, and future of a woman's personal journey. DeBeers' marketing arm, the Diamond Trading Company (DTC), launched print ads featuring women studying overseas, running a café, and taking up photography. "The market was about accumulation of past life, but also rediscovery [of themselves] and an ever-evolving journey. This was an emotional hook for us," explains Peter Bromwitz, the account director at DTC's ad agency J. Walter Thompson in Japan.[18]

Indeed, senior citizen advocacy groups such as AARP and specialized marketing firms such as the San Francisco-based Age Wave are striving to convince companies and advertisers to dispense with the stereotype that the elderly are too set in their ways to explore new brands and products. "If that notion were real, I would be sitting here in Thom McCann shoes, have a Chevy Impala parked in my garage, be wearing a Timex watch, have brushed my teeth with Crest and, for a little arthritis in my shoulder, I would have taken St. Joseph aspirin," complains Ken Dychtwald, the president at Age Wave. "All of which is ridiculous," he adds. "There's not one product that I use today that I was using in my late teens."[19]

Even though young people tend to be the first to buy new products, consumers over 50 may also do so. The Global Consumer Innovation Study, which links consumer personality traits to a variety of demographic and adoption factors, shows that about 12 percent of consumers 50 and over are innovators or early adopters of new products, especially high-tech products. The study was cosponsored by A.T. Kearney, the Marshall School of Business at the University of Southern California, and the Judge Institute of Management at Cambridge University.

Perhaps the most self-defeating assumption among marketers is the belief that the elderly are technophobes wary about using the Internet for any purpose beyond sending e-mails to the grandkids. In truth, a rising number of "silver surfers" are reaching for the computer mouse. Nielsen/Net Ratings reports that senior citizens are the fastest growing age group online in the United States, surging 25 percent per year to 9.6 million web surfers from home and work in October 2003.[20] In the United Kingdom, this age bracket represents 12 percent of all online users.[21] A 2002 survey found that 52 percent of older consumers are using the web to make purchases, while 38 percent research stocks and check investments.[22] Banks have begun actively courting this group of consumers, making them aware of the advantages of online services. As more and more retirees take to the road, they appreciate the convenience of being able to monitor their finances and pay their credit card bills from a cyber café in Venice or Las Vegas.

Targeting the Young and the Younger

Corporations are also adopting new strategies to confront a fickle youth market that celebrates its freedom of choice and individualism even as pressure from society and peer groups demands conformity. In 2001, the Swiss company Nestlé went global with a message of empowerment when it launched a $30 million marketing campaign to promote Nescafé to coffee drinkers aged 16 to 24. "Coffee is now the beverage of choice amongst young people," notes Andrew Ward, worldwide account director on Nescafé. "The role of coffee for young people has fundamentally changed from one based around functional needs to one which allows them to participate in an exciting and provocative world, and which offers friendship and sociability, inspiration and creativity, opportunities and possibilities."[23]

Mobile phones have also found global resonance among the youth market. But instead of using the phones to speak to one another, young people from Europe to Asia have embraced the medium of text messaging, which concurrently taps into desires for individualism, empowerment, and acceptance. "Teens adopt phones massively because they want to communicate, but texting can convey codes—the private intimate communication," observes Jerome Traisnel, the CEO of Freever, a mobile community services provider.[24]

Short messaging systems (SMS) provide on-the-go young people with a unique opportunity to keep in contact with one another and organize their social lives. Research by Virgin Mobile shows that in the United Kingdom, half of these young phone owners spend a substantial portion of their monthly phone bill on text messaging.

In fact, mobile phones are the biggest monthly expense for a quarter of these youngsters—more than fashion, music, and social activities.[25] South Korea-based LG helped lead the way by producing mobile phone handsets offering an assortment of ring tones, cartoon characters, and individual "wallpaper" applications that appealed to its young customers' need for personalization and customization.[26] Chinese mobile phone users sent more than 100 billion text messages in 2003 to stay connected with friends and family, not to mention other popular services like joke downloads.[27]

It appears that the young consumers keep getting younger. The mail order catalog dELiA*s, aimed at young women from 10 to 24, has successfully marketed merchandise for preteen girls, offering whimsical, age-appropriate denim, printed t-shirts, and iridescent nail polish, fulfilling these young consumers' need for fun, self-confidence, and acceptance by peers. Yet the line refrains from make-up and fashion designs that look too mature. Likewise, Pottery Barn Kids and PBTeens have been primary drivers of revenue growth for the furniture chain Pottery Barn, capitalizing on the premise that the ability to influence one's room décor enhances young people's self-identity and allows expression of their personal tastes.[28]

Rich Consumer, Poor Consumer

In addition to learning the distinctive attitudes, needs, and values underlying different age groups, some corporations are also tapping into broad social and economic trends as a way of appealing to changing groups of consumers. With per capita incomes rising in North America, Europe, and Japan, there is a growing demand for luxury brands and prestige products. Journalist and commentator David Brooks foreshadowed this trend in his witty book on upscale culture, *BOBOs in Paradise: The New Upper Class and How They Got There.*[29]

Brooks described *bobos*, or bourgeois bohemians, as the new information age elite. They have "one foot in the bohemian world of creativity and another foot in the bourgeois realm of ambition and worldly success." This group has established the now familiar consumption patterns of the up-and-coming: luxury cars, kitchens lined with granite and stainless steel, microbrewed beers, free-range chicken, and dainty $5 bags of heritage lettuce.

This new elite has its own "code of financial correctness," which transforms conspicuous consumption into a statement of personal values and an expression of self-worth. Like today's growing class of choosy consumers, bobos want to be associated with the highest quality products available. That's why they eagerly buy goods labeled "professional quality," from kitchen equipment to stereos, even when they have no professional association. Bobos also spend heavily in pursuit of "perfect" items packaged in small doses, from miniature French potatoes to $5 bottles of water.

Brooks points out that the sport utility vehicle is testimony to the new ways Bobos think about their possessions, especially tools. In the past, people either played or worked, but the modern worker who deals in abstract concepts, data, or images all day likes to come home and haul people, animals, and stuff around in a mega-cruiser. Utility is turned on its head into sport.

Corporations that can tap into these consumption desires with enhanced brand images and differentiated products reap the largest gains. That's why some of the financial analysts' favorites are companies that sell luxury in small doses, such as Starbucks, Panera Breads, and high-end appliance makers.

Paradoxically, demand for consumer products is not only growing and evolving among the nouveau riche, but also among the very poor. C. K. Prahalad, a professor of corporate strategy at the University of Michigan, and Allen Hammond, of the World Resources Institute, generated considerable buzz with their *Harvard Business Review* article, "Serving the World's Poor, Profitably."

Prahalad and Hammond argue that the four billion people earning less than $2000 per year (65 percent of the world's population) represent a vast untapped market for corporations.[30] India, for instance, has some 13 million customers who are middle income or above, but 800 million who fall into the lower-income bracket.[31]

In presenting their case, Prahalad and Hammond debunk several misconceptions about selling to the poor. Take, for instance, the simple proposition that the poor don't have much money. While that might be true at an individual level, it is not true when you consider the aggregate buying power of entire communities. In rural Bangladesh, the average villager has a per capita income of only $200. Yet, they collectively pool their resources to invest in telecommunications. "Grameen Telecom's village phones, which are owned by a single entrepreneur but used by an entire community, generate an average revenue of roughly $90 a month—and as much as $1000 a month in some large villages."[32]

As we mentioned in the last chapter, megacities are mushrooming throughout the developing world. As these metropolises grow, so will the aggregate purchasing power of the poor. Already, the total purchasing power of the poor in Rio de Janeiro is $600 per person, or $1.2 billion. Rapid urbanization offers another benefit to firms—these megacities already offer an extensive commercial infrastructure for marketing and selling products to the poor.

Another myth Prahalad and Hammond deflate is that those with modest income are too preoccupied with fulfilling basic needs (such as food and clothing) to waste their money on nonessential luxury items. As they point out, in the Mumbai shantytown of Dharavi, 85 percent of

> In the Mumbai shantytown of Dharavi, 85 percent of households own a television set.

households own a television set and 75 percent own a pressure cooker and mixer.[33] Because people with modest income do not expect to be able to purchase a home, fear the risk of theft, or have little access to banking, they tend not to save their money. Instead, they spend it on products and services that will make a genuine improvement in their lives right now. Consumers and households in rural India or Thailand who cannot afford a car may instead buy a motorcycle or scooter, as Japan's Yamaha Motor aptly identified. Young consumers in India purchase moderately priced products such as wristwatches from Timex with an MP3 music-playing function, the sleek Philips India MP3 key ring that can be worn as a neck pendant, and the new iPod, the digital music player by Apple Computer. Such products meet their individual style and leisure needs but are still affordable for those of modest means.[34]

Hindustan Lever, the Indian subsidiary of Unilever, stands out as a leader in providing high-quality, affordable products to the bottom of the income pyramid. In 1999, the company announced the nationwide launch of its "Max Uno" ice-cream candies, available in two flavors (orange and cola), selling for only one rupee each.

In marketing the product, Hindustan Lever touted the ice cream's delicious taste and affordable price, as well as the company's high standards of hygiene and safety. Hindustan Lever even obtained an endorsement from the president of the Bangalore South Consumer Protection Society, who proclaimed: "Ice candies from recognized manufacturers of ice cream, at an affordable price, is a welcome initiative. It provides children, even those from the lower income groups, with an option for healthier food. The same money which children would otherwise spend on ice cream products that could harm their health can now be spent on hygienic and unadulterated ice candies."[35] Such confections emerged as the fastest-growing products in

Hindustan Lever's portfolio. The company has enjoyed similar successes with laundry detergent packaged in small, affordable quantities, and iodized salt that provides health benefits for children and does not boil away in Indian cooking.

One Size Fits One

As global migration trends make countries more heterogeneous, retailers have also targeted the needs of growing ethnic populations. Businesses that seek to expand their share of the Hispanic market have studied attitudes and values of these consumers and have learned that one-size-fits-all sales strategies are doomed to failure.

For instance, Dan Vargas, the executive vice president of Pinnacle Associates Group, an Atlanta-based advertising agency that specializes in targeting Hispanic and African-American consumers, warns that some types of bargains aren't universally appealing. For instance, the coupons that mainstream Americans love tend to fall flat among the Latino community, as some people think using them makes them look cheap.[36]

Similarly, Latinos are uneasy with promotions along the lines of "Buy one, get one free," since such offers imply the manufacturer has been taking advantage of them all along. Instead, Vargas emphasizes the importance of establishing grassroots connections with the community—a sentiment echoed by Sonia Maria Green, who was hired by GM as its director of Hispanic sales and marketing after the automaker's share of the Latino market fell by 11 percent. Green re-educated GM about Latino culture, encouraging the company to enhance its image by sponsoring local events and getting executives to speak Spanish in 30-second commercials. She even went to dealerships to retrain salespeople. "Latinos don't go into a dealership by themselves," explains Green. "They'll bring their father, their mother . . . their sister, whatever. They come in a group. So how can a dealer put them in a cubicle with two seats?" GM's strategy paid off, as it saw its market share within the Hispanic community rise by five points. "We advertised to their heart," Green said. "The people love it."

Another company appealing to this consumer group is Kmart, which introduced its Thalia Sodi Collection—named for the international pop star—at 335 stores in cities such as Los Angeles, Phoenix, and Miami where there is a large Hispanic population. The collection includes branded apparel for women and girls, as well as footwear, jewelry, and bed and bath products. Nationwide sales to Hispanics now account for 17 percent of Kmart's revenue.[37]

Other businesses have sought to appeal to untapped religious niche markets, for instance, Muslim communities in the United States and around the world. Some foreign companies have sought to ride the wave of anti-Americanism—the most notable example being Mecca Cola, a soft drink launched by French-Muslim entrepreneur Tawfik Mathlouthi to challenge the dominance of Coca-Cola. Promising consumers that 20 percent of the profits will go to charities operating in Palestinian territories and nongovernmental organizations in Europe, the bottles bear the slogan, "No more drinking stupid, drink with commitment."[38] Similarly, local franchises operating in the Arab world have sought to adapt to the shifting political landscape: In Saudi Arabia, some McDonald's restaurants pledged to donate 25 cents earned on every sandwich to the Al Quds Intifada Fund, which supports Palestinian children's hospitals.[39]

Yet, politics alone do not drive consumption patterns, and it is possible to tap into the Muslim market, as with any other community, by appealing to its unique needs and values. For instance, since *sharia* (Islamic law) forbids paying or collecting interest, banks are seeking to accommodate Muslims who can't take out loans to pay for cars, homes, or education. The Islamic branch of HSBC bank provides a mortgage service that allows the borrower to enter a lease-to-own arrangement with the bank.[40] Dow Jones launched an "Islamic Index" that, in keeping with religious law, reassures Muslim investors by excluding firms whose products include tobacco, alcohol, pornography, and weapons, as well as companies in the conventional financial-services industry that collect interest.

Other examples of Muslim-oriented marketing include Canadian outlets of the Swedish home furnishing company Ikea, featuring products such as trays for serving sweets during the holiday of Ramadan. Hallmark introduced a line of greeting cards to commemorate Eid ul-Fitr (the Feast of Fast-Breaking), which marks the conclusion of Ramadan.[41] LG Electronics Inc., the second largest mobile handset manufacturer in South Korea, has launched a new cellular phone that, using global positioning system technology, will allow Muslims to locate the position of Mecca for prayer, no matter where they are in the world.[42] Heineken has purchased a majority stake in Egypt's Al-Ahram Beverages Co. in the hope that the brewer's nonalcoholic malt beverages might serve as a venue into other Muslim countries.[43]

As always, companies must avoid cultural insensitivities. McDonald's inadvertently offended Muslims when, as part of its 1994 World Cup promotion, its paper bags featured the flags of 24 nations competing in the summer playoffs. One of those countries was Saudi Arabia, whose flag bears the Arabic passage, "There is no God but Allah, and Mohammed is his Prophet." Devout Muslims were not pleased to see this declaration of faith stained with ketchup and crumpled up in trash cans.[44]

Cracking the Cultural Code

Serving the unique needs of different consumer groups is just one way to reach the consumer in a nonthreatening, personal way, but cracking each targeted consumer group one at a time can turn into an uphill battle as these groups become more fragmented.

Another strategy is to make a broad appeal to groups that seem diverse on the surface but actually share underlying values. The key to this approach is to employ psychographics that decipher archetypes and break the cultural codes of markets. Archetypes are deeply rooted concepts and form what Swiss psychologist Carl Jung called the "collective unconscious." Arts, sports, business, politics, and social customs are outward manifestations—shadows, if you will—of these broad, widely shared archetypes. By using them, easily recognizable stories and images can provide emotional impact, while performing an end-run around cultural defense mechanisms.

For instance, archetype researcher G. Clotaire Rapaille has found that emotional responses dictated by cultural mores play a greater role in food choices than cost and nutrition. In the United States, some consumers think of their bodies as machines and view food as fuel to fill up the tank and get ready for the day. In contrast French Canadians—vive la difference—tend to see their bodies as instruments for pleasure and believe eating should be an enjoyable experience. As a result, Americans are more amenable to food advertising that promotes value and quantity, while French Canadians may prefer the association of food to quality of life.[45] According to the international marketing firm Young & Rubicam, companies enjoy greater economic benefit when their brands are aligned with archetypes. The market value-added of brands closely defined with an archetype rose 97 percent over more confused brands. The economic value-added rose 66 percent more than weakly aligned brands.

Archetypes help deepen emotional connections that underlie brand loyalty and retain consumers. It is up to five times less expensive to sell to a loyal customer than it is to create a new one. Archetypes improve retention by identifying basic human desires. Firms do not create archetypes; they play to them. Archetypes are part of societal consciousness, and many firms have successfully built solid brand names by appealing to them. Nike's name and marketing evoke "the hero," while Harley-Davidson's bad-boy image evokes "the outlaw," and status-conscious American Express consciously plays to images of "the ruler."

America particularly loves "the hero" archetype, best epitomized by the cowboy. The spirit of adventure associated with taming the West is an important feature of America's historical consciousness. In addition to the famous "Marlboro Man" cigarette ads, Japan's Mitsubishi effectively plays to this cowboy spirit through the deft marketing of its Montero SUV ("conquer the road less traveled"), inviting consumers to use its four-wheel drive to vanquish the West all over again.

Similarly, in China, BMW associated itself with Bao Ma, the mythological treasure horse. To modern Chinese familiar with folklore, Bao Ma evokes a sense of wealth, power, and influence. This helps to explain why Chinese consumers are willing to pay for the cars, despite import duties that raise prices to twice their level in Germany. Lueder Paysen, senior vice president at the sales division of BMW Group, estimates that there are now 1.3 million middle class Chinese consumers who can afford a BMW. "These people want to show that they are successful and buying a BMW is one way to show it," he observes.[46]

> *Firms do not create archetypes; they play to them.*

Starbucks' success can partly be attributed to its alignment with the "explorer" archetype, which seeks to convey the joy of discovery and new ideas. Starbucks' seafaring logo, earthy colors, and even the name (taken from a character in *Moby Dick*), play into this imagery. Howard Schultz, who spearheaded the purchase of Starbucks in 1987, was in part inspired by the book *The Great, Good Place*, by sociologist Ray Oldenburg, which described the human need for a "third place" beyond home or work. Starbucks helps fulfill the desire for learning about others by providing a venue for friends and even strangers to meet and interact. It is also a natural fit with bookstores and universities, places where people seek self-improvement and new ideas. Starbucks' archetype-focused branding has paid off, with *BusinessWeek* reporting that the coffee juggernaut saw the biggest jump in brand value among global brands between 2000 and 2001.[47]

One of the most daring examples of marketing to a psychological niche is the Chrysler PT Cruiser. Emotional reactions tend to be quite strong, as some people love the car's style while others despise it. ("The #1 ugliest car on the road," declares one of many online auto enthusiasts.) But that's precisely the point—a certain segment of the population is intensely enthusiastic about the PT Cruiser, making the car an unmitigated success. It won the Motor Trend 2001 Car of the Year Award, and its psychographic design has captured imaginations worldwide. The car is bursting with personality and flavor, touching on several key archetypes: the 1920s gangster hood and fenders (rebellion), the 1950s hot rod body (freedom), the "Mad Max" rugged design (survival), and the SUV features (exploring and conquering).[48] Not surprisingly, it has crossed demographic boundaries and is exciting teenagers and 80-year-olds alike. In the first year after its March 2000 introduction, 175,000 Cruisers were sold. Moreover, at a time when worldwide auto sales were expected to contract, demand for the car was so strong that Chrysler invested $300 million in 2001 to boost worldwide production from 180,000 to 310,000 units.[49]

Advertising Without Ads: Marketing Revisited

Unearthing archetypes or identifying unique needs of consumers—old or young, American or Chinese, Hispanic or white, Muslim or Catholic, rich or poor—is just one piece of a much larger puzzle. As consumers become more diverse and demanding, they will become more powerful as well. True, corporations retain tremendous resources, but the consumer market scales are tipping in favor of assertive customers.

More importantly, as big corporate brands seek to bond with consumers on a more emotional level, they are also falling prey to the rising tide of consumer activism, with ordinary consumers in some places resisting what they see as corporate messages that do not show sufficient sensitivity to their way of life. The backlash against intrusive global brands is fraying the relationship between corporations and consumers, presenting a tremendous challenge for global brand management. Consumers in industrialized countries already feel saturated by marketing that infiltrates every aspect of their personal lives. Consumers in Europe and Asia see U.S. brands as an assault upon their cultural identity. Consumers in the youth market reject obvious attempts to manipulate their buying habits and transform them into walking billboards. Consumers in the Middle East and throughout the developing world see corporate brands as icons of U.S. political and economic hegemony.

As Harvard Business School marketing professor John Quelch explains it, "we are witnessing the emergence of a consumer lifestyle with broad international appeal that is grounded in a rejection of American capitalism, American foreign policy and Brand America."[50] Corporate marketing tactics must reach fragmented, savvy consumers—but not overwhelm them.

Fortunately, newer tools can help corporations to establish or rekindle the bond with the consumer and make their brands less intrusive, less culturally threatening. Chief among these is "viral" or "buzz" marketing, which targets early adopters or "bees" who act as the critical link between a new trend and its ultimate emergence in the mainstream. These early adopters build brand loyalty through word-of-mouth or (by way of the Internet) word-of-mouse techniques.

For instance, when Hotmail started in 1996, it spent only $50,000 on advertising, a fraction of the $20 million spent by Juno, Hotmail's closest competitor at the time. Hotmail grew through viral marketing by offering free e-mail addresses and services, and attaching a simple tag at the bottom of every free message sent out that read: "Get your private, free e-mail at http://www.hotmail.com." Every person who sent an e-mail through Hotmail became a de facto salesperson for the product. In just 18 months, the company went from zero to 12 million members.[51] Even more astonishing, Hotmail became the largest e-mail service in countries such as India and Sweden, where the company had done no advertising at all.

Evite is another successful web-based company employing a viral technique: All Evite event invitations use their own product and software, and each invitee must use the company's software to respond to the invitation, thus becoming familiar with the product. Evite's parent company, Ticketmaster, offers the following pitch to advertisers: "With

Evite, advertisers reach social influencers who love to entertain and who take the initiative to plan social gatherings. The viral nature of Evite allows a marketing message to travel further than just the immediate audience. With an average of 36 guests per invite list, marketing exposure on Evite multiplies naturally without any effort or additional expenditure on your part." Evite offers advertisers an enviable upscale demographic: 68 percent of customers earn $50,000 or more per year, 48 percent earn $75,000 or more per year, and 88 percent attended or graduated from college.[52]

Blogs and chat rooms are other online venues for "word-of-mouse" marketing. *Blogs* (web logs) are online diaries that can be openly viewed. Frequent net users who are more familiar with new electronic products share a variety of insights, including product evaluations (an especially pronounced trend among teens and twenty-somethings). Public relations firm Burson-Marsteller says that these "e-fluentials" represent over 10 percent of the online population (more than 11 million users). Yet, although 45 percent of online shoppers choose e-commerce sites based on word-of-mouth recommendations

> *Blogs blur the line between commercial and noncommercial commentary.*

(according to a survey conducted by Jupiter Media Metrix), only 7 percent of companies are implementing tools that allow them to identify viral influencers through e-mail pass-along rates. Some companies are even including blogs on their websites. Blogs blur the line between commercial and noncommercial commentary, yet they often build greater customer loyalty. While there is a risk that a blogger will criticize a product, frank comments even when negative can build a stronger relationship than mindlessly positive ones.

According to MSN, the Internet can help marketers reach an additional 25 percent of their target audience who are heavy online users that cannot be reached via television, and online advertising campaigns are even more effective when coupled with television commercials. In one study conducted by the European Interactive Advertising Association, recall of ad details increased by 14 percent among people exposed only to television commercials relative to those who were not—yet when people were exposed to both television and online ads, recollection increased by 44 percent. In the case of Colgate-Palmolive's Total tooth-paste, dedicating 11 percent of the overall budget to online advertising generated an increase in purchase intent of 4.3 percent, compared with a 3.4 percent rise when only offline media are used. (It costs 23 percent more to encourage consumers to purchase using television alone.)

One of the most successful examples of TV-web synergy was Reebok's creation of a fictional character named Terry Tate, the "office linebacker," an American football player who keeps inattentive employees in line by tackling them. Terry Tate was first introduced in a third quarter U.S. Super Bowl commercial in 2003, prompting a surge in web traffic to Reebok.com where the company set up a Terry Tate site with a four-minute film (modeled after the much-admired BMW Films campaign). In the three days following the game, 800,000 people visited the site with 750,000 downloading the film (which required registration from viewers, most representing the almighty 18- to 34-year-old male demographic). Within a week, 1.2 million films had been downloaded.

Star Power

If corporations are not inclined to make films of their own, they can arrange for a guest appearance of their product in Hollywood movies or television programs. Product placement is now a common way to build brand equity. While some publicity-hungry advertisers pay for screen time in movies, most product placement works on a barter system: Products are supplied free of charge (often with support services) in exchange for exposure in the movie. Deals often include the right to use the movie name in other advertising, such as print media, which, in turn, enables movie makers to spend less themselves on advertising. This approach offers several advantages over conventional advertising: the implied endorsement of celebrities, low cost (an estimated less than $1 per thousand to reach a target audience), far reach (feature films and top-rated sitcoms have increasing global distribution), long lifespan (movies and hit TV shows go to DVD and reappear on TV for years afterwards), and a reduced level of obtrusiveness (although excessive use can lead to a backlash—the 20th James Bond film *Die Another Day* had so many product placements and tie-ins that it became known as "Buy Another Day"). Also, in the case of TV programs, product placement does an end-run around digital recording technology (such as TiVo) that automatically deletes commercials.

Product placements and commercial tie-ins can also help reinvent or upgrade a product's image. In an effort to convince younger beer drinkers worldwide that Heineken was not just the beer their parents drank, the company created a marketing blitz around *The Matrix: Reloaded* and arranged for a product placement in *Austin Powers: The Spy Who Shagged Me* (wherein our hero declares "Get your hands off my Heiny, baby!").

Then there's the BMW Mini Cooper. "Boxy" and "cute" are two of the adjectives that *BusinessWeek*[53] and others used to describe the car upon its 2002 release. But, with the 2003 premiere of the film *The Italian Job*, the car took on an edgier, more exciting image as three of the film's stars drive the Minis in a frantic chase scene. (The Mini was also featured in the original 1969 version of the same film.) The Mini Cooper's website included a link to the movie's web page, telling Internet surfers: "[C]lick below for an appetizer of the most exciting driving scenes ever seen on the streets of Venice and Los Angeles. Including a chance to explore the streets of L.A., to indulge in your own Mini gold bullion heist—and to win a trip to Venice."[54]

Another way to subtly hype products and generate buzz is to take a cue from Shakespeare's Macbeth: "All the world's a stage." Undercover marketing is product placement in the real world. Nobody tries to overtly sell you anything; they only try to get you to want it (and, of course, buy it later). When the energy drink Red Bull was first released in the early 1990s, the company littered empty cans of the drink in high-traffic trashcans to pique curiosity. Young video gamers were hired to use the P5 gaming glove in a Starbucks coffee shop and invite those who seemed interested to try it out.

The Downside: The Backlash

While such tools have enabled powerful and cost-efficient use of marketing dollars and made consumer products more ubiquitous than ever, companies risk a backlash if their covert attempts to promote a product suddenly become too overt. For instance, to introduce their new cigarette brand "Legal," Freedom Tobacco went undercover by hiring attractive women to sit at trendy bars with the cigarettes on the counter. The women asked various bar patrons for a light, all the while alluding to their recessed filters and commenting when asked, "They're pretty good." Freedom Tobacco's hubris went a little too far when it actually publicized an offer they made to supply celebrity smokers with a life-time supply of Legal cigarettes. The ploy was ill received by anti-smoking groups, as were their undercover marketing efforts, which were ultimately exposed on the U.S. news program *60 Minutes*.[55]

The perils of turning a blog into an overt marketing tool, as opposed to a forum for honest grassroots communication, were revealed when Dr. Pepper/Seven-Up created "Raging Cow"—an online diary chronicling the fictitious adventures of a disgruntled bovine whose in-your-face life motto is "pasteurize this." The blog was launched with the intent of promoting a new line of flavored milk drinks. Executives flew five of the world's most popular bloggers and their parents to the company plant in Dallas for free samples of the product. The bloggers were not obligated to mention their opinion of the product, but were invited to include links to the site on their own blogs.

It seemed a good idea at the time, but it prompted a backlash among other bloggers who saw the site as an underhanded advertising ploy and an attempt to leverage the influence of online commentators without offering them anything in return. Some net activists even set up a highly publicized boycott campaign against Raging Cow. "The people who make the cash decisions need to know that charging into our arena expecting it all for nothing is a very bad idea," declares the boycott's homepage. "This is a rare chance for us to play the game on our terms. To change the rules. If people want to reach us, they need to know that it's going to be on our terms, and that we will not be insulted by offers of cheap freebies. Commercial influences will always be a part of life, but this kind of campaign sets a very dangerous precedent—and a very low price on our complicity (if, indeed, any is forthcoming)."[56]

These newer marketing tools and the backlash they sometimes create is yet another dimension of a world rife with paradox. Individuals have become more vulnerable to exploitation by large corporations, but at the same time corporations have never been more exposed to fragmented, sophisticated, and empowered individuals than they are today. Firms that take a fresh approach to marketing may increase emotional attachment, but they can also trigger strong negative sentiments, incense consumer activists, and instigate cultural angst.

The New Consumer: Three Possible Scenarios

Consumption patterns are greatly influenced by purchasing power, which has risen globally, but most acutely in emerging markets. Future global economic growth will significantly influence the levels of wealth and purchasing power among consumers in different countries, as well as the continued spread of technological use among consumers. But the direction and speed of this growth between now and 2015 remain uncertain, since the rise and fall of economic cycles ultimately depend on how other macro factors unfold. In addition, while technology has already penetrated many aspects of modern life, the potential of technological developments to further transform consumer behavior is less than certain. Will the convenience and experience of online shopping equal or exceed that of conventional shopping? If so, how enthusiastically will consumers embrace these technologies?

Rice and Beans

The first possibility, *rice and beans*, would be weak economic growth worldwide—or worse yet, a prolonged global recession or a global economy disrupted by unpredictable events (*see Figure 3.3*). Such a scenario would restrain the rise of the global middle class in emerging markets and elsewhere. Consumers in developing countries would be empowered and demanding, but possibly unable to afford the quality products they want.

If this scenario materializes, companies must find innovative ways to price quality goods at very low prices for mass consumption in order to get a piece of the shrinking consumer pie. Domestic, homegrown companies in developing countries may be more agile and capable of supplying such products, and may also be viewed as less culturally intrusive. By contrast, global companies entering these markets may find themselves targets of a serious backlash, as they may be viewed as exploitative of poor consumers. This backlash could gain momentum if small groups of technologically savvy, discontented consumers coalesce to take on large corporations. Under this scenario, global corporations may increase their likelihood of survival by scaling back intrusive marketing efforts, toning down their brands, and operating as smaller, regionalized companies that partner with domestic brands.

Figure 3.3 The New Consumer: Three Possible Scenarios

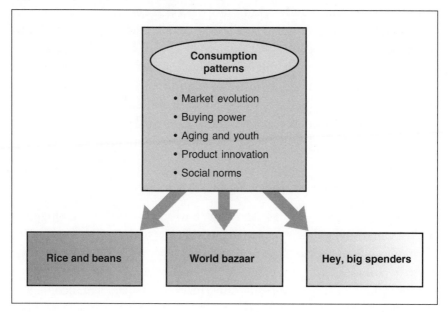

Source: A.T. Kearney

World Bazaar

If the global economy maintains moderate and stable growth, allowing consumption patterns to remain similar to those today, consumer demand will continue to span a wide spectrum from customized, quality goods to subsistence basics. The scenario that unfolds would be a *world bazaar*. Increased fragmentation of consumer groups could confer a competitive advantage upon global companies that have already established themselves in emerging markets, as they can more easily command loyalty among existing customer groups. Companies that wish to enter these markets must strive to quickly win the hearts of fragmented consumers and repackage products to reach masses of lower-income consumers.

Internet usage will continue to increase moderately and reach saturation in developed markets, where online channels will increase consumer leverage, but not revolutionize buying behavior. However, continued lack of Internet infrastructure in parts of the developing world will limit companies' ability to reach those consumers in the lower-income brackets through electronic marketing tools. Instead, companies are more likely to break into those markets through word of mouth or community networks in more rural areas.

Companies that manage to be all things to all people through multiple, differentiated product lines that offer high-end to low-end merchandise may be more uniquely capable of reaching a broad consumer base. The backlash against culturally intrusive foreign brands will continue within developing countries, but this backlash will be somewhat alleviated as dissatisfied, marginalized consumers are counter-balanced by consumers who have experienced rising living standards and purchasing power.

Hey, Big Spenders

The third scenario, *hey, big spenders*, envisions savvy, technologically sophisticated, and affluent consumers worldwide, with new concentrations of middle-income consumers in developing countries. Global economic growth continues to surge, spreading wealth across different income groups in both advanced and emerging markets. As personal income levels continue rising, affluent consumers dominate consumer markets. Demand for premium products swells across the globe, with virtually all consumer segments seeking higher quality, more upscale products that they are now able to afford.

Most of the nouveau riche will be found in the modernized cities of rapidly developing countries like China and India. These affluent consumers, younger and more technologically adept, will demand products that display their newfound status and fit with their lifestyles. They may also have developed pre-established loyalty to certain powerful domestic brands. As a result, consumer goods offered by global corporations—ranging from technological gadgets to furniture—may be characterized by more culturally sensitive designs, small sizes, and multifunctionality, together with customizations and unique experiences for consumers.

With consumers in emerging markets wielding such power, customers in developed markets in North America and Western Europe may have to start adapting to designs geared toward Chinese consumers. In addition, companies will be compelled to devise creative marketing tactics to reach increasingly sophisticated consumers, who frequently conduct their purchases online and also exchange product evaluation information with other consumers worldwide via multiple media. Companies that sustain global technological infrastructure and networks as well as optimize the use of new marketing tools—such as blogs, product placement, and advertising via mobile phones and computing devices—will find themselves well positioned to reach their consumers.

In any of these cases, global corporations must take the cue from their empowered consumers. Companies may find themselves fending off negative media and risking vandalism if they are too aggressive or intrusive in their marketing efforts. But they will watch market share slip away if they treat themselves as mere providers of goods and fail to tap into new demands and growing markets. Given the instability of this environment, leaders of today's corporations will find themselves in an elaborate balancing act.

CHAPTER

Natural Resources and the Environment

Stretching the Limits

Nature understands her business better than we do.

—Michel de Montaigne

As the world population grows and societies become more prosperous, our most fundamental natural resources—water, air, and oil—are coming under intense strain. More than a quarter of the people living in the world today still lack access to electricity, and within 50 years, nearly half of them may not have enough water. Meanwhile, our continued reliance on finite supplies of fossil fuels both raises the stakes of geopolitics and accelerates the process of global climate change. So far, technology has allowed us to defy predictions that population growth will outstrip the supply of natural resources. But staying ahead of the Malthusian trap will require better management and new governance structures. Governments must create policies to protect vital resources without compromising economic growth, and corporations must carefully monitor the full spectrum of pressures on natural resources. Those that minimize energy and water use within their own operations will develop a critical edge over their competitors.

Water Scarcity: A Lesson in Trickle-Down Economics

Since water covers more than 70 percent of the Earth's surface, we can perhaps be forgiven for taking it for granted. Yet fresh, drinkable water comprises only 2.5 percent of our total supply, and nearly 80 percent of that drinkable water is locked away in the polar ice caps and glaciers. Groundwater represents another 20 percent, which means that only 1 percent of fresh water (or 0.000008 percent of the Earth's total water supply) is easily accessible.[1]

Water is a unique substance. It is essential for life, it has no substitutes, and it is finite. It is also renewable, meaning that it can be purified and recycled but, to borrow Will Rogers' famous observation about land, "God ain't making any more of the stuff."

Today, the water supply situation may not seem that dire. The majority of the world's population, approximately 90 percent, enjoys relative water sufficiency, as defined as an adequate amount of fresh water per person for all purposes, including agriculture, industry, and household use. Five percent of the world experiences water scarcity, meaning there is insufficient water to satisfy these normal requirements. Another 5 percent of the world is suffering from "water stress," a situation in which water supply problems are chronic and widespread, and there is mounting competition among water's various users.[2]

Looking ahead to 2050, however, the situation is far more alarming. Because of growing populations, industrial growth in emerging markets, and continuing environmental degradation, some form of water scarcity will affect almost half of the people in the world.[3] These populations will not have sufficient water resources to maintain their current level of per capita food production. To sustain their needs, water may have to be transferred out of agriculture into other sectors, making certain countries or regions increasingly dependent on imported food.

Already, there are more *water refugees*—people who have left their homes in Mexico, Somalia, northern China, Nigeria, and Iran to find water—than there are war refugees in the world. Among the countries expected to experience water stress or scarcity in the coming decades are India, Turkey, Nigeria, Poland, the United Kingdom, parts of China, and the western United States.

Not a Drop to Drink: The Evolution of Water Scarcity

The causes of water scarcity are varied. Population growth is certainly a key factor, not just because more people need water to drink—household consumption represents only a small percentage of water use—but because of rising demands for food. Approximately 1000 tons of water are required to grow one ton of grain. The amount of water required to grow a single ounce of rice is equivalent to the amount needed to do a load of laundry in a typical washing machine.[4]

Also, as living standards rise around the world, diets are changing to include more meat. Few economic endeavors are as water-intensive as meat production. Grain-fed beef production consumes around 12,000 gallons of water for every pound of meat, while grain-fed chicken requires about 420 gallons of water per pound.[5]

Agriculture accounts for some 70 percent of all fresh water use, and in some areas of the developing world—North Africa, South Asia, and West Asia—agriculture accounts for between 85 and 95 percent of total water consumption.[6] Many agricultural systems throughout the world are extremely inefficient: An estimated 60 percent of the water used for irrigation never reaches the crops it is intended for and is instead lost to runoff and evaporation. Farmers have little incentive to adopt more efficient techniques, such as *drip irrigation*, whereby water is slowly applied to the soil surface through small, low-discharge emitters, owing to generous government subsidies that artificially lower water prices. In the western United States, for example, total water subsidies are between $2 and $2.5 billion per year. Farmers in arid Tunisia get their water at one-seventh of its actual cost.[7]

Various industrial sectors—including manufacturing, iron and steel, computer hardware, chemicals, food and beverage, paper, and textiles—also utilize extensive amounts of clean water. At present, industry accounts for 22 percent of fresh water use, although that number can be as high as 59 percent in some advanced economies.[8] An automobile coming off the assembly line will have consumed 31,700 gallons of water.[9]

It takes a lot of water to make everyday products in the United States (*see Figure 4.1*). It requires as much as 14,400 gallons of water to produce one ton of whiskey and up to 38,000 gallons to produce one ton of paper.[10] The average facility that manufactures silicon chips generates around one million gallons per day of wastewater, due to the multiple washings that

Figure 4.1 Water Use of Various Industries

Industry	Range of flow (gallons/ton product)
Cannery Green beans Peaches and pears Other fruits and vegetables	 12,000–17,000 3,600–4,800 960–8,400
Chemical Ammonia Carbon Lactose Sulfur	 24,000–72,000 14,400–21,600 144,000–192,000 1,920–2,400
Food and beverage Beer Bread Meat packing Milk products Whiskey	 2,400–3,840 480–960 3,600–4,800* 3,600–4,800* 14,400–19,200
Pulp and paper Pulp Paper	 60,000 –190,000 29,000–38,000
Textile Bleaching Dyeing	 48,000–72,000** 7,200–14,400**

Source: ITT Industries **Live weight*
**Cotton

each wafer must undergo to remove residue. As a result, Philips Semiconductors, Motorola, and Intel are among the manufacturers that have begun to implement water conservation technologies. By installing a water purification process, improving chip washing and rinsing techniques, and using water-efficient landscaping, an Intel facility in Albuquerque, New Mexico has reduced water use by 47 percent since 1994.[11]

Tough Choices in Emerging Markets

Looking ahead, a significant portion of rising water use will be attributed to industrial growth in key emerging markets, notably India and China. Already, water scarcity is taking a toll on industries in these and other developing countries. In India, for instance, Harihar Polyfibres Limited, which processes pulpwood, and Indian Rayon, a textile company, had to shut down operations completely for a few days due to the unavailability of water in 2002.

A joint study conducted by the Confederation of Indian Industry and the World Bank in 2003, which surveyed more than 1000 manufacturing companies—including consumer electronics, textiles, garments, and pharmaceuticals—concluded that water scarcity could prove to be a major roadblock to future industrial growth in the country.[12] In the spring of 2002, the Taiwanese stock market fell 4.5 percent in one day, the largest single-day drop since the 1999 earthquake, amid fears that a water shortage would cripple industrial production on the island. Water shortages continue to pose a constant threat to high-tech manufacturers in Taiwan's Hsinchu Science-based Industrial Park.[13] Similarly, commenting on economic growth in southern Africa, the South African government issued a report noting, "Given the continuing vulnerability of the economies in the region to drought and water scarcity, potential investors that require assured access to water resources will therefore attach a higher risk rating to those countries that either lack the will or the capacity to plan and execute policies and programs aimed at decreasing this vulnerability."[14]

As the water situation tightens, emerging market countries may face an unenviable choice: Should water be used to grow food for their swelling populations, or should priority be given to industries that help fuel economic growth? Nowhere is this dilemma more acute than in China, where the World Bank estimates that by 2010, the country's industrial water demand will surge by 62 percent, from 127 billion cubic meters to 206 billion cubic meters.[15]

It is generally supposed that water will flow to where the money is. So when agriculture and industry vie for scarce water in China, agriculture is usually on the losing side. One thousand tons of water can produce one ton of wheat, valued at around $200, or expand industrial output by $14,000. "In a country desperately seeking economic growth and, even more, the jobs it generates, the gain in diverting water from agriculture to industry is obvious," notes Lester Brown, founder of the Worldwatch Institute and president of the Earth Policy Institute. As such, Brown thinks it's unlikely that the Chinese government will increase the price of water anytime soon.[16]

Even as industry and agriculture compete for water, the two sectors effectively reduce the overall water supply by contributing to pollution. Although the problem of industrial pollution is well known (and often the subject of protests and legislation), agriculture also contributes to environmental degradation as pesticides, manure, and chemical fertilizers contaminate water sources. Over-irrigation of crops can cause the salination of croplands by leaching dissolved salts from alkaline soil. This salt not only kills crops and reduces yields, but it also makes ground water undrinkable. It takes just one liter of wastewater to pollute about eight liters of fresh water. Every day an estimated two million tons of waste is dumped into lakes and rivers.

Tensions Boiling Over: A Future of Water Wars?

Insufficient access to water will affect the world's health, living conditions, and even prospects for war. Water availability has a direct impact on food security. By 2025, sub-Saharan Africa may face a 23 percent shortfall in crop yields due to insufficient supplies of water.[17] The total annual losses could, at the extreme, be as high as the entire grain crops of the United States and India combined.[18] Consequently, these already poor countries may end up becoming increasingly dependent on foreign aid to import food. Some countries, such as China, will most likely purchase grain from nations such as the United States. But with an estimated shortfall of 40 million tons of grain per year, Chinese consumers could drive up global grain prices, thus complicating efforts to feed millions of impoverished people in developing countries that already spend 70 percent of their income on food.[19]

Shortages of clean water also have a direct effect on human health. Over 80 percent of disease and infection in developing countries can be traced to unsafe or inadequate water supplies. For instance, contaminated drinking water is responsible for the gastric infections that cause as many as one billion episodes of diarrhea per year. Diarrheal diseases are one of the major causes of infant and child deaths in the developing world.

These are vast, but preventable, problems. Companies are beginning to develop products and services to address water issues, citing both ethical and economic reasons. In June 2003, Procter & Gamble, in collaboration with the International Council of Nurses and the U.S. Centers for Disease Control and Prevention (CDC), announced the development of a new product that provides clean drinking water for people in the developing world. The product, called PuRPurifier of Water, has been shown to significantly reduce diarrheal illness in two trials in Guatemala. P&G has begun to work with relief agencies to provide the product for emergency water use. The International Rescue Committee was among its first customers, buying enough PuR to provide 3.5 liters of drinking water to the people of Iraq in the summer of 2003.[20]

Water scarcity can also threaten a company's profitability, as PepsiCo learned in 2003 when it came under pressure from a group of shareholders. "We strongly believe that companies and their shareholders face emerging new business risks from global water scarcity," said Steve Lippman of Trillium Asset Management, a Boston-based socially responsible investment group, which filed a shareholder resolution, one of the first of its kind. The investment group argued that water shortages pose a threat to PepsiCo because they could increase the cost of a key input, as well as harm the corporate brand and reputation via community protests, legal challenges, and government scrutiny.[21]

The resolution received only 8 percent of the vote, but the investment group has vowed to resubmit the resolution next year. Shortly afterwards, the *New York Times* reported that the village government of Pudussery in southwestern India revoked the local bottling plant's water-use license, which was not due to expire until 2005, due to concerns that Pepsi was overutilizing local water resources.[22]

Tensions Across Borders

Dwindling supplies of water will not only cause tension in the boardroom, but also introduce new fissures in international relations as nations compete to hold onto their share of this increasingly scarce resource. This could create opportunities for countries such as Canada, which alone controls 7 percent of the world's fresh water and 25 percent of global wetlands.[23]

Water may be tomorrow's equivalent of oil for a thirsty world. But today, water scarcity seems more likely to lead to tension and conflict. For instance, the Aral Sea is an ecological and political nightmare with no regional solution in sight. Back in the 1960s, Kremlin planners designed a system of canals to suck water from the Syr and Amu Rivers

> *One scientist even called the Aral Sea "a liquid Chernobyl."*

for new cotton fields in Uzbekistan and Turkmenistan. At the time, the Aral Sea was an enormous lake, only smaller in size to the Caspian Sea, Lake Superior, and Lake Victoria. Over the years, however, the Aral's surface area has shrunk by half and its water volume by three-quarters. As water tables have dropped, poor farmers and city-dwellers alike have been forced to rely on either brackish wells or tank trucks from afar for drinking water. The blotted shoreline has become a source of poisonous salts and pesticides. Researchers blame exposure to agrochemical wastes from the Aral seabed for a high incidence of anemia, stillbirths, and eye and lung disease among Kazakhstan's 16 million people. One scientist even called the Aral Sea "a liquid Chernobyl."

Despite this ongoing tragedy, Central Asian governments have been unable or unwilling to cooperate on this problem. Instead, the countries have been bickering over water usage as they hold meetings twice a year to coordinate the allocation of water from the Aral. Upstream countries such as Kyrgyzstan want to increase their water quota for hydroelectric power. Downstream countries such as Turkmenistan and Uzbekistan demand the water for the irrigation of their cotton crops, which are vital to their economies. Disputes over water allegedly caused a military standoff between Turkmenistan and Uzbekistan in 1995 and could further inflame this volatile region in the future.[24]

Similar water disputes are percolating in other politically volatile areas of the world. The Middle East and North Africa represent 5 percent of the world's population but have access to only 1 percent of global water supplies. Jordan and Israel routinely bicker over access to water from the Jordan River. Palestinians claim that Israel's controversial security fence is depriving West Bank villages of access to water. Turkey's massive water project launched in the 1980s for its southeast region of Anatolia, involving 22 dams and 19 hydroelectric plants, cuts the flow of the Euphrates into Syria by almost a quarter. The Turkish government has promised Syria that it would always provide at least 15.7 billion cubic meters of water per year from the Euphrates, but has refused to put this in writing by signing an actual treaty. Syria's anger at the Turkish refusal to commit has strained relations, complicating political solutions to conflicts as diverse as the Kurdish insurgency and reconstruction in Iraq.

In Asia, Bangladesh is concerned over India's plans to build water-diverting dams that link its northeastern rivers, the Ganga and Brahmaputra, claiming that the project will transform vast tracts of the flood-prone country into desert. Singapore's water resources are so limited that it is forced to import over half its water from Malaysia. In 1997, then Malaysian Prime Minister Mahathir Mohamad threatened to cut off Singapore's supply of water in retribution for criticisms by Senior Minister Lee Kuan Yew. This incident has elevated the water issue to a top national security concern for the Singaporean government, which has announced plans to build two additional seawater desalination plants by 2011 to replace the water supplied by Malaysia.

In Africa more than two-thirds of the continent's 60 river basins are shared by more than one country. Egypt's recent efforts to divert 9 percent of the Nile's flow to irrigate its western desert are eliciting concern among the seven other African countries that share the river. Upstream countries have begun challenging Egypt's traditional dominance over the Nile. Ethiopia is starting to exploit the Blue Nile with small dams for electrical power and irrigation, while Tanzania launched a $27.6 million project in 2004 to draw water from Lake Victoria despite previous agreements that countries must get permission from Egypt before initiating projects that would affect the volume of Nile waters.[25]

Even the United States is facing tension over one of its most important rivers, the Colorado River, which provides the U.S. southwest and northern Mexico with water and power. The seven states and two nations that compete for the Colorado River have often been likened to "thirsty dogs fighting over a wet sponge." Mexico has been on the losing end of the bargain—most years the Colorado River never reaches the Gulf of California. The once lush mile-wide Colorado Delta is now a barren salt flat.

"The question of the Colorado River is very serious," notes Victor Lichtinger, head of Mexico's Secretariat of Environment and Natural Resources. "The fact that the part of the river that belongs to us arrives contaminated is a serious problem for biodiversity and also for the marine ecology . . . this has important implications for agriculture, in the availability of water in all the Mexicali Valley and the Colorado River Delta."[26]

Finding Common Ground

Could these simmering water disputes boil over into full-fledged wars? Opinion on this subject is divided. There hasn't been a war explicitly about water since 2500 B.C., when two Mesopotamian city-states clashed in the region now known as southern Iraq. By contrast, between the years 805 and 1984, nations signed more than 3600 water treaties. Two hundred such treaties were signed during the last 50 years alone.[27]

Because water is such a vital resource, countries frequently have had little choice but to find a common solution. The 1960 Indo-Pakistani treaty on sharing the water of the Indus has endured two wars between the feuding countries. The Mekong Committee established in 1957 exchanged data even during the Vietnam War. As the U.N.'s *World Water Development Report* notes: "Once international institutions are in place, they are tremendously resilient over time, even between otherwise hostile riparian nations, and even when conflict is waged over other issues."[28]

The key phrase here is *once international institutions are in place*. The problem is that the growing competition over water is outpacing the number of existing treaties and organizations created to share water equitably. Water researchers Sandra Postel and Aaron Wolf have identified 17 "basins at risk," highlighted on the global map, where countries are unilaterally implementing dam projects and other diversion schemes, and there is no mechanism for resolving water disputes (*see Figure 4.2*). Getting countries to the negotiating table might prove harder and harder in the years ahead since water stress is creating more zero-sum situations in which one party's gain is perceived as another's loss.[29]

One Drop at a Time: Managing Water Scarcity

Dealing with water scarcity will require several actors and multiple solutions. One recommendation is to apply the market-based approach used with other commodities. An eight-ounce glass of water can be refilled for 2500 times less than the cost of a can of soft drink. Under these conditions, consumers have little incentive to conserve. A 1998 survey by the American Water Works Association indicates that 33 percent of the 60,000 public water systems in the United States encourage waste by offering volume discounts.[30] Virtually no governments have adopted sys-

Figure 4.2 Water Basins at Risk

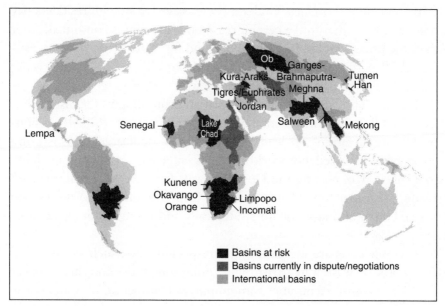

Source: *Basins at Risk, Transboundary Freshwater Dispute Database, Department of Geosciences, Oregon State University, July 2001; cartography by Greg Fiske & Becci Dale*

tems that would allow water rates to rise automatically as reservoir levels fall. Such a mechanism would send signals to businesses and consumers well in advance of an emergency, just like the price system for natural gas and other resources. There's some evidence that water demand is responsive to price changes. When Boulder, Colorado, moved from an unmetered to metered system, water use per person dropped by 40 percent.[31]

A modified market-based approach to water could even work in the developing world. In many countries, consumers are charged a flat rate for household water use. Yet the poor, especially those in rural areas, often end up paying more. In Karachi, for instance, residents connected to municipal supplies pay on average 14 cents per cubic meter of water, while the poor have to pay private vendors up to six times that price. In Manila, the poor pay vendors 42 times more for water for household use.[32] One solution to this problem would be to develop a progressive pricing scheme whereby water prices rise per unit consumed. For example, in 2002, municipal authorities in Beijing set quotas on residents' water use and adopted a progressive water pricing system in order to prevent worsening shortages. Under a progressive fee system, residents pay one price for water until a certain reasonable amount is consumed. After that, the price goes up. In Beijing, demand for water dropped by an estimated 20 percent.[33] The money saved from eliminating wasted water could be reinvested in developing more water-efficient technologies.

Business also will have a role to play in promoting water sustainability. The Global Environmental Management Initiative (GEMI), a nonprofit organization of leading companies dedicated to fostering environmental excellence worldwide, has launched a water sustainability tool called "Connecting the Dots: Towards Creative Water Strategies." Under the leadership of Coca-Cola and ConAgra, GEMI's Water Group has laid out a business case for strategically addressing water challenges:

- Water costs are increasing in unexpected ways, such as the rising costs of wastewater treatment, pollution mitigation, and worker absenteeism stemming from employee contraction of water-borne illnesses.
- Business disruption risks are growing and there is the potential for water-related constraints on business activity. Current water allocations are not assured into the future.
- Customer expectations related to water use and impacts are evolving. For example, companies report that they are increasingly hearing from customers—shareholders and those who buy a company's products and services—about the growing importance of water issues.
- Business' "license to operate" and ability to expand are increasingly tied to water-related performance by financial markets, suppliers, neighbors, nongovernmental organizations, and regulators.[34]

The Benefits of Going Green

Companies that rely heavily on water are learning that it pays to be proactive. For instance, since the mid-1990s, a Coca-Cola plant in Brazil has invested more than $2 million in a partnership with other local businesses and the municipality to protect the Jundiaí River watershed, which is the main source of water for the community. As a result, GEMI reports, "two key sanitation projects (a new solid waste landfill and a new wastewater treatment plant) were built, dramatically improving the quality of the water reaching the reservoir. The plant, which is the largest in the Coca-Cola system, also improved water use efficiency by lowering its usage ratio from 2.9 to 1.7 liters of water per liter of beverage."[35]

Similarly, Abbott Laboratories found that it makes good business sense to invest in clean drinking water in communities where it operates. In Puerto Rico, many rural communities' drinking water systems don't meet current standards set by the U.S. Safe Drinking Water Act. Abbott has supported local efforts to improve rural drinking water systems in order to improve the health and well being of company employees, decrease employee absenteeism, and increase productivity.[36]

Companies are also recognizing that this resource, often taken for granted, can actually be very costly. In 2003, Dow Chemical Company determined that it was using roughly 900 billion pounds of fresh water to produce 43 billion pounds of products. Dow projected that over time its demand for water would expand, the cost of water would rise proportionately, and some of its major sites around the globe would face water shortages in the near future. A Dow company executive warned that "over 10 years, this may represent some $100 million in additional operating costs and perhaps an additional $1 billion in future capital."

As a result, Dow began to rethink its water management system, first by consolidating its water needs—including water rights, conveyances, quality, use, and treatment for discharge—into a single business. The results have been positive, including up to a 5 percent reduction of water use in a single year. As just one illustration, Dow saves $1.2 million annually by recycling treated fresh water at its Terneuzen site in the Netherlands, as opposed to importing fresh water.[37]

Finding Opportunity in Scarcity

Successful corporations not only understand the costs of future water scarcity, but also recognize its opportunities. The market for bottled water is increasing at a vigorous pace, and most of this industry's growth opportunities are in the emerging markets, where safe tap water is not available.

While some companies make money by bottling trendy water such as Evian, others can find profit in purifying it. The global demand for providing clean water for industrial and municipal use has sparked a potential $100 billion revenue industry that has attracted big businesses such as General Electric and Pentair.[38] General Electric is (literally) tapping into this water market, having expanded its holdings to include Betz Dearborn (a company specializing in water treatment chemistry) and Osmonics (which manufactures membranes used in water treatment). GE Water Technologies is now a $1.4 billion unit of GE Infrastructure.

"Auto companies want paint to stick. Power plants want to run boilers at higher pressure. Soda companies want global consistency. Everyone wants lower disposal costs," explains George Oliver, the VP of GE Infrastructure Water Technologies. "Of course water is a growth business."[39]

Breakthrough technologies might also help quench the planet's thirst. Researchers at the University of Illinois at Urbana-Champaign in the United States are investigating the possibility of extracting potable water from gas hydrates. These crystalline materials, also known as clathrates, are found on the ocean floor. They form when water molecules create a cage-like structure around "guest molecules," such as methane and propane. When the clathrates form, the salt from the seawater separates out. Consequently, the technology might soon be available to split the clathrates into their component molecules, leaving behind an abundant source of fresh water.[40]

However, desalination technology is probably a more feasible solution in the near future. In addition to removing salts and other dissolved solids from water, some desalination techniques also remove suspended material, organic matter, and bacteria and viruses. Desalination has tremendous potential. Although cost still remains an important factor, the prices of this technology are continuing to drop. Already in Saudi Arabia, the cost of bringing water by tankers is twice the cost of producing it by water desalination methods. Looking ahead, desalination shows even greater promise.

Hungry for Power: The New Energy Crisis

An estimated 1.6 billion people, or 25 percent of the global population, do not have access to electricity or gasoline.[41] As shown in the global energy poverty map, 80 percent of these people live in South Asia or sub-Saharan Africa (*see Figure 4.3*). They can't flick a switch to light their

Figure 4.3 Global Energy Poverty

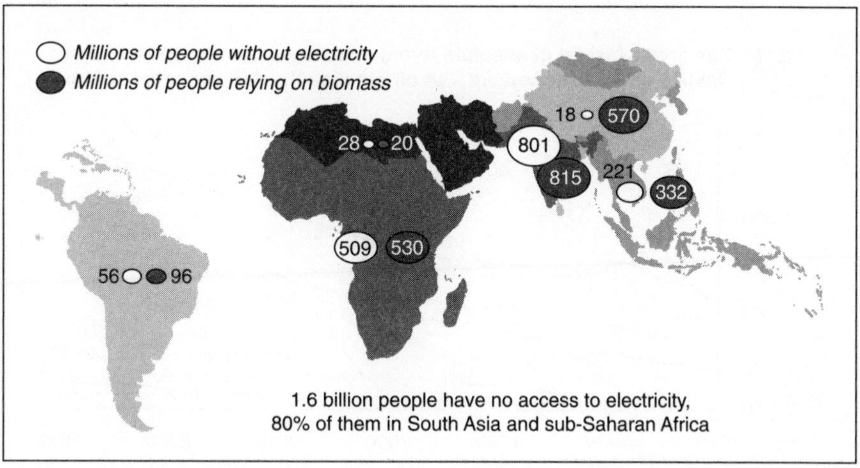

○ Millions of people without electricity
● Millions of people relying on biomass

28 ● ○ 20
18 ○ 570
801
815 ● 221 ○ 332
509 ○ ● 530
56 ○ ● 96

1.6 billion people have no access to electricity,
80% of them in South Asia and sub-Saharan Africa

Source: International Energy Agency

schools or homes, use a telephone, run mechanized farm equipment, or refrigerate food and medicine. Instead, they still depend on energy generated inefficiently by burning fuel, wood, and plant and animal wastes.

Energy consumption goes hand in hand with economic development. A lack of energy perpetuates the cycle of poverty, while sufficient access to energy drives economic growth. In South Africa, 10 to 20 new businesses are created for every 100 households that become electrified.[42] In Tanzania, when BP Solar began importing inexpensive solar power facilities, rural communities were able to extend the productive workday, refrigerate lifesaving vaccines, improve education, and stem urban migration.[43]

Looking ahead to the year 2030, the International Energy Agency (IEA) predicts that the global demand for energy will grow by two-thirds. This surge in demand, shown here by energy type, will require an investment of up to $16 trillion dollars—including $5 trillion in developing countries (*see Figure 4.4*).[44]

By 2020, the Far East, largely driven by China, will likely consume more energy than the United States and Europe combined.[45] As an indicator of what's to come, China's demand for energy surged 15 percent in just one year, triggering brownouts in half of its provinces during the summer of 2003.[46] China's demand for energy is not driven just by its

Figure 4.4 World Primary Energy Demand, 1970–2030

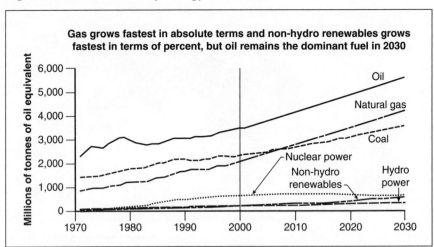

Source: *International Energy Agency,* World Energy Outlook, *2002*

industrial output, but also by rising household incomes. Many Chinese citizens, who only two decades ago could not imagine having an electric light, are now filling their homes with television sets and air conditioners. General Motors anticipates that China will account for 18 percent of the world's growth in new car sales through 2012, compared with 11 percent in the United States.[47]

Filling Up the Tank: Potential Sources of Energy

Where will the world find all this energy? Oil, like water, is a finite resource. However, unlike water, we have been reasonably successful in finding more of it. Thanks to intensive exploration, the world's proven oil reserves grew from 660 billion barrels in 1980 to more than 1 trillion in 1990. Despite consumption, oil reserves have hovered over 1 trillion barrels ever since.[48] Technology makes it possible to stretch existing oil fields further than ever before. While conventional drilling techniques can leave up to 70 percent of oil in the ground, more sophisticated drilling techniques can help lower this "leave rate" to below 30 percent.[49] Deepwater drilling ships are extracting oil from the shores of Texas, Brazil, and West Africa at ocean depths of 8000 feet.[50] All told, technologies that have already been developed could increase the world's recoverable oil supply by another 50 percent.[51]

Although the world is not about to run out of oil, our continued reliance on this fossil fuel carries several hidden costs. For starters, there are the environmental effects. Oil use contributes to local air pollution and climate change. Pipeline and roadway construction, seismic testing, or the routine operation of oil facilities can disrupt sensitive natural habitats. Oil spills are extremely damaging to rich marine environments, harming fish, aquaculture, and marine mammals, as well as polluting beaches and marinas. The journal *Science* reported in December 2003 that the Exxon Valdez oil spill continues to have an impact on the ecosystem in Alaska's Prince William Sound, 15 years after the disaster took place.[52]

Second, while we have become more adept at finding and extracting oil, most of the world's proven crude oil reserves (67 percent) remain in the politically volatile Middle East (*see Figure 4.5*). The IEA estimates that by 2030, 43 percent of the world's oil will come from the region—a 50 percent increase from today.[53] Saudi Arabia alone sits atop of 25 percent of the world's oil reserves and maintains a large amount of excess production to manage sudden price shifts. It was the rapid release of excess Saudi oil in 2003 that kept prices from rising exponentially in the aftermath of the U.S. invasion of Iraq and political turmoil in Nigeria and Venezuela.[54]

That much oil concentrated in just one country has some analysts worried. Saudi Arabia's King Fahd is 81 years old and not in good health, and his brother Abdullah, 80, is next in the line of succession, followed by another brother, Sultan, who is 76. Beyond that, it's anyone's guess who will be the next Saudi leader.

The uncertain succession of the monarchy is coupled with economic malaise. While 12,000 Saudi princes live richly off the national output of oil and taxes, the country has an unemployment rate of 20 percent. As a result, Saudi Arabia, a conservative religious country, is full of young people who don't have enough to do, truly resent the dominance and incursion of Americans into their society, and have learned from their textbooks about the duty of Muslims to wage jihad.[55]

Opinion is divided as to whether a reactionary, anti-Western regime in Saudi Arabia would go so far as to refuse selling oil to the United States or Europe again, as occurred during the oil embargo of

Figure 4.5 Crude Oil Reserves and Production by Region

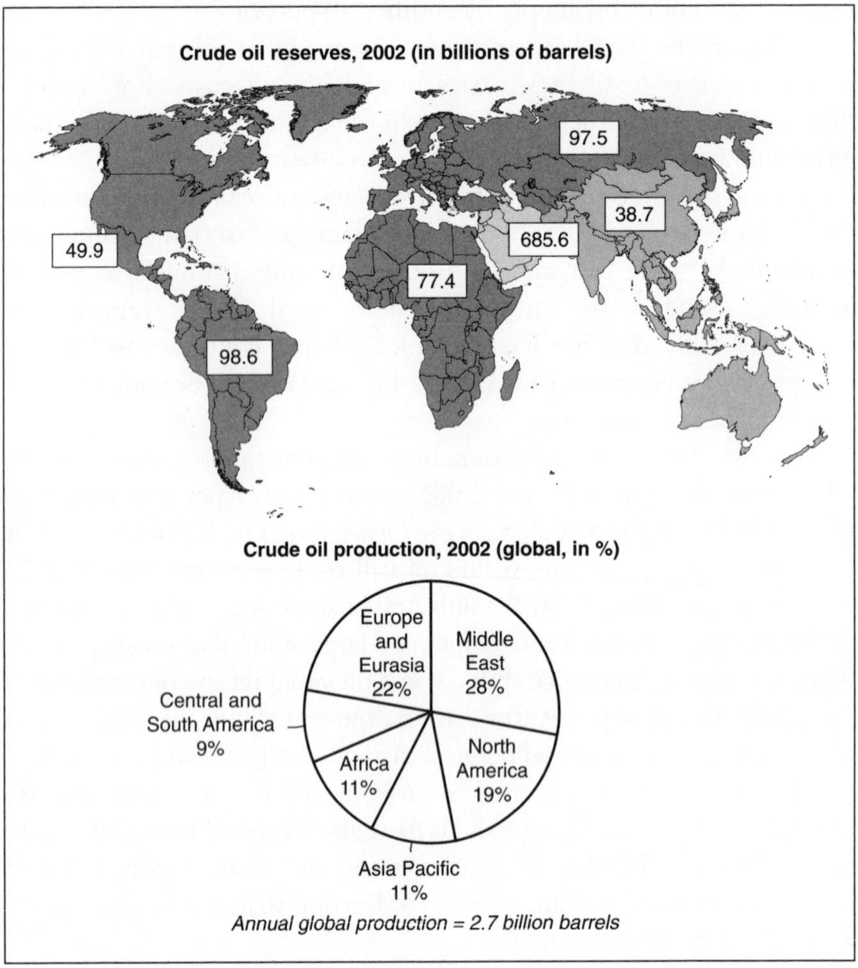

Crude oil reserves, 2002 (in billions of barrels)

97.5

38.7

685.6

49.9

77.4

98.6

Crude oil production, 2002 (global, in %)

Europe and Eurasia 22%

Middle East 28%

Central and South America 9%

North America 19%

Africa 11%

Asia Pacific 11%

Annual global production = 2.7 billion barrels

Source: BP 2003 Statistical Review of World Energy

1973. It's not outside the realm of possibility. Nor is it unthinkable in the post-9/11 world that militants could strike at the heart of the monarchy's power by decimating the oil fields with weapons of mass destruction.

Similar risks are at play in Central Asia, where conservative estimates indicate there could be some 100 billion barrels of oil in the Caspian basin. However, the oil wealth in the region could prove more of a curse than blessing. The region is already home to a number of authoritarian regimes. As we've seen elsewhere, oil brings with it the possibility of political instability, corruption, environmental degradation, and civil wars.

Russia, which at 60 billion barrels has the largest oil reserves of any country outside the Middle East, is the "X factor" in the great oil supply equation.[56] Russia's daily oil output is comparable to that of Saudi Arabia's. However, to continue to be an oil power after 2010, Russia will need to invest in new fields, which will require a huge influx of foreign investment. Foreign investors, however, remain somewhat skittish about pouring money into Russian oil development, owing to the country's endemic corruption, bureaucratic infighting, weak laws protecting property rights, and economic volatility.

"The rule of law is not widespread; corruption is widespread," observes BP CEO John Browne.[57] BP lost $200 million in what it claims was a rigged Russian bankruptcy case in 1998.[58] But Browne believes that the risks of investing in Russia are still less than doing business in the politically turbulent Middle East or West Africa. In February 2003, the company announced it had returned to Russia in a $6.75 billion deal to acquire a 50 percent stake in a newly merged company formed from Tyumen Oil and Sidanco Oil. "Where everything is cut and dried there is no opportunity," Browne notes.[59] Even if Russian oil production rises to its full potential, it is far from clear that the country could be a surplus swing producer like Saudi Arabia.

Given all of the volatility surrounding oil, it is fortunate that oil's share of the world energy pie continues to decline, from 50 percent in 1975 to 40 percent in 2003.[60] This trend is due to consumers substituting natural gas, coal, and other more efficient, stable, and cheaper fuels for oil. For example, the Royal Dutch/Shell Group is likely to expand its natural-gas operations to take advantage of rising demand in the United States and the Asia-Pacific region. According to Shell's former Chairman, Sir Philip Watts, "demand for gas as a fuel may outstrip oil in the next two decades, and Shell is moving aggressively to establish positions in regions that are already experiencing that growth."[61]

Coal: A Return to "Black Gold"

In China, the Shenhua Group, China's top coal producer, plans to double its coal output capacity to 200 million tons per year by 2010.[62] In Guangdong province, growth in fuel oil demand will likely be restrained by the province's policy to encourage power plants to switch from expensive, imported oil to domestically available coal.

The good news about coal is that there is plenty of it left in the world, and it's much cheaper than petroleum. Unfortunately coal is the dirtiest of fuels and emits considerably more carbon dioxide and other pollutants than oil does. Coal burning also contributes to water scarcity, since it is the principal source of poisonous mercury deposits in lakes and streams. The process of mining coal also releases an additional greenhouse gas, methane, into the atmosphere.

Although coal usage has been declining in North American and Europe, it is surging in the high-growth economies of China and India. The IEA estimates those two countries will drive two-thirds of the global demand for coal by 2030.[63] China is already the world's largest consumer of coal, since it has no oil of its own. The country is burning coal faster than its railroads can deliver it from domestic mines. As a result, China has begun importing coal from Australia.

Natural Gas: Demand on the Rise

Natural gas, one of the cleanest fossil fuels, was the fastest-growing energy source in the 1990s. Demand for natural gas increased nearly 30 percent between 1990 and 1999. Projections show that the demand for gas will nearly double by 2020, increasing at 3.2 percent per year, as opposed to oil's 2 percent per year growth. Emerging markets will cause much of this increase—some 12 percent per year in Brazil alone.[64]

Natural gas is the most environmentally friendly fossil fuel, and it's economical, efficient, and relatively easy to extract. Unfortunately, some nations are already confronting an imminent natural gas shortage. In 1990, gas represented less than 1 percent of Great Britain's energy market. As of 2004, it was the country's main source of electricity, accounting for 39 percent of its energy needs. The problem is, Great Britain's own source of natural gas, the North Sea reserves, might be depleted by 2011. As a result, the British will soon have to import their natural gas, and they are concerned that two of their likely principal suppliers, Algeria and Russia, could be prone to future political instability.[65] China and Japan, which lack domestic supply, are already in a heated competition to cut deals for oil and natural gas pipelines from Russia.

In the United States, where natural gas accounts for 24 percent of energy consumption, gas prices climbed 70 percent in the three years leading up to 2004. Top American officials have warned that the United States must expand its supply of natural gas to prevent future price shocks that could drive up utility bills, raise the prices of consumer goods, and threaten jobs in energy-intensive industries. The United States could meet its rising demand for gas by piping it in from Alaska. However, that plan would require constructing a 3270-mile pipeline to the upper Midwest, which would cost $20 billion and would not be finished until 2013 or later.[66] More likely, the United States will once again seek out energy on familiar turf: the Middle East. Qatar alone sits atop 900 trillion cubic feet of gas, enough to keep the United States supplied for four decades.[67]

The key challenge in meeting the world's growing demand for natural gas is developing a cost-efficient way of delivering it. Unlike oil, gas cannot simply be pumped aboard tankers and shipped abroad. The gas must first be liquefied by chilling it to minus 160 degrees Celsius, loaded aboard tankers equipped with special cryogenic tanks, and unloaded at terminals that can convert the gas back into vapor and pipe it to consumers. The cost of a liquefaction plant is $1.5 billion, while the price tag for a specialized tanker is $250 million.[68] Daniel Yergin, cofounder and chairman of Cambridge Energy Research Associates, estimates that it will require over $200 billion of investment to allow this nascent industry to reach its full potential.[69]

Clean Energy: Promise and Problems

Another source of power that has yet to reach its full potential is clean, renewable energy, such as hydroelectric, solar, and wind power. The U.S. Department of Energy estimates that renewable energy use will increase by 56 percent by 2025, accounting for 8 percent of the world's commercial energy consumption.[70] However, most of this will be in the form of hydroelectric dams, which have their own environmental drawbacks, such as disrupting ecosystems, decreasing biodiversity, and displacing human populations.

But even without considering large hydroelectric dam projects, the market opportunity for clean energy is vast. GE Energy said its activities in the global wind industry produced more than $1.2 billion in revenues for 2003, a 150 percent increase above the previous year's total. "The growth of this business within the GE Energy portfolio is a clear indication of the tremendous interest in wind power, which has become the world's fastest growing energy source," said Steve Zwolinski, CEO of GE Energy's wind operations.[71] Investments in clean energy technology have made it the sixth largest venture capital category, according to Cleantech Venture Network, a New York City–based research and information firm. Venture firms pumped $488 million into U.S.-based clean energy deals in 2002 alone.[72]

Despite the investment buzz, solar and wind power are problematic for two reasons. First, government subsidies for fossil fuels create a market disincentive to invest in developing renewable technologies. Second, Mother Nature is a very fickle source of energy. Consumers expect energy on demand, and it is not possible to command the wind to blow and the sun to shine 24 hours a day with the flick of a switch. ExxonMobil Chairman and CEO Lee Raymond notes: "Wind and solar power will likely continue to grow very rapidly, but only due to government policies and incentives, not market forces or economics. However, even with double-digit growth rates, wind and solar are unlikely to exceed a 1 percent share of the world's energy needs by 2020."[73]

> *It is not possible to command the wind to blow and the sun to shine 24 hours a day.*

Wind and solar power might prove to be a more viable source of energy if we develop an efficient way to store their electricity for consumption on the proverbial rainy day. One solution to this dilemma is hydrogen. As a potential energy resource, hydrogen exists everywhere on Earth. However, it needs to be harvested from existing chemical compounds such as hydrocarbons (coal, oil, natural gas) or water (H_2O). The hydrogen is then fed into fuel cells, which convert it into electricity through a noncombustible process that does not produce harmful emissions. Wind and solar power can provide the energy to harvest the hydrogen, which is then stored for use whenever the consumer demands it.

The technology to develop efficient, low-cost fuel cells is still under development, but significant progress has been made. In the 1960s and 1970s, the power generated by fuel cells cost $600,000 per kilowatt. The next generation of fuel cells now under development could cost less than $1000 per kilowatt, making them competitive for utility-level power generation.[74] Automotive companies are already actively pursuing this technology. In 2002, DaimlerChrysler's Necar 5 completed the first transcontinental journey of a fuel cell-powered vehicle, a 3262-mile trip across the United States.[75] According to GM spokesman Scott Fosgard: "We expect to have a commercially viable fuel cell by 2010, a vehicle that can be bought by consumers. It won't cost more than the other vehicles in that category on that day."[76]

Roadblocks Remain

Yet, for all its promise, the hydrogen economy is not about to dump fossil fuels into the dustbin of history. Robert Olson, the research director of the U.S.-based Institute for Alternative Futures, has identified several obstacles that could turn the nascent hydrogen boom into a bust. One possibility is a public backlash. Some environmentalists have denounced government-funded research-and-development programs as a "dirty energy plan," since much of the research is focused on producing hydrogen from oil, coal, and natural gas and will do little in the long run to reduce our dependence on fossil fuels. This concern, coupled with mounting budget deficits in industrialized countries, could prompt politicians to cut off public funding for these research initiatives.[77]

Another roadblock on the road to hydrogen efficiency is the fear of premature lock-in. Olson notes that history is littered with premature commitments to technologies that could otherwise have been supplanted by better ones—as when VHS conquered Betamax, or when the awkward "QWERTY" keyboard format became the bane of typists for generations.[78] Because the technology is not yet fully developed, automakers may decide to downplay further research on fuel cells and jump on the gasoline-electric hybrid vehicle in light of the tremendous success of existing models, such as the Toyota Prius. The Prius' demand in early 2004 was so great that some dealers had a waiting list that extended as far as orders for the 2006 model.[79]

Premature lock-in may also come in the form of fuel cell cars that are designed to convert gasoline into hydrogen and then into power. This approach allows automobile companies to make use of the existing infrastructure for producing and distributing gasoline, avoiding the risks and expenses associated with creating an entirely new hydrogen infrastructure.

However, as Olson warns: " . . . if cars with onboard fuel processors do succeed in the marketplace, the auto market could lock in on them for decades, denying society the benefits of more advanced cars that run directly on hydrogen. Direct hydrogen vehicles would cut dependence on imported oil, improve vehicle energy efficiency, and completely eliminate exhaust and carbon-dioxide emissions."[80] The failure to develop direct hydrogen fuel cells for cars would also intensify the competition for energy between consumers and the industrial sector. The IEA estimates that, in the 2020s, the demand for energy in the transportation sector will overtake the industrial demand for energy.[81]

But the future of hydrogen is not entirely grim. The barriers to developing cost-effective hydrogen fuel cells are not scientific but in the realm of engineering. As such, Olson suggests that the most feasible approach might be an Apollo Project-type initiative, wherein government would issue a challenge to industry to develop hydrogen power and invest upwards of $100 billion to fund the R&D. While that price tag might seem high, it is comparable (in today's dollars) to what the United States spent to reach the moon, and the benefits of hydrogen power—curbing global climate change, reducing air pollution, ending dependency on foreign oil, and promoting sustainable development worldwide—certainly suggest that it is a worthy investment.[82]

At the same time, we should not rule out the potential for a technological quantum leap. For example, progress in the development of nanotechnologies could lead us closer to hydrogen power by improving membranes and catalysts that make fuel cells cheaper and more efficient and revolutionizing hydrogen storage, making it possible to safely store highly compressed gas. Nanomaterials could also generate cheap solar energy that could cost-effectively liberate hydrogen from renewable sources such as water. A nanorod solar cell constructed with miniature semiconducting crystals would cost considerably less than today's solar cells made from silicon.

While some scientists contemplate the power of the sun, others are looking toward the moon. In September 2003, Norwegian engineers completed the world's first working prototype of an underwater power station that harnesses the power of ocean tides. This station generates electricity from the rise and fall of the sea (caused by the moon's gravitational pull on the Earth) much in the same way that windmills generate power from wind currents. Tidal power has an advantage over other forms of renewable energy, such as solar and wind, in that it never fluctuates, since tidal movements occur 24 hours a day. This prototype station produces 300-kilowatts of electricity, enough to power 30 Norwegian homes. The European Commission has identified 106 ideal sites for tidal mills off the coast of Europe. The tidal currents around the United Kingdom alone could produce 48-terrawatt hours of electricity per year.[83]

The moon offers another potential source of energy in the form of helium-3, an element deposited on the lunar surface as it is struck with supercharged articles from the solar wind. Helium-3 is very rare on Earth, where it is filtered out by the atmosphere and magnetic field. But, if extracted from the lunar soil, helium-3 could be a potent fuel source for fusion power, which fuses atoms to create energy (as opposed to nuclear fission, which splits atoms). Helium-3 provides one million times more energy per pound than a ton of coal. "If we could land the space shuttle on the moon, fill the cargo with canisters of helium-3 mined from the surface and bring the shuttle back to Earth, that cargo would supply the entire electrical power needs of the United States for an entire year," notes Gerald Kulcinski, the director of the Fusion Technology Institute at the University of Wisconsin-Madison.[84]

The Heat Is On: The Rising Costs of Climate Change

Our increasing dependence on nonclean energy sources has come at a cost. Global warming is caused by an increase in the concentration of greenhouse gases. These gases allow direct sunlight, or ultraviolet light, classified as *short-wave energy*, to reach the surface of the Earth. As this sunlight heats the surface, longer-wave infrared energy (otherwise known as heat) is radiated upwards into the atmosphere. Greenhouse gases absorb this energy and prevent the heat from escaping into space, effectively trapping it in the lower atmosphere and forming a blanket that warms the planet.

Several greenhouse gases, such as water vapor, carbon dioxide, and methane, are naturally occurring. Indeed, their presence is vital to life on this planet. Without them, the entire Earth would be a frigid wasteland, with a temperature hovering at around minus 18 degrees Celsius.[85] But recall that old axiom about "too much of a good thing." Human activity has been increasing the concentration of naturally occurring greenhouse gases in the atmosphere—especially carbon dioxide—through the combustion of oil, gas, and coal. The U.S. National Oceanic and Atmospheric Administration reports that levels of carbon dioxide prior to the industrial revolution were about 280 parts per million by volume (ppmv). Since the industrial revolution, that number has increased by more than 30 percent to 370 ppmv. That's higher than at anytime in the last 420,000 years.[86]

As a result, parts of the world are beginning to feel the heat. Global surface temperatures have already increased by about 0.6 degrees Celsius since the late nineteenth century, with a rise of 0.4 degrees Celsius in just the last 25 years.[87] North America alone has seen its average temperature rise by 1.0 degree Celsius since 1900, with 80 percent of that increase occurring since 1970.[88] Researchers at the University of Bern have found that average summer temperatures in Europe from 1994 to 2003 were the hottest they have been in five centuries. And the 30-year average from 1973 to 2002, for both winter and annual temperatures, also topped the 500-year record.[89] At this rate, the average global temperature will increase by 1.0 or 1.5 degrees Celsius by 2050. The Intergovernmental Panel on Climate Change, which advises countries around the world, warns that the average temperature could rise by 5.8 degrees Celsius by the end of the century.[90]

A temperature increase of even a few degrees could have catastrophic effects as large ice sheets melt and raise global sea levels. The hydrologic cycle—the constant circulation of water from the sea, through the atmosphere to the land, and then back to the atmosphere by way of evaporation—would undergo drastic changes that could affect the water supply, as well as patterns of floods and droughts all over the world.

> A temperature increase of even a few degrees could have catastrophic effects.

As the scientific evidence of global warming mounts, even confirmed skeptics have become devoted environmentalists. The American Geophysical Union, the United States' most broadly based professional organization in earth and space science, which had long adopted a neutral stand on the issue, officially declared in 1999 that there was a "compelling basis for legitimate concern" about climate change.[91]

Even defense experts worry that the fallout from global warming could pose a greater threat to national security than terrorism. A 2004 report commissioned by the Pentagon—written by Peter Schwartz, a CIA consultant and former head of planning at Royal Dutch/Shell Group, and Doug Randall of the California-based Global Business Network—warns that sudden climate change within the next two decades could lead to widespread droughts, famine, and rioting. Nations seeking to hoard and protect their dwindling food and water supplies might increasingly resort to nuclear weapons as the ultimate deterrent. "Disruption and conflict will be endemic features of life," Schwartz and Randall conclude. "Once again, warfare would define human life."[92]

The Hardest Hits

Although climate change is a global problem, particular regions are likely to be at a greater risk. Since the driest air masses (which are also the coldest) respond first and most strongly to global warming, northernmost regions, such as Siberia and northwestern North America, may be among the most affected. Swiss experts note that if climate change remains unchecked, many ski resorts in the Alps may face bankruptcy. The precise economic losses facing a country like Switzerland are uncertain, but some experts have suggested that tourism losses in that country could eventually be as high as $1.6 billion annually. Some ski resorts are already making contingency plans against global warming by constructing all-season hiking facilities and convention centers.

Yet that will be small comfort to countries that hope to host future Olympic winter games. In late 2003 the International Olympic Committee reported that resorts in Canada, Italy, Switzerland, Austria, and the United States might be unviable hosts by 2030.[93]

Alternatively, some parts of the world may face more winter than they can handle. The rising temperatures that melt the glaciers and snow in Europe could eventually usher in a mini-Ice Age throughout much of the Northern Hemisphere. Ocean currents that flow northward from the equator warm the eastern United States and northern Europe. As this current, known as the *Great Conveyor Belt*, cools down, it grows denser and sinks into the North Atlantic, thereby drawing more water from the tropical south as it makes its return journey to the equator. However, if global warming prompts arctic glaciers to melt enough fresh water into the Atlantic, the salinity of the Great Conveyor Belt would decline, which would lower the currents' overall density. At a certain threshold, scientists still aren't sure when this tropical pump would shut down entirely. Switzerland would once again see snow on the Alps; however, the crop failures throughout the United States and Europe would likely make finding food a higher priority than skiing.

Meanwhile, as melting glaciers cause sea levels to rise, coastal populations would begin to see the land beneath them disappear. Current estimates indicate that about half of the world's population lives in coastal zones, which have been growing at double the national rate of population growth.

The U.S. Environmental Protection Agency estimates that a one-foot rise in sea level is likely by 2050 and could occur as soon as 2025. A two-foot rise, projected within the next century, would eliminate approximately 10,000 square miles of land, an area equal to the combined size of Massachusetts and Delaware, and subject major port cities in the United States at below-average elevation (such as Boston, New York City, Charleston, Miami, and New Orleans) to major flooding and shoreline retreat. Professor Robert Mendelsohn at Yale University estimates that by 2065, the cost of protecting the U.S. coastline from rising sea water could be as high as $1 billion per year.[94]

China's 11,185 mile-long coastline is home to about 70 percent of the country's large cities, more than 50 percent of its population, and nearly 60 percent of the agriculture and industry that drives the national economy. Ding Yihui, a climate expert at the China Meteorological Administration, warns that, "With comparatively advanced social, economic and cultural developments, China's off-shore regions will suffer great losses if the sea level doesn't cease rising."[95]

Globally, some of the biggest losses will be in the area of insurance. According to Munich Re, one of the world's biggest reinsurance companies, flood defense schemes to protect homes, factories, and power stations from rising sea levels and storm surges may cost on average $1 billion per year.[96]

Changes in the hydrological cycle mean that rainy seasons may become shorter and more intense in some regions, while droughts in other areas may grow longer in duration. Brutal storms, typhoons, cyclones, and hurricanes may also become more frequent. The effects are already being felt. The number of major flood disasters has steadily risen over the last half-century: six in the 1950s, seven in the 1960s, eight in the 1970s, 18 in the 1980s, and 26 in the 1990s. Between 1971 and 1995, floods killed 318,000 people and left more than 81 million homeless. The World Water Council estimates that up to 45 percent of reported deaths from natural disasters between 1992 and 2001 were the result of droughts and famines.[97]

Developing nations have been the hardest hit, accounting for 96 percent of the deaths resulting from natural disasters, owing to poor infrastructure, higher population density in vulnerable areas, and the tyranny of geography that locates many of them in humid tropical zones where storms are especially severe.[98] By 2025, half the world's population is projected to be living in high-risk areas vulnerable to extreme weather.[99] For instance, more than half of Egypt's industrial capacity is located within a one-meter zone of sea level and would be devastated by even an 11-inch rise in ocean waters.[100] Ghana's Akosombo Reservoir, a huge manmade lake that at one time supplied 95 percent of the country's power needs, has been depleted to less than half its size due to intermittent rainfall, prompting the country to ration electricity.[101]

The economic losses from floods and other weather-related catastrophes have been doubling every decade, reaching a total of $1 trillion between 1987 and 2002. The United Nations Environmental Programme's (UNEP) Financial Initiatives taskforce—a partnership between UNEP and 295 banks, insurance, and investment companies—estimates that economic losses will surge to nearly $150 billion per year by 2010 if current trends continue and warns that, "The increasing frequency of severe climatic events, threatening the social stability or coupled with significant social costs, has the potential to stress insurers, reinsurers, and banks to the point of impaired viability or even insolvency."[102]

Fifty Years to Extinction?

Plants and animals may also become victims. Warmer seas have already killed 25 percent of the world's coral reefs due to the loss of temperature-sensitive algae that the corals feed upon.[103] In addition, as the world's oceans absorb more and more of the carbon dioxide produced by human beings, the concentration of carbonate ions (an essential element for coral growth) is falling. Just as the Swiss face a future without ski resorts, the Australians might witness the death of the Great Barrier

Reef, which attracts two million tourists a year and has an estimated value of $40 billion.[104]

Ocean coral might just be the canary in the coalmine. In 2004, a landmark study in the journal *Nature* predicted how global warming would affect plants and animals in six biodiverse regions, from Australia to South Africa. The researchers plugged field data into computer models that simulated how temperature changes would alter natural habitats, taking into account the ability of species to move to better climates and thrive. The results of the simulation were, to say the least, distressing: More than one million of the world's plant and animal species could be at high risk of extinction by 2050.[105]

These findings are worrisome to more than nature lovers. One group of ecologists estimates that the value of biodiversity is $3 trillion per year due to the goods (crops, genetic material from plants) and services (air and water purification, climate regulation) that healthy ecosystems provide.[106] Complicating the dilemma, while several species face extinction, disease-carrying pests such as rats, mosquitoes, and ticks would thrive in an environment of increased temperatures, flooding, and higher humidity. Scientific models project an increase in the proportion of the world's coastal population affected by malaria to increase from 45 percent to 60 percent by mid-century.[107]

Big Oil: Going Green

In light of the growing scientific evidence and wide-reaching impacts of climate change, corporations are also beginning to feel the heat. For instance, ExxonMobil publicly rejected the connection between the consumption of oil and gas and climate change for years. Activists in Europe reacted with a Stop Esso campaign (Esso is the company's European brand name), encouraging consumers to boycott ExxonMobil's gas stations in order to push the company to change its environmental views.

In 2002, top energy analysts at Deutsche Bank warned that ExxonMobil was risking its brand and business reputation due in part to its views on climate change and opposition to the Kyoto Protocol to reduce global greenhouse gas emissions. "Being handed a reputation as environmental enemy number one for such a big consumer-facing business has to be considered a brand risk," wrote analyst JJ Traynor of

Deutsche Bank. Traynor put ExxonMobil's shares on a "hold" rating, questioning, "[H]ow nimble has the current management been in terms of . . . communicating a detailed strategy to shareholders, and dealing with the new environmental age?"[108]

At the company's annual meeting in May 2003, two shareholder proposals—one suggesting that the company conduct a climate change report and another urging a report on renewable energy— won more than 20 percent of the vote. Dave Ebner of the *Globe and Mail* suggests that as the current CEO, Lee Raymond, heads toward retirement, ExxonMobil will likely select a CEO more open to environmental concerns.[109]

Cooler Heads Prevail: Managing Climate Change

Since the consumption of fossil fuels is the main source of greenhouse gases, mitigating the impact of global warming will be intimately tied to how we consume energy. As is the case with water scarcity, the best solution might be to use the invisible hand of the market to prod countries toward more efficient energy use and the accelerated development of breakthrough technologies.

One proposal advocated by the Earth Policy Institute's Lester Brown is lowering income taxes while increasing taxes on environmentally destructive activities. "The basic idea is to establish a tax that reflects the indirect costs to society of an economic activity. For example, a tax on coal would incorporate the increased healthcare costs associated with breathing polluted air, the costs of damage from acid rain, and the costs of climate solution."[110]

Previous experiments with environmental taxation have proven effective. Finland, for instance, adopted a tax on carbon emissions in 1990 that led to a 7 percent decrease in emissions by 1998.[111] In Europe and the United States, opinion polls reveal that 70 percent of the public would be willing to support environmental taxes, as long as they did not increase their overall tax burden.[112]

In recognition of the spiraling costs associated with changing weather patterns, the insurance and financial services industry, in cooperation with the UNEP, has issued a detailed list of recommendations on how companies can better cope with environmental problems and remain solvent. Among the proposals:

- All financial services companies should incorporate climate change considerations into their business practices by developing carbon risk management and benchmarking tools.
- Asset managers, such as pension funds, should develop more robust, quantitative tools to assess the potential implications of climate change and use these tools to conduct portfolio-wide assessments of risk exposures arising from equity and debt holdings and asset allocation decisions.
- Insurance companies should strive for greater clarity on the potential threats and opportunities from altered climate conditions through cooperation with scientific research.
- Commercial banks should fully price the risks associated with climate change into loan agreements and provide incentives to develop cleaner energy sources.[113]

Corporations are also committing to better controlling and reducing greenhouse gas emissions. BP was a pioneer in this endeavor. In 1996, it broke ranks with other industry leaders and threw its support behind the Kyoto Protocol. Then, in 1998, BP CEO John Browne upped the stakes further when he pledged to cut BP's carbon dioxide emissions by 10 percent below its 1990 levels by 2010, a steeper cut than the Kyoto Protocol itself prescribed.

To obtain this objective, BP consulted with nongovernmental organizations such as the Pew Center on Global Climate Change, which advises Fortune 500 companies. BP gave each one of its 150 business units in 100 different countries a designated quota of emissions permits. Each unit was given the freedom to decide how to bring itself into compliance, whether by reducing emissions, buying credits from other BP units, or selling leftover credits to BP units that failed to meet their quota. Business units that successfully reduced emissions or decreased fuel consumption would see cost savings reflected in pay scales and bonuses. By 2002, BP had not only exceeded its target, but announced a net gain of $600 million thanks to greater fuel efficiency.[114]

For BP and other companies striving to reduce global warming, their motivations are not simply altruism and public relations. Rather, it is the growing recognition that if they do not act, governments may act for them. Companies are also seeing that environmental sustainability and the growing "green" sentiment of consumers can be a competitive advantage. Mauricio Reis, Environment Systems Manager of the Brazilian-based CVRD, the largest diversified mining company of the Americas, with a market capitalization of approximately $10.5 billion, admits that, "we at CVRD are not doing what we are doing because we love the monkeys, birds, and butterflies—but in order to keep the company competitive . . . our ecosystems are under the spotlight . . . our clients, particularly from Europe, demand that our production uses clean methods."[115]

Corporations have also recognized that acting in a more environmentally friendly manner can cut costs. Acer Incorporated, a Taiwanese company that is chiefly involved in manufacturing and marketing of personal computers, motherboards, multimedia products, and peripherals, has made significant efforts to reduce pollution and lower its impact on the environment. In addition to demanding that its employees strengthen end-of-pipe treatment and reduce their use of resources, Acer also considers the impact of every step of the production process on the environment—from green design, green production, green packaging, and green reuse to industrial waste reduction and environmental initiatives in the office. As a result of the environmental improvements, Acer saved costs to the extent of approximately $2.5 million.[116]

Natural Resources and the Environment: Three Possible Scenarios

When we consider all the variables that determine the availability of natural resources—political, technological, economic, and regulatory—three possible future scenarios emerge (*see Figure 4.6*).

Constrained Energy

The first is *constrained energy*, which envisions a world where there is little in the way of international cooperation and countries rely on their own unique energy assets. The world becomes increasingly polarized between those who have, or can afford, access to natural resources and those who cannot. Oil prices rise sharply due to increased demand, inadequate development of alternative energy sources, and an OPEC monopoly with renewed strength.

The United States and Europe reluctantly pay the higher prices, but turn increasingly inward to protect their own economies. The United

Figure 4.6 Natural Resources and Environment: Three Possible Scenarios

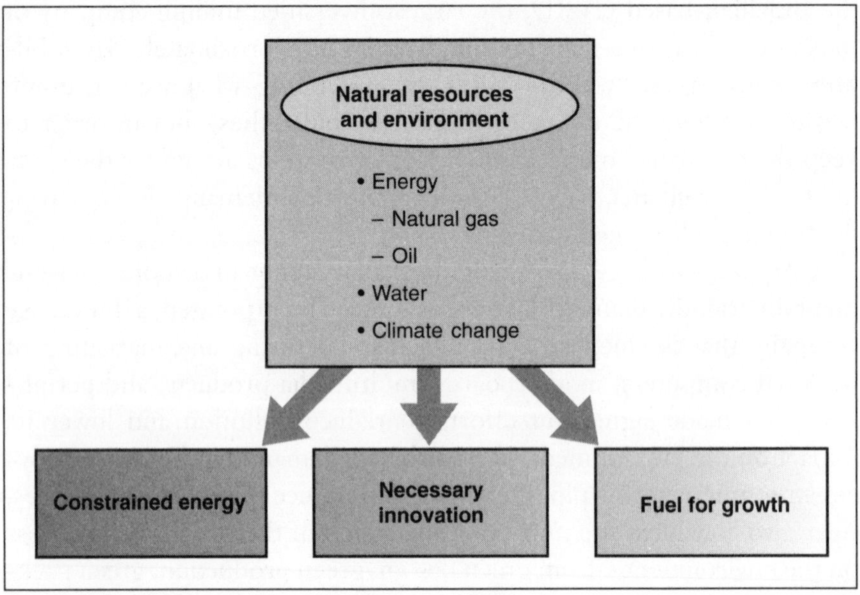

Source: A.T. Kearney

States seeks to safeguard its supply by providing significant military assistance to the resource-rich countries in the Middle East. The European Union imports oil and natural gas from neighboring Russia and cultivates relations with "rogue states" such as Iran. As Asia struggles to meet its energy needs, economic development slows throughout the region. China, with its insatiable demand for energy, depends increasingly on "dirty" coal as the only affordable energy resource. China also increasingly flexes its political and economic muscles to spearhead projects to construct oil and natural gas pipelines from Central Asia.

Despite warnings from scientists about rising greenhouse gas emissions, Western corporations successfully roll back environmental regulations, claiming they need to keep a lid on rising prices. At the same time, the higher oil prices lead to technological breakthroughs in alternate energy sources, including some clean energy solutions, such as more efficient solar power and hydrogen fuel cells. The net effect on the environment, however, is still overwhelmingly negative.

Water supplies deteriorate amid unchecked pollution and accelerating global warming. Up to three billion people—mostly in Africa, the Middle

East, South Asia, and northern China—suffer from inadequate water. Small, but deadly, armed clashes break out in Africa and the Middle East over insufficient water. Farmers lack enough water to irrigate their lands and food prices rise. Industries in the developing world are forced to close for days at a time when they can't receive the water they need.

Necessary Innovation

In the second scenario, *necessary innovation*, countries strive to lessen their dependence on foreign energy. The oil and natural gas markets remain volatile, and when prices swing sharply upward, governments and companies seek alternate energy sources. The United States and Canada exploit oil reserves in the Arctic, construct a new generation of coal-fired power plants, and introduce legislation requiring more energy-efficient vehicles. European countries share declining reserves of the North Sea and Scandinavian oil more efficiently, but they also develop more expansive, environmentally friendly renewable sources of energy, such as wind and solar power. Japan, which possesses scant natural resources, builds more nuclear power plants and develops new technologies to tap into geothermal and hydroelectric sources of energy. China continues to remain heavily dependent upon coal to meet its soaring energy needs.

However, when oil and natural gas prices are low, enthusiasm for alternatives wanes. As fossil fuels serve as the world's primary source of energy, global greenhouse gas emissions continue to rise. Water quality and availability worsen. Governments recognize the seriousness of the problem, although the increased demand for energy coupled with the ineffectiveness of international institutions precludes effective multilateral solutions. Nevertheless, growing public concerns about environmental degradation—particularly in crowded urban centers—creates a strong market niche for "green" products. Fuel cells emerge as a cost-effective option for large-scale applications such as stationary power generators, but are still not able to compete with lower-cost hybrid systems in automobiles.

Fuel for Growth

In the third scenario, *fuel for growth*, surging economic expansion has made countries in emerging markets and industrialized countries more dependent on foreign supplies of oil and natural gas than ever before. Industrialized nations and key emerging markets form strategic alliances with resource-rich nations to meet their soaring energy needs. The United States maintains close ties with Mexico and Venezuela, and seeks non-confrontational relations in the Persian Gulf. The European Union, Japan, Korea, and China offer economic assistance to key allies in Russia, Central Asia, and the Persian Gulf.

New technologies allow companies to cost-effectively tap previously inaccessible sources of oil with less environmental damage. As a result, oil production in the North Sea, Canada, and the United States surges significantly, the power of OPEC weakens, and oil prices remain moderate. The political environment in Central Asia and Russia remains open to Western firms, helping to guarantee that production of oil remains high and that prices remain low. New pipelines link Central Asia to eastern China, and developing Asia continues to grow rapidly. This strong economic growth in China, however, triggers tensions with Western countries that fear the competition for limited natural resources will ultimately raise prices or lead to shortages.

> *As surging industrial growth takes its toll on the environment, water supplies deteriorate further.*

Renewable energy sources have gained market share, but are still more expensive to develop than the market can bear. As countries, particularly those in the developing world, continue to burn fossil fuels with abandon, climatologists and environmentalists step up their warnings about global climate change. By 2015, governments in industrialized countries agree that climate change is a serious problem, requiring a multilateral solution. Despite their efforts, they cannot agree on a mechanism to reduce emissions, but they are actively trying. The European Union and Japan take the lead in promoting international efforts to modernize "dirty" production systems in emerging markets through bilateral aid and multilateral funding. These efforts further boost their substantial lead over the United States in developing cutting-edge environmental technologies.

As surging industrial growth takes its toll on the environment, water supplies deteriorate further. Governments provide incentives for corporations to reduce greenhouse gas emissions and conserve water.

Companies recognize that protecting the environment means protecting their bottom line; they develop innovative ways to harness technology to ensure ample water resources and reduce environmental damage. Developing countries benefit from the technological spillovers and are able to leapfrog over some of what the developed nations experienced during their Industrial Age.

The Price of Admission

These three scenarios, or parts of each, are all plausible. However, the future state of natural resources and the environment will not be resolved in isolation. Indeed, as we'll see in the next chapter, activists, regulators, and shareholders will play a key role in determining how natural resources are allocated and how governments and corporations respond to the challenges of environmental degradation.

Whether or not companies agree with the speculative effects of global warming, everyone will be affected by the political juggernauts that impose monitoring requirements and taxes on carbon emissions. Corporations must not only worry about climate change, but also confront a perfect regulatory storm that is sweeping across the private sector. As Browne himself put it, companies now face the choice of either standing in the wings or gaining "a seat at the table, a chance to influence future rules."[117]

Regulation and Activism

A New Breed of Challenges

Thank God we don't get all the government we pay for.

—Will Rogers

An era of liberalization and deregulation may have come to an end. Not so long ago, governments around the world were renouncing interference in the marketplace and racing to reduce barriers to trade and investment. But the new millennium marked a turning point, with governments diving into markets with renewed vigor. The emergence of international terrorism and heightened security concerns has given rise to increasingly stringent regulations in many countries. Meanwhile, the public has grown disillusioned after a string of botched efforts to deregulate industries including airlines and energy utilities. At the same time, a spate of corporate scandals has undercut faith in the private sector. The rise of increasingly savvy and effective activist movements further complicates the equation for corporations. But a new era of regulation appears set to stay, and as the issues and controversies grow more complex, corporations may have little choice but to play along and demonstrate their commitment to social responsibility.

We're from the Government, and We're Here to Help

Marketing experts argue that products often sell as much for their functional capabilities as for their ability to generate brand loyalty by tapping into the emotional needs of consumers. In recent years, some political scientists have reached the same conclusions about governments. Harvard University professor Joseph Nye, author of the book *Why People Don't Trust Government*, concludes that faith in government is not only determined by how well government actually performs, but also how the public perceives its performance.[1]

By these standards, "government" may be among the most improved brands of the decade. Between 1994 and 2002, the share of Americans who said they trust government "most of the time" or "just about always" increased from 21 percent to 56 percent (*see Figure 5.1*).[2] Confidence in the government was rising even before the deadly September 11th terrorist attacks—although those events and the subsequent war on terrorism have strengthened the bond between governments and their constituents to a degree that few other institutions can achieve. After all, as Francis Fukuyama put it, "Microsoft or Goldman Sachs will not send aircraft carriers and F16s . . . to track down Osama bin Laden; only the military will."[3] A similar trend can be found in Europe, where confidence in national governments and the European Union (EU) increased significantly in the aftermath of the terrorist attacks. Although support for governments has slipped somewhat, Europeans still have broad confidence in supranational organizations. In fact, they place more confidence in the EU and the United Nations than in their own national governments.[4]

Growing security concerns, however, may be a double-edged sword. They have raised faith in governing institutions and given them a free hand to deal with national security issues. The United States and Europe have spent billions to implement new national counter-terrorism measures, including enhanced airport security, passport control, and response teams for biological and chemical weapons attacks. European nations have also moved to create uniform banking standards and enhanced judicial cooperation within the EU. Germany has tightened tax-evasion laws and curtailed rights of association, and France has empowered police to access, monitor, and seize computers. These trends are underscored by rapidly growing budgets for government agencies in

Figure 5.1 Public Trust in U.S. Government

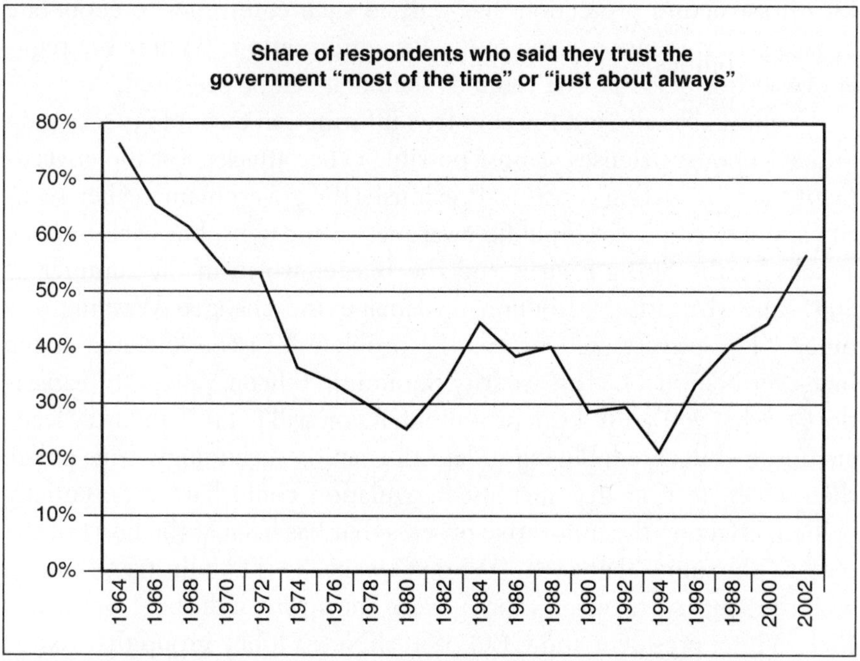

Source: National Election Studies, Guide to Public Opinion and Electoral Behavior

the front line. The 2005 budget for the new U.S. Department of Homeland Security totaled $40 billion, exceeding the annual budget for the U.S. Department of State.[5]

A Free Hand or a Strong Arm?

Where governments have a free hand, however, they are increasingly using it to strong-arm the private sector. In 2003, U.S. President George W. Bush directed the Department of Homeland Security to compile a list of vulnerabilities to the nation's critical infrastructure, including public monuments and government facilities as well as transportation and telecommunications systems, dams, chemical plants, power and water utilities, and banking and financial institutions. Private companies, which own 85 percent of the designated infrastructure, have sometimes been reluctant to cooperate because they are fearful that revelations about potential weak spots might drive away investors or expose secrets to competitors. Robert Liscouski, the department's assistant secretary for infrastructure protection, has warned such companies to cooperate or face government coercion to disclose information. "Where the regulatory authority exists," he reminds them, "it can be exercised."[6]

Liscouski has also put the country's information technology sector on notice to boost defenses against possible cyber attacks, lest the government start mandating controls. Previously, the government's cyber-security strategy emphasized public-awareness campaigns, but back-to-back attacks by the SoBig.F virus and the Blaster worm in the summer of 2003 caused nearly $40 billion in damage and changed Washington's tune.[7] "The private sector owns the problem," Liscouski noted at the first-ever National Cyber Security Summit in Silicon Valley. "If [legislation] is what you want, I can promise that you will get it."[8] Industry leaders, meanwhile, are lobbying to let information technology firms police themselves, fearing that increased regulation could have a potentially chilling effect on the innovative process that has been at the heart of the sector's phenomenal growth. "We don't want the [IT] industry to end up with the same sorts of rules that govern the airline industry," complains Rick White, president and CEO of TechNet, a lobby group that represents more than 200 senior executives from top technology companies.[9]

A Tangled World Wide Web

As information technology continues to develop, however, the airline analogy may prove uncomfortably prophetic. Even beyond security concerns, the industry has become an inviting target for new rounds of regulation. Simply put, e-mail communication, electronic commerce, and digitized information have become so central to daily life that they need new "rules of the road," even if standards were not terribly important when the industry was still carving out its niche. With questions about privacy, intellectual property rights, and tax liabilities clamoring for answers, the authorities are likely to step in as traffic cops. Take, for instance, the growing amount of "spam" messages clogging the world's e-mail inboxes. The United Nations Conference on Trade and Development estimated that, since the end of 2003, spam constituted 50 percent of all e-mail messages in circulation and cost as much as $20.5 billion in wasted technical resources.[10] As the number of junk messages grows, trust in e-mail communications suffers, and many users report less frequent or less enjoyable use of their e-mail accounts. "Some legitimate commercial or business communications are simply not read anymore," notes Erkki Liikanen, member of the European Commission responsible for Enterprise and the Information Society. "The overall result is that spam undermines consumer confidence, while consumer confidence is a prerequisite for the success of e-commerce and, indeed, for the Information Society."[11] Even typically trustworthy corporations are under pressure to limit their use of e-mail to contact potential customers. A series of two e-mail newsletters from IBM asking subscribers to forward offers to their friends and colleagues in exchange for free speech-recognition software was perceived as unwelcome spam by many recipients.[12]

As a result, governments worldwide are implementing an ever-increasing amount of anti-spam legislation. South Korea bans unsolicited wireless advertisements between 9 p.m. and 8 a.m. Japan now has a law that requires commercial wireless text messages to be labeled as "unauthorized advertisements." The EU has issued an e-communications directive that requires companies to have an "established business relationship" including previous sales of goods and services, before sending e-mail messages to customers. The U.S. law firm of Wiley Rein & Fielding has warned that, "U.S. companies with a presence in Europe should analyze their exposure to the e-communications directive. EU authorities could attempt to extend the law to spam originating outside the EU." Some EU member states are already contemplating hefty fines: Ireland may charge up to €3000 ($3700) per unsolicited e-mail, and Sweden may fine spammers as much as €558,000 ($690,000).[13]

The EU and the United States are also at loggerheads over extraterritorial Internet taxation. As of July 1, 2003, the EU requires all foreign Internet firms with customers in its member countries to impose a value added tax (VAT) on services and products sold on their websites. The intent is to level the playing field for European businesses, since Europeans could shop duty free online with U.S. and other firms and thereby avoid paying taxes that range from 15 percent in Luxembourg to 25 percent in Sweden.[14] In effect, foreign companies have become tax collectors for the European Union. These companies argue that the new rules discriminate against them, since they have to accommodate 15 different national VAT codes if they do not set up a European office. By contrast, EU-based companies only have to charge the VAT rate of the country in which they are located. American firms are particularly nervous about being accused of noncompliance, since U.S. law now requires companies to disclose any potential tax liabilities.[15] The online auction company eBay has already said it would comply with the new regulations, although its annual report acknowledges that this could slow the expansion of its international operations, which accounted for 30 percent of its sales in 2003.[16]

Barriers at the Frontiers of Science

Government intervention is being felt throughout the economy, from basic manufacturing to the most sophisticated telecommunications services. Nowhere is the effect stronger than at the frontiers of science and technology, where a host of new discoveries and developments is confounding existing regulations and rendering old ways of doing business irrelevant. Competing technical standards are on the rise and new ethical quandaries seem to be popping up everywhere, giving rise to increasingly complex regulatory issues that virtually beg governments to wade into the mix.

Perhaps the most intense ongoing debate surrounds the growing sophistication of biotechnology, where the ability of scientists to splice and manipulate genes has moved much faster than public acceptance for genetically modified (GM) organisms and "designer foods." The United States gives broad latitude to scientists and companies seeking to develop new, disease-resistant plants and has quickly taken the lead as the world's largest grower of GM crops.[17] The European Union, where the public views the latest biotech developments with increasing suspicion, has put strict limits on imports of these so-called Frankenfoods, a move that may cost American farmers $300 million a year in lost corn sales alone.[18] In response, the United States has filed a lawsuit against Europe in the World Trade Organization. For its part, the EU has retaliated through the U.N. Cartagena Protocol, which stipulates that a nation may reject genetically modified imports (even without scientific proof) if it believes such

> Competing technical standards are on the rise and new ethical quandaries seem to be popping up everywhere.

imports threaten traditional crops or reduce the value of biodiversity to indigenous communities. At a February 2004 conference on the Cartagena Protocol, the EU bloc successfully lobbied for more stringent labeling of genetically modified exports—a move the United States contends could disrupt trade by unfairly stigmatizing biotech products.[19]

Activists further complicate the picture as they mount successful publicity campaigns, calling into question the health and safety of GM foods. In the United States, the Genetically Engineered Food Alert coalition protested against the presence of an experimental corn variety used in Kraft's Taco Bell corn taco shells several years ago, and has since raised public sentiment against other Kraft products tested for such ingredients.[20] German-based Bayer Crop Science abandoned its plans to grow herbicide-resistant corn in Great Britain following anti-biotech campaigns by green and consumer groups.[21]

This debate is also raging in developing nations, where lawsuits have emerged as just one tactic to delay the introduction of GM foods. As early as 1998, the Monsanto Company, a pioneer of genetically modified crops, thought it had won official approval in Brazil for five varieties of soybeans that could withstand applications of the company's Roundup herbicide, which kills troublesome weeds. But a local consumer group and the Brazilian office of Greenpeace filed suit, and a judge issued an injunction that stopped the approval. While the case winds its way through the Brazilian court system, planting GM seeds in the country remains illegal.[22] In Zambia, nongovernmental organizations (NGOs) were instrumental in convincing the country not to accept GM products in 2002 for humanitarian food relief, even though 2.5 million Zambians were hungry and at risk of famine.[23] Expressing the frustration of the $3.5 billion GM food industry in the United States, Mark Mansour, an attorney representing several multinational food companies, complains that, "There is no harmony to the legislation being enacted by countries. This makes it very difficult and expensive for food companies to comply."[24]

Tinkering with the Human Genome

Similarly, stem cell research and human cloning promise huge health advantages, but have also been subject to scrutiny from governments and citizens. On this issue, at least, Europe and the United States are closer together on the need to hammer out ethical ground rules. Europe's reluctance to tinker with the human genome is driven by lingering historical trauma over fascist-era eugenics programs and the continent's strident environmentalism. Despite government reluctance, privately funded research in the United States is proceeding at university-based centers like the Harvard Stem Cell Institute, which aims to develop medicines for degenerative diseases derived from human embryonic stem cells.[25] But U.S.- and EU-based corporations considering future investments in such research will continue to be constrained by public uneasiness.

Elsewhere, however, companies may be in a more comfortable position. Francis Fukuyama, who served as a member of the Bush administration's Bioethics Council, believes the real wild card is Asia, which for cultural and historical reasons is not as concerned about the ethical dimensions of biotechnology. "If there is any region that is likely to opt out of an emerging consensus on the regulation of biotechnology, it is Asia," he argues. "A number of Asian countries are not democracies or lack a strong domestic opposition. Asian countries like Singapore and South Korea have the research infrastructure to compete in biomedicine and strong economic incentives to gain market share in biotechnology at the expense of Europe and North America."[26] Indeed, in South Korea— where researchers announced in 2004 that they had been the first in the world to successfully clone a human embryo—nationalist pride almost entirely drowned out the country's debate over the larger ethical issues. "This [cloning] proves that South Koreans are ahead of everyone else in the world in this field," declared project leader Moon Shin-yong. "I hope future South Korean scientists will build on what we have achieved."[27] But while some companies are able to operate in less constrained environments, they may encounter regulatory obstacles as they seek to expand abroad.

Governments Stretched Too Thin?

As governments become more assertive in imposing regulations and the range of regulatory issues grows more complex, it is worrisome to consider the shrinking pool of talent among the officials who will manage the whole situation. Governments are not immune to aging populations and the shrinking workforce that (as discussed in Chapter 2) will soon become common throughout the developed world. In the United States,

53 percent of the government workforce will be eligible for retirement by 2007.[28] Nearly 40 percent of the federal civil service were born during the first 10 years after World War II. Similar demographic trends are apparent throughout the aging, developed world.

Efforts to downsize big government have also taken their toll. A survey conducted by the U.S. Merit Systems Protection Board (MSPB) in 2000 revealed that 62 percent of federal employees worked in units that had been downsized within the previous five years. Even among agencies with the least reported staff shortages (such as the Departments of Energy, Treasury, and the Navy) almost 40 percent of respondents reported insufficient numbers of employees to get their work done. Almost half of all federal employees worry that downsizing had "seriously eroded the institutional memory" of their work unit, and 48 percent of all federal workers feel they have insufficient training to perform their duties—up 16 percent from 1992.[29]

Adding to the problem is the dwindling number of talented young people seeking careers in the public sector. A 2004 poll revealed that only one-third of young Americans found the ideas of a government-service career appealing, as compared to two in five just two years earlier.[30] This is a strong sign that the post-September 11th patriotic jump in U.S. federal job applications was ephemeral. The public sector is no longer able to recruit from as large a pool of Americans preferring government jobs as compared to a decade ago, and governments in North America and Western Europe are not the only ones facing these personnel challenges. With issues like low pay, lack of training, and limited advancement opportunities threatening to erode public sector talent, governments in emerging markets such as Hungary have implemented performance-based pay, while South Korea and Poland have promoted open competition in recruitment.[31] These programs promise to revive interest in and improve the quality of public service in the future, but the results may be long in coming. Meanwhile, given the host of increasingly complex regulatory issues on the horizon, the ongoing public sector "brain drain" could not come at a worse time.

Dirty, Rotten Scoundrels: The Corporate Image Under Siege

While governments begin to grapple with their new empowerment, a deregulatory era in which corporations had an increasingly free hand may have reached its end. How the mighty have fallen. During the 1990s, CEOs were hailed as saviors of companies and the fearless architects of the New Economy. But these days, the CEO is just as likely to be depicted in the media as a handcuffed and disgraced corporate executive. One scandal after another has taken a toll on the image of corporations worldwide: Enron, WorldCom, Imclone, Merrill Lynch, Qwest Communications, Tyco International, Rite Aid, Parmalat, and Ahold.

As anyone who lived through the 1980s can attest, corporate scandals are not entirely new. Yet, this time around, the impact is not limited to just the financial markets. The collapse of Enron left thousands of workers without jobs, pensions, and health insurance, even as corporate executives paid themselves generous bonuses and unloaded their stock prior to the crash. And many investors and activists alike consider it indefensible that top-level corporate salaries continue to rise while share prices tumble. Public outrage over the amount of money paid to Jean-Marie Messier, the former chairman of Vivendi, prompted the French government to implement regulations that require top executives to fully disclose their compensation.[32] The former directors of the German telecom Mannesmann are being sued for payouts of nearly $140 million when the company was taken over by Britain's Vodafone.[33]

> One scandal after another has taken a toll on the image of corporations worldwide.

"I'm working with one CEO who said that for the first time in his life he's embarrassed to tell people in a casual conversation that he's a CEO," says Marshall Goldsmith, a consultant who coaches chief executives.[34] When Goldsmith sought to write an article profiling icons of corporate ethics for the *Harvard Business Review*, he could not even find a CEO who was willing to be interviewed for the article. "They felt the publicity would make them targets," Goldsmith explained. "They said it would just inspire someone else to look under every rock to find something to prove they weren't that good. There's almost this implicit assumption of guilt today."[35]

Why the recent outbreak of so many corporate scandals? Luigi Zingales, a professor at the University of Chicago, suggests that fraud has become both easier and more lucrative. "It is easier because the increased complexity of organizations makes it simpler to divert resources. Between 1996 and 2001, the number of foreign subsidiaries of Tyco, for example, grew from 154 to 1750, making it impossible for all but a handful of people in the company to understand the whole picture."[36] Fraud has become more profitable due to the increase in market valuations. Twenty years ago, a fraudulent profit of $1 would have increased company value by $7. At the height of the dot-com-driven economic boom, the value had increased fivefold.[37]

Adam Smith Takes a Hit

Most people no longer believe that a few bad apples are to blame. Rather, they are beginning to feel that corporations are often rotten to the core. A survey conducted in the United States in 2002 revealed that only 13 percent of the American public was confident that chief executives make job-related decisions that are "morally appropriate."[38] Corporate leaders scored lower than journalists, TV producers, and elected government officials. Not surprisingly, portrayals in the popular media only worsen these perceptions. "Scandals Grow Out of CEOs' Warped Mind-set," declared one especially pointed headline in *USA Today*. "The hit parade of corporate scandal isn't about money. It's about boredom," staff writer Bruce Horovitz wrote. "It's not about wealth. It's about loneliness. It's not about power. It's about insecurity. And it's not about greed. It's about unrealistic fantasy."[39] When such perceptions gain traction, the pressure for stronger government oversight builds.

Botched attempts at privatization in both developed and developing countries have further undermined the sort of confidence that the private sector once enjoyed. Not long ago, turning moribund public services over to the private sector was seen as a silver bullet that would improve quality and lower costs. However, the large-scale privatization of the British railway system only lowered service quality and was widely blamed for a series of serious accidents in the late 1990s. Russia's "loan for shares" privatization of state enterprises led to poor corporate management with little accountability and "asset tunneling" by corrupt officials. Privatization of water utilities in South Africa prompted price hikes that forced the country's poor to draw water from lakes and streams, leading to the country's worst-ever cholera outbreak.[40]

Often, the role of a foreign corporation in a privatization scheme only further fuels the ire of consumers. For example, the Bolivian government turned to the private sector in the late 1990s to operate the water and wastewater system in Cochabamba, the country's third largest city, where the local utility was inefficient and out of funds. When Aguas del Tunari, a local water company partially owned by Bechtel Corporation, raised rates beyond what residents could afford, the locals took to the streets by the tens of thousands. A citywide strike and ensuing violence eventually forced Bechtel to leave, and the incident became a public relations disaster for privatization in the developing world, suggesting that multinational firms were interested only in profits and not in the well being of the people they served.[41]

Efforts at economic liberalization and deregulation have not always fared well, either. The most notable example in recent years was capital market liberalization in emerging markets such as South Korea, Thailand, Indonesia, and Malaysia that invited "crony capitalism" and left national regulators unprepared, ultimately paving the way for the Asian financial crisis in the late 1990s. Other efforts at deregulation have fueled grassroots consumer anger by disrupting utility, transportation, and telecommunications services.

In the United States, deregulation of the market for cable television led to market concentration, skyrocketing prices, and complaints about program quality among TV viewers. At a 2003 conference, Federal Communications Commission Chairman Michael Powell warned telecommunication executives that a growing consumer backlash—combined with public outrage over corrupt practices at companies like Qwest and Adelphia Communications—had profoundly changed the political climate. "In Washington, I see a rise of a regulatory ethos, a belief that regulators can do it better."[42]

Similarly, electricity market deregulation in the United States and Canada has given rise to big price hikes with very little investment in capacity. Some critics even held deregulation responsible for the blackout across the Northeast United States and parts of Canada in the summer of 2003. Among state governments, California's experiment in electricity deregulation was a spectacular failure that cost taxpayers billions of dollars. "This version of competition was a disaster," said James Hoecker, the former Chairman of the Federal Energy Regulatory Commission, the U.S. government agency that regulates wholesale power distribution.[43] In India, the Maharashtra State Electricity Board's contract with Dabhol Power Company encountered a host of problems, including environmental pollution and allegations of human rights violations and financial mismanagement, effectively shattering the notion that deregulation could solve infrastructure problems in the developing world.[44]

The Regulators Strike Back

Amid corporate scandals and unpopular reform schemes, the public is increasingly skeptical of the ability of private sector to manage itself responsibly without the government looking over its shoulder. In early 2001, nearly 80 percent of the American public thought government regulation of the private sector was either too high or just the right amount. By the end of the year, after terrorist attacks and a string of high-profile corporate scandals, the ratio dropped to 62 percent, while the share of people who thought government intervention was too little increased from 17 percent to 33 percent.[45] At the same time, a 2002 *BusinessWeek* poll found that only about 25 percent of respondents agreed with the assertion that corporations could reform themselves without new laws and regulations.[46]

Growing distrust of the private sector and rising faith in the public sector have empowered governments to initiate sweeping new regulations designed to control not just particular industries but the behavior of all corporations. In the aftermath of the Parmalat scandal in Italy, Frits Bolkestein, the European Commissioner responsible for Financial Services, delivered a blistering speech to the European Parliament. He warned that, "We need some real industry leadership to stand up and take charge, to clear out the crooks, expose their unscrupulous practices and curb excessive greed. If industry leaders are not prepared to do this, then regulators will have to do much more than perhaps they or we would like. If that is the result, then industry leaders can't whine about regulation from Brussels—they will have brought it upon themselves."[47] Declaring that "Scandal upon scandal will cumulatively weaken financial markets like the corrosive drip of a leaking fuel tank," Bolkestein announced a series of tough new measures in early 2004, including stronger sanctions for corporate malpractice and the compulsory rotation of auditing firms to undermine the links between auditors and the companies they monitor.[48]

In the United States, the Sarbanes-Oxley Corporate Reform Act significantly redesigns federal regulation of corporate governance and reporting obligations, while tightening accountability standards for directors, auditors, securities analysts, and legal counsel. Reflecting the widespread suspicions of corporate management, Sarbanes-Oxley requires that independent directors comprise the majority of corporate boards and the full membership of audit committees. Not only has this requirement set off a scramble to find new talent at dozens of companies, but critics say it will create a more timid corporate culture. "The independent directors of a company are part-timers," argues Peter J. Wallison, a resident fellow at the American Enterprise Institute in Washington, D.C. "No matter how astute in the ways of business and finance, they know much less about the business of the companies they are charged with overseeing than the CEOs and other professional managers who run these enterprises day to day. Unfamiliarity in turn breeds caution and conservatism. When asked to choose between a risky course that could result in substantial increases in company profits or a more cautious approach that has a greater chance to produce the steady gains of the past, independent directors are very likely to choose the safe and sure."[49]

A Long Paper Trail

Corporations are also chafing under Section 404 of the Sarbanes-Oxley Act, which obliges auditors and executives to perform an annual evaluation of internal controls and procedures for financial reporting, while requiring companies to assess and guarantee the efficacy of these controls.[50] As *BusinessWeek* reports, in practical terms this means that, "[M]anufacturers will have to prove that they can trace their products from assembly line to customer. Temp agencies will have to show that the hours they bill match those worked by their employees. And public companies in all industries will have to document that they have similar systems to keep their books in order."[51]

To keep pace with demand, auditors are already charging 50 percent to 100 percent more for their services.[52] In one of the first cost estimates publicly revealed by a large company, GE estimated it would spend $30 million on additional paperwork and professional service fees.[53] The

total cost of compliance for all companies in the first year alone could
reach up to $7 billion.[54] On the bright
side for the IT sector, the market for
Sarbanes-Oxley compliance software
could be worth between $1 billion

> *Few overseas companies are ready for Sarbanes-Oxley.*

and $4 billion within three years. The sticker shock will also be felt
across the Atlantic, since foreign auditing firms overseeing European
companies listed in the United States must also comply with Sarbanes-
Oxley as of 2005.[55]

Already, the new regulations have had a chilling effect on global
merger and acquisition activity. Few overseas companies are ready for
Sarbanes-Oxley. Compliance has suddenly risen from the sidelines to
the center of the executive agenda. Tighter corporate governance
requirements not only compel corporations to deal with the increasing
complexity of already complex processes such as mergers and public
offerings, they also force executives to align their companies' reputation
and their own careers with these rules.

Shoot the Messenger: Activists Target Corporations

Against this backdrop of corporate scandals and declining faith in the private sector, corporate leaders face another kind of pressure: increasingly
powerful activists bent on highlighting alleged abuses by multinational
firms. These activists are part of a growing movement of people frustrated
by the invasion of foreign influences and the perception that outside forces
have taken control of their economic destinies and damaged the fabric of
their societies. The infamous "Battle of Seattle," when anti-globalization
activists effectively shut down a pivotal World Trade Organization summit, is widely acknowledged as the movement's coming-out party. Protests
against national governments and multilateral institutions continue, but
activists are increasingly focusing on corporations. By deftly tapping into
the public's resentment of corporate power and wealth, these activists are
painting a picture of widespread injustice and inequality.

The foot soldiers of this movement are international NGOs, who
have seen their numbers quadruple from about 6000 to more than
26,000 in the 1990s alone.[56] They are creating a movement that is not
just a replay of the 1960s social unrest and boycott movements: These

activist groups have made important advances in coordination. They are technologically savvy, using the Internet to transform small, local campaigns into international social movements with incredible speed—and very little cost. Protestors use cell phones as a basic means of communication and control during protests, and they carefully videotape their events to document police abuses that might win more public sympathy. When today's protestors head off to activists' camps, they learn not only how to combat police tactics, create banners, and scale walls, but also how to use websites, text messaging, and video cameras. As a result, they are forming new and much more powerful international networks. Global activist umbrella organizations such as the World Social Forum, which is held every year as a grassroots response to the World Economic Forum, show the emergence of cross-border strategic activist alliances. Because of the anti-globalization movement, First World consumer activists are shaking hands with Third World labor union leaders.

Skip the Molotov Cocktail; Bring Your Blackberry

Corporations are most vulnerable to this form of anti-globalization activism. As a result, they spend millions of dollars on sophisticated advertising designed to build highly emotional relationships with customers. Naomi Klein, author of the worldwide best seller, *No Logo*, argues that this marketing blitz is the modern corporation's Achilles heel. Brands can work against corporations when customers feel mistreated, exploited, or betrayed—a phenomenon she calls *brand boomerang*.[57] Remember, for instance, the Coca-Cola commercials featuring adorable, computer-animated polar bears frolicking in the snow, with the tagline, "Enjoy Coca-Cola"? In the summer of 2000, Greenpeace launched a boycott against the company, protesting the company's use of hydrofluorocarbons (a type of greenhouse gas) in its refrigerated dispensers. As part of the campaign, Greenpeace Australia designed downloadable posters with the slogan "Enjoy Climate Change," picturing a pitiful family of polar bears struggling to keep cool on a melted polar ice cap (*see Figure 5.2*).[58] The boycott and the bad publicity struck home, and an embarrassed Coca-Cola Company agreed to end the use of hydrofluorocarbons several years later. Nike, BP, and many other organizations were similarly targeted by activists who used companies' brand images to lobby for change.

Figure 5.2   Exploiting the Power of Brands

Source: www.adbusters.org

When activists waged a similar boycott campaign against ExxonMobil in 2001, *New York Times* columnist Thomas Friedman observed that savvy environmental protesters "don't waste time throwing stones or lobbying governments. That takes forever and can easily be counter-lobbied by corporations. No, no, no. They start with consumers at the pump, get them to pressure the gas stations, get the station owners to pressure the companies, and the companies to pressure governments."[59]

Activists know how to exploit the media and create publicity to build momentum in boycott campaigns. Perhaps that is why corporate executives stay up at night worrying about public relations. A 2002 survey conducted by *Chief Executive* magazine asked 600 corporate presidents and chief executives to identify the biggest threats to the reputation of their businesses. The most common response was "media criticism."[60] Publicity campaigns can hit corporations right in the pocket. Mass protests against highly visible retail chains such as The Gap and Wal-Mart—where activists picket stores, distribute leaflets, hang banners, and threaten boycotts—are little more than a decade old. Yet, according to one Greenpeace organizer, it was like "discovering gunpowder."[61] These days, the mere hint of an embarrassing consumer backlash orchestrated by NGOs is enough to get some corporations to cry uncle. Within days after the group Global Exchange assembled a televised protest against Starbucks, executives of the coffee retailer met with the NGO to develop a plan to offer customers fair-trade coffee, which is certified to be made from coffee beans grown and picked under more humane conditions.[62]

Other campaigns may take NGOs more time and effort. It took the Rainforest Action Network (RAN) more than three years to convince the Boise Cascade Corporation, the largest logger of public lands in the United States, to withdraw from old-growth forests worldwide by 2004. When the company did not react to a publicity campaign, the activists focused on the companies that purchase large amounts of wood products from the Idaho-based multinational. "When you're up against a very recalcitrant target, you don't have a whole lot of choice but to hit them in the pocketbook," says RAN's campaign director Jennifer Krill. "It wasn't until we showed Boise's largest customers who they were buying from that we could make that change." When customers such as Kinko's, Levi Strauss, Patagonia, and LL Bean started canceling contracts, Boise caved and became the first major U.S. forest products company to adopt a comprehensive environmental statement for its operations.[63]

Corporations have begun to fight back. Some companies, such as Sony, Burger King, and BMW, hire web detective agencies to monitor their brands. For example, when Ben & Jerry loyalists began to criticize parent-company Unilever for not upholding the brand's socially responsible agenda, online sleuthing company Infonic Ltd. quickly alerted the company about a potential boycott. By the time the story emerged in the press, Unilever was well prepared to address the concerns.[64] In an effort to bring clarity and accountability to the burgeoning world of NGOs, the American Enterprise Institute and the Federalist Society launched NGOWatch, a website which aims to "compile factual data about non-governmental organizations . . . [with] cross-referenced information about corporations and NGOs, mission statements, and news about causes and campaigns."[65] The U.S. company eWatch services 900 companies, alerting them to Internet rumors, campaigns, and chat room web-discussions that may threaten their reputations. Clients include H. J. Heinz and Northwest Airlines. "You'll hear rumors before they start to spread," assures its website. "You'll be among the first to find out about negative or inaccurate information—instead of the last."[66]

Corporations are also becoming more media-savvy, sometimes by learning from their mistakes. A case study of how *not* to defuse a crisis was the response of Shell UK to the Brent Spar controversy in 1995. When Greenpeace launched a campaign against the oil giant's intent to dispose of a 14,500-ton oil storage facility in the North Sea and sent activists to occupy the facility, Shell forcibly expelled them. But activists reoccupied Brent Spar, prompting a three-week showdown with images of water-soaked eco-warriors playing out on TV news. A consumer boycott ensued, compelling Shell to back down. Looking back on the incident, Peter Duncan, the former chairman and CEO of Shell Australia, reflected, "[W]hat Shell should have done when Greenpeace occupied Brent Spar was not to try and expel them but to say, 'Clearly, there is an issue here of a dimension that we hadn't fully realized: Make yourself at home, and by the way, we are also going to bring others on so that you can together establish what is there—and given the dimensions of this thing—let us have a more open process of discussion about whether it is right to sink it in the Atlantic, or is it better to spend money doing something else.' And that would have been seen as a huge public relations coup by Shell . . ."[67]

Targeting a New "Mass Class"

Despite these attempts to be proactive, corporations remain vulnerable at a number of pressure points beyond the media. Activists who find it difficult to convince governments and multilateral institutions of the justice of their causes often have better luck swaying shareholder opinion. With more people owning stock today than ever before, this target audience is increasingly large. In 1965, 10 percent of Americans owned stock. By 1980, the number had doubled to 20 percent. Today, nearly half have investments. This new "mass class" of shareholders is different than their predecessors because they have a wider set of interests. Once inside the annual shareholder meetings, they can affect the agenda, table shareholder resolutions, and issue proxies. Shareholders forced Ford to change its position on global climate change. Energy giant BP faced major challenges from two activist groups: Greenpeace wanted the company out of the Arctic, while Free Tibet wanted it out of China. Both concerns resonated with the wider audience of shareholders and captured nearly 15 percent of the vote.[68]

In the United States, more than 300 shareholder resolutions were filed in 2002, up from just over 220 in 1999. According to the *Financial Times*, "Calls for companies to produce sustainability reports received more than 20 percent of the votes on average, while resolutions about climate change, human rights, and labor standards attracted more than 10 percent of votes."[69] The power of U.S. shareholders might soon increase considerably, owing to a new rule being considered by the SEC that aims to further strengthen corporate oversight: Shareholders would be allowed to put forward their own nominee for a board of directors if they can demonstrate widespread discontent with either management or the proxy process. The rule would not lead to a change of control, since only a limited number of seats could be contested—but it's not unthinkable that an incumbent director could be voted off the board.

> Corporations remain vulnerable at a number of pressure points beyond the media.

Although shareholder activism has traditionally been concentrated in the United States, it is growing in Europe and even Japan. In a 2003 survey, more than 50 percent of European fund managers and analysts said that social and environmental issues would strongly influence mainstream investment decisions during the next few years.[70] In March 2003, the Mutual Aid Association for Tokyo Metropolitan Teachers and Officials launched the first socially responsible investing (SRI) pension fund in Japan.[71] Although Japan's SRI funds are less than 1 percent of total investment in the country, the percentage is expected to rise, particularly on environmental topics.[72]

Shareholders are also increasingly focusing on the activities of companies that operate in developing nations. Faced with a shareholder proposal that would link executive pay to fair labor practices overseas, Mattel Inc. adopted an unusual monitoring plan under which outsiders, such as community groups, would inspect production sites to weed out labor abuses in their factories in developing countries.[73] After three years of shareholder resolutions, oil company Atlantic Richfield Corp. (Arco) announced it would withdraw its operations from Myanmar (formerly known as Burma), which was widely condemned for its systematic use of forced labor and other human rights abuses.[74] Most companies followed suit, with the exception of a few holdouts, such as U.S. oil giant Unocal. At Unocal's 2002 annual meeting, Amalgamated Bank (a bank that primarily serves trade unions) put a proposal before shareholders, urging the company to adopt and implement fundamental principles and rights at work. The proposal received 32.8 percent of the votes cast, the highest ever vote on a human and labor rights shareholder proposal. In the face of rising shareholder concerns, Unocal agreed in 2003 to include these principles and rights of work in its company code of conduct.[75]

Social Responsibility: Sincerity or Spin?

Over the past decade or so, companies have realized that they are being closely evaluated—by consumers, investors, and analysts—on social issues and environmental standards, as well as on financial performance. As Thomas d'Aquino, President and CEO of the Canadian Council of Chief Executives, describes the situation, "The new expectations of corporate governance sweeping across the world are based on a simple reality—you can run, but you cannot hide."[76] Corporate social responsibility (CSR) is a concept with a growing currency around the world. In an effort to preempt activists and defend their reputations among consumers, more and more multinational firms are implementing certification schemes, including codes of conduct, environmental statements, and labor standards. As of 2001, the OECD listed nearly 250 such certification schemes, covering almost every major industrial sector targeted by activists, such as chemicals, textile and apparel, forest products, oil, mining, nuclear power, and coffee.[77]

Some of these initiatives are industry-specific and combine the efforts of companies and NGOs. For instance, the Fair Labor Association (FLA), a nonprofit organization for the textile and apparel industry, consists of large global companies, such as Nike, Eddie Bauer, Liz Claiborne, and Phillips-Van Heusen, in addition to NGOs from around the world and more than 175 colleges and universities. The FLA was founded to develop a monitoring system for multinationals' global supply chains and to promote adherence to international labor standards. The FLA's Workplace Code of Conduct is truly global in scope and is available in 22 languages, including Hindi, Khmer, and Vietnamese.[78] Other industries that have adopted similar codes of conduct include coffee, forest products, diamonds, toys, and handmade rugs.

At the company level, firms are trumpeting their particular commitments to corporate social responsibility in an effort to preempt NGO wrath and appeal to consumers on an emotional level. Almost any website of a large corporation has a section on the firm's CSR program prominently displayed on its homepage, whether they call it "Good Works" like Ford, "In the Community" like Bank of America, or "Global Citizenship" like HP. Japanese companies dutifully fill out as many as 30 questionnaires a year, some 10 to 20 pages long, touching upon such diverse topics as whether they do business in undemocratic countries such as Myanmar and disclosing the ratio of disabled employees. "We can't avoid dealing with corporate social responsibility, since we live in an age when a single scandal can lead to the sudden death of a company," says one beleaguered official at a Japanese electric appliance manufacturer.[79]

Some companies are very targeted in their CSR schemes. BC Hydro in British Columbia, Canada, deals with 168 First Nations in its dam construction and energy transmission business. BC Hydro's statement of principles recognizes Aboriginal aspirations, expresses the company's willingness to consult early on any planned company activities, and articulates its commitment to Aboriginal employment, culture, and economic opportunities. As of 2002, it had trained 4500 Hydro employees in cross-cultural relations. As a result, BC Hydro has been very successful in obtaining the permissions it needs to operate its power generating and transmission business while avoiding conflict.[80]

Is corporate social responsibility an effective response to these threats? Advocates claim that CSR protects stakeholder interests. They believe it will create a new basis for achieving competitive advantage. However, it is far from clear that embracing CSR will silence globalization's most strident critics. Activists often dismiss such corporate activities as too limited and deride them as little more than public relations or "greenwashing." In addition, corporations can get caught in a cycle of rising expectations and find it increasingly difficult to fulfill the long list of NGO demands once they pledge to become better corporate citizens. For example, responding to pressure from activists, pharmaceutical company GlaxoSmithKline (GSK) began dropping the price of its leading AIDS drugs Combivir and Retrovir for AIDS patients in Africa. NGO groups continued to accuse the pharmaceutical industry of greed, and eventually GSK offered the AIDS drugs to African countries at cost, on a not-for-profit basis. Nevertheless, in November 2003, the U.S. activist group AIDS Healthcare Foundation launched a $150 million lawsuit against GSK's HIV/AIDS drug prices, effectively blaming the company for the millions of deceased AIDS victims who could not afford antiretroviral drugs. As a result, GSK decided to allow generic drug makers in South Africa to produce generic versions of Combivir and Retrovir, lowering their prices even further.[81] Responding to the criticism, GlaxoSmithKline's CEO Jean Pierre Garnier claims that "I think the public has much higher expectations of multinational companies than they did 10 years ago. I think they have lost their confidence in the ability of governments and large international institutions to solve the world's problems." Although Garnier believes companies have a responsibility to be good corporate citizens, he also explains there are limits to what his firm could do for AIDS in Africa, since "to be fair, we are a for-profit organization."[82] NGO demands for drug donations from GSK and other pharmaceutical companies are simply unsustainable given the millions of AIDS patients in Africa.

Yet, while CSR might not appease the harshest critics of globalization, the practice is not without benefits to the corporation. Morale is higher at companies that make a serious commitment to socially responsible causes. Employees want to be proud of the companies they work for and do not want to be associated with corporations that are branded as polluters or sweatshop manufacturers. For instance, employee turnover at Starbucks is one-third the norm in the retail food industry, owing at least partly to the company's commitment to social responsibility through programs that support small coffee growers and assist victims of violence.[83]

When companies support noble causes, it helps to build a stronger emotional bond with consumers. One 2002 survey found that 84 percent of Americans would likely choose a brand that was associated with a good cause over other brands of similar price and quality.[84] "Smart marketers no longer sit on the sides," says Carol Cone, the CEO of a cause-marketing company in Boston. "They want to be a heartfelt, soulful brand that's relevant to consumers."[85] Indeed, Tony Wright, Ogilvy & Mather's Director of Strategy, warns that cause-based marketing can backlash if it is viewed as a gratuitous public relations scheme. Such marketing works best when companies choose a cause that is clearly connected to their mandate.[86] The pharmaceutical company Merck, for example, developed a treatment for the tropical disease river blindness. Although the drug has no commercial applications in the West, the company spent millions of dollars developing it, and collaborates with the World Health Organization to distribute it for free in developing countries.[87]

> *Cause-based marketing can backlash if it is viewed as a gratuitous public relations scheme.*

Winning Hearts and Minds—Worldwide

Surprisingly, multinational corporations have been slow to deepen their bond with consumers overseas. Writing in the *Harvard Business Review*, John Quelch and V. Kasturi Rangan report that increased sales and operations in foreign markets have not been matched by proportionate increases in overseas philanthropy. In an era when an American brand no longer automatically commands a price premium, Quelch and Rangan argue, "These multinationals need to win hearts and minds, but they won't unless they implement their value statements with equal commitment worldwide."[88] The authors cite IBM as a paragon of overseas philanthropy. The computer company gives more than 30 percent of its charitable donations to non-U.S. residents, sponsoring technology education programs for 10 million children and 65,000 teachers worldwide. This initiative not only created local goodwill but helped IBM get a better sense of how consumers in different parts of the world interact with computers. By encouraging technology development in poor countries, IBM is sowing the seeds for new markets. When properly implemented, corporate social responsibility is proof positive that nice guys don't necessarily have to finish last.

Corporations confronted by grassroots activists might also consider cooperation in place of confrontation. Stanford business school professor David Baron notes how, in the early 1990s, McDonald's decided to work together with environmentalists who were upset with the fast-food company's waste-disposal policies. McDonald's created a joint taskforce with one of its harshest critics, Environmental Defense. Working together, they identified 40 steps to reduce solid waste by 80 percent. Instead of a damaging boycott, the initiative resulted with a settlement that left both sides happy.[89]

Likewise, fruit company Chiquita upgraded its environmental and labor practices in accordance with standards set forth by the Rainforest Alliance's Better Banana Program in 1997. The company spent $20 million to improve its facilities to reduce the use of chemicals and protect water sources. Chiquita became the first multinational company to sign an accord with unions in the southern hemisphere.[90] "Rather than simply respond to criticism, my hope was to define leading standards for our business and to prove to myself and others that we could indeed live up to them, everywhere they operate," noted Steve Warshaw, Chiquita's former chief executive in the company's first corporate responsibility report. "This was not to be a public relations exercise but a management discipline."[91] Chiquita claims its policies are paying off. In 2002, it reported $4.8 million worth of savings by relying less on agrochemicals.[92]

Similarly, as governments grow more powerful, companies must learn to adapt. Jeffrey Garten, the dean of the Yale School of Management, argues that multinational corporations will need to work with federal regulators to achieve the delicate balance between "openness" and "security" for a sustainable profitable environment. One area that requires collaboration is the creation of workable rules and procedures for the global commercial system, which is now under heavy duress and subject to severe regulations, particularly if terrorist attacks continue. Joint efforts in drafting regulations on customs inspections and other logistical matters are essential.

Echoing that sentiment, Ray Gilmartin, the CEO of Merck, notes that "There is definitely the potential for these [security] regulations to raise costs and make things more difficult for companies . . . That's why the private sector needs to take the initiative to work with government. It's counterintuitive, but we believe you can have greater security and lower costs."[93] Gilmartin cites shipping as an example where private-public sector partnerships can enhance both security and corporate efficiency. "By streamlining the distribution process and using global positioning systems, we can ensure the integrity of supply lines and enhance the productivity of the supply chain."[94]

Companies can also grow their bottom line by tapping into the new wave of government spending and fulfilling the growing demand for innovative technologies that can give the United States and other Western countries the vital edge in the war against terror. InVision Technologies is adapting its medical CAT scan equipment to scan luggage for explosives.[95] Bismuth Cartridge, which sells specialized duck-hunting bullets that shatter on impact, is marketing its product for airport security, as sky marshals could shoot the bullets in an airplane cabin without fear of penetrating the body of the plane.[96]

As former U.S. deputy undersecretary of commerce David Rothkopf notes in *Foreign Policy* magazine, it is the nimble private sector, not bureaucratic government behemoths, that has always been the source of such innovation. It is venture capitalists, researchers, and corporate program managers who will "provide the software, systems, and analytical resources that will enable the United States to track terrorists. It is they who will develop the sensing systems to detect biological, chemical, and cyber threats. And it is they who will perfect the biometric devices, such as retinal scanners or thumb-print readers or facial-recognition technologies, that will be critical components of next generation security systems and that will close the gaps Mohammed Atta and his associates revealed."[97]

Regulation and Activism: Three Possible Scenarios

How regulatory patterns unfold in the future will be determined by how corporations respond to the new dynamics of regulation and activism emerging today. Companies already manage a diverse array of constituents, including governments, nongovernmental organizations, consumers, and the public, in addition to their own shareholders. As such, value-building companies that find creative ways to address broad social concerns and cooperate with interest groups may be better positioned for future success than those with a single-minded pursuit of the bottom line. But regulatory trends will also depend on the power and reach of governments. As regulatory issues grow increasingly complex and overstretched, governments run headlong into their own demographic crises. The result is that quality and efficiency could decline, and regulators may see eroding public support for government oversight. At any rate, corporate executives looking for a single prescription are not likely to find one (*see Figure 5.3*).

Figure 5.3 Regulation and Activism: Three Possible Scenarios

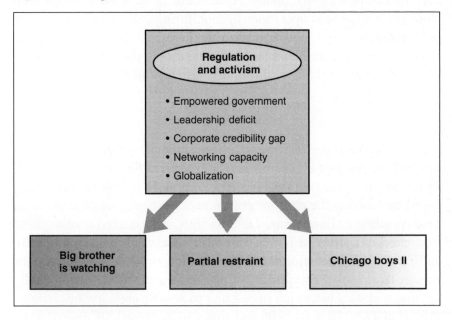

Big Brother Is Watching

Instead, business leaders must prepare for a range of possible scenarios. The first scenario, *big brother is watching*, envisions a hardening of the trend toward empowered governments and strident anti-corporate activists around the world. Periodic scandals at prominent global corporations do not help. Thousands of people see jobs disappear as their companies suffer market setbacks, and stockholders watch as their investments shrink. The stock markets remain unfriendly territory for the majority of corporations—and between a wary public and outraged advocacy groups, the rest of society does not provide much support, either.

In response, governments expand their oversight and impose increasingly tight restrictions over the private sector, at the same time that taxes and fiscal spending are on the rise. The growing clout of regulatory agencies helps them recruit talent and overcome the retirement-driven brain drain, often by hiring directly away from industry. Compliance costs for most companies rise dramatically, and companies that survive find they are in a cost-cutting race to the bottom. Some escape offshore to take advantage of less cumbersome costs and restrictions, but the difficulty of selling goods and services back to highly regulated home markets makes this a limited option. At the same time, activist groups keep close tabs on overseas operations by monitoring corporate activities and publicizing anything untoward through the media. In short, firms face intense pressure from above and below, and only those that are able to cut back and make their organizations "lean and mean" survive.

Partial Restraint

A second scenario, *partial restraint*, offers a more hospitable environment in which corporations, governments, and activists find a middle ground. Occasional threats to national security continue to bubble up around the world, reinforcing the need for government oversight, while at the same time revealing its limitations. Tight budgets and a limited pool of talent help check government power, and most regulation remains moderate and rational. While efforts at self-regulation produce a mixed bag of results, large global companies become more attuned to volatile public opinion and do a better job of reacting to activist pressure, by strategically choosing times to fight and times to concede. An uneasy truce develops, with activists monitoring corporate behavior and corporations tinkering with a wide range of partnership, certification, and charity efforts, in addition to better business practices. As scandals wane, public attitudes toward corporations gradually soften.

Chicago Boys II

A third possible scenario is called *Chicago boys II*. It imagines a future in which global corporations experience a new boom and largely unfettered markets abound. As notions of corporate social responsibility spread throughout the ranks of business, corporations overcome the cynicism greeting them at the turn of the century. Big companies project increasingly transparent, responsible images, convincing larger segments of society that the private sector is aware of important issues and stands ready to act as responsible players in their communities. Having overreached in previous years, once-powerful government regulatory agencies are cutting back. With no major security concerns on the horizon, they reduce both budgets and personnel and begin streamlining regulation, often in cooperation with the private sector. Activists remain a powerful force, but they more often work in partnership with corporations, who look to third parties to validate their sound business practices, adherence to emerging social and environmental norms, and socially responsible community initiatives.

As is the case with all of our scenarios, each outcome depends upon multiple, interacting factors. Strict regulations and a reversal in globalization, for instance, could create an inhospitable climate for global business. Alternatively, regulatory flexibility and strong consumer confidence could create powerful conditions for global business to reach new consumers in far-flung markets. The next chapter pulls these threads together, painting more detailed portraits of three possible scenarios for the world that will emerge in 2015.

Visions of the Future

If you don't know where you are going, every road will get you nowhere.
—Henry Kissinger

THE PRECEDING CHAPTERS offer a glimpse of the future through the prism of five principal drivers of the global business environment: globalization, demographics, consumer preferences, natural resources, and regulation and activism. As the scenarios at the end of each chapter reveal, the trajectory of each driver can lead to multiple outcomes. Global integration may intensify further, generating stronger economic growth and creating more closely connected societies, but barriers to trade and investment could also rise as concern about globalization's less benign aspects grows. Changing demographic patterns may well shift middle-class purchasing power toward emerging markets but could also raise tensions over immigration and create explosive conditions in some overpopulated regions. The diversity of possibilities is the whole point of scenario planning, a structured process that illuminates possible future conditions through careful examination of factors likely to shape those conditions.

Until now, however, we have only considered each driver on an individual basis. The next step is to bring them together, using the multiple possibilities revealed by each driver to craft more comprehensive views of what the world might look like further down the road. If the first chapter encouraged business leaders to pick up a telescope, look at the landscape, and gain a better sense of the strategic context within which they operate, then business leaders are now ready to view that information through the lens of a kaleidoscope. Scenario planning helps them consider how these constantly evolving drivers are likely to interact and yield new patterns of the future.

Yet the output from scenario planning is only as good as the input that supports it, and the specific methodology used to analyze and assess that input should be specific to the corporation and uniquely tailored to its needs. When designing their own processes, companies must avoid the two extremes to which planning exercises often fall prey: either focusing so much on the detailed input that they fail to see the big picture, or failing to have sufficiently detailed input to bring the right picture into focus. Nevertheless, the basic scenario planning process is the same. As Figure 6.1 illustrates, each driver raises its own range of future possibilities and scenarios. These interact with one another in countless ways to help paint complex and dynamic scenario pictures of the future environment, each of which has implications for the ways in which businesses will operate in the years to come.

The kaleidoscope metaphor is used advisedly. Particularly in this era of "information smog," millions of data points alone do not form a coherent analytical structure. A proper scenario-planning process involves continuous monitoring of the external environment and the rapid updating of critical data, based on the best available assessment of current and likely future conditions. This process often requires external expertise from strategic partners in academic institutions, think tanks, or trade organizations (and even from consultants). Corporate strategic planners must be able to elaborately orchestrate multiple networks of information focused on illuminating a limited number of worst-case to best-case possible futures. Otherwise, they risk failing to anticipate gathering storms that, in retrospect, they should have seen coming. Such was the case in 1979, for example, when most major forecasts failed to foresee the Shah's fall from power and the extraordinary impact that the subsequent rise of the Islamic regime had on the course of history. In fact, this extraordinary oversight helped undermine the credibility of corporate strategic planning in that era.

Now, a quarter of a century later, debates rage over another failure to understand and anticipate a fundamental series of events and forces

Figure 6.1 Process for Arriving at Three Final Scenarios for the World in 2015

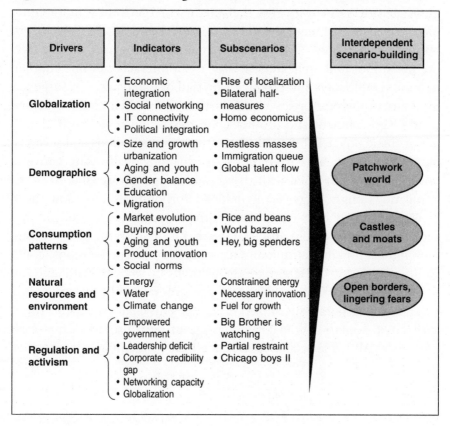

Source: A.T. Kearney

shaping the global business environment through the rise of global terrorism. Accurately forecasting *when* and *how* such disruptive events will occur might well be beyond the reach of even the most sophisticated and effective planning process. However, the ability to acknowledge the prospect of such events and work through their possible consequences should be part and parcel of today's planning process. Without it, companies lack "shock absorbers" when they hit bumps in the road. The notion of using scenarios to aid strategic planning is neither new nor foolproof. It is simply a way to organize a diverse mix of data and analysis to bring clarity to possible future events, conditions, or developments, and to do so in a way that makes sense for each company, given its unique character and concerns.

The scenarios that follow are designed to illustrate the kind of global business environments that might emerge from a more complete scenario-planning assessment, and are based on the five drivers outlined in this book. Like a chess game played in three dimensions, the possibilities inherent in each driver can interact with one another in innumerable ways and produce a myriad of outcomes. A resurgence in international terrorism could further strengthen the regulatory hand of government and prompt countries to embrace "go it alone" nationalistic policies that weaken multilateral institutions and severely curtail the ability of corporations to expand globally. Alternatively, governments confronted with rising public expenditures due to aging populations might increasingly defer to corporations and allow them to assume control over a number of formerly public sector obligations, such as law enforcement and healthcare. Or, if a surging global economy intensifies competition among multinational corporations, companies may seek to differentiate their brands by working with activists to convince their shareholders and the general public that they are paragons of corporate social responsibility. This chapter presents three speculative scenarios that cover a range of best-case and worst-case outcomes. All three scenarios are based on a certain combination of

Figure 6.2 Full Spectrum of Scenarios for the World in 2015

Dimension	Full-spectrum scenarios		
	Long winter	Bipolar world	Long boom restored
Globalization	• Rise of localization	• Bilateral half-measures	• *Homo economicus*
Demographics	• Restless masses	• Immigration queue	• Global talent flow
Consumption patterns	• Rice and beans	• World bazaar	• Hey, big spenders
Natural resources and environment	• Constrained energy	• Necessary innovation	• Fuel for growth
Activism and regulation	• Big Brother is watching	• Partial restraint	• Chicago boys II

Source: A.T. Kearney

subscenarios that offer a view of the global business environment in the year 2015 (*see Figure 6.2*).

Scenario One: Patchwork World

The state of the world and the business environment is characterized by a muddle-through mentality: Few governments show much leadership or vision, or even have enough high-quality talent to try to do so. The corporate sector responds in kind, seeking growth and profits by working their relationships and seeking advantage wherever they can find it in a fairly chaotic and turbulent world. Large patches of the globe are mired in poverty and violence, although the good news for North America, Europe, and Australasia is that much of the trouble is localized and does not spill over excessively into the zones of affluence, though they would be getting even more affluent if global growth rates were higher (*see Figure 6.3*).

By 2015, the global economy is stagnant. Certain countries record several quarters of above-trend performance. Yet, industrialized economies and key emerging markets remain subject to the swings of

Figure 6.3 Scenario One: Patchwork World

Dimension	Full-spectrum scenarios		
	Long winter	**Bipolar world**	**Long boom restored**
Globalization	• Rise of localization	• Bilateral half-measures	• *Homo economicus*
Demographics	• Restless masses	• Immigration queue	• Global talent flow
Consumption patterns	• Rice and beans	• World bazaar	• Hey, big spenders
Natural resources and environment	• Constrained energy	• Necessary innovation	• Fuel for growth
Activism and regulation	• Big Brother is watching	• Partial restraint	• Chicago boys II

Source: A.T. Kearney

Indicates the combination of subscenarios that comprise the patchwork world scenario the business cycle. The United States and the expanded European Union prove to be more resilient than others, given their vast internal demand and relative self-sufficiency. However, trade barriers in export markets have a damaging impact on key industrial sectors in Japan, China, and Southeast Asian nations, curtailing overall macroeconomic growth in these countries. Government aid and emergency financing grow more scarce, leaving the developing world to fend for itself amid worsening economic, political, and social conditions, even as high fertility rates add to severe population pressures in the poorest countries. Africa, the Middle East, and Central Asia occasionally witness localized explosions of unrest. This turmoil does not typically extend into nearby countries. However, as the cases of Afghanistan and Somalia revealed, failed states can pose a threat to the entire international community, since such countries emerge as locus points for transnational terrorist networks, money laundering, arms deals, and narcotics trafficking.

Meanwhile, as industrialized and emerging countries seek to maintain their competitive advantage in the global marketplace, governments adopt strategic protectionist measures to shield important industries and safeguard jobs from foreign competitors. This emerging parochialism makes it difficult to achieve international consensus and paralyzes the decision-making process at key institutions such as the World Trade Organization. Multilateral trade and investment agreements are supplanted by bilateral and regional treaties among nations whose interests most closely converge. The world becomes a patchwork quilt of contrasting regional and national norms.

> *Companies that seek to expand globally are hindered by a complex regulatory obstacle course.*

As countries, particularly those in the developing world, continue to burn fossil fuels with abandon, climatologists and environmentalists step up their warnings about global climate change. Governments are slow to address the problem, since they are reluctant to put the brakes on economic growth by tightening energy conservation rules. Absent coherent global standards on issues such as the environment and biotechnology, companies are burdened with longer research and development periods, lower economies of scale, and higher consumer prices in new areas of technological development. Companies that seek to expand globally are hindered by a complex regulatory obstacle course. As a result, all but the largest corporations limit their expansion to a specific region, opting to dominate in one local standard while competing in other parts of the world on a more limited basis.

The world's wealthiest consumers account for a greater share of global spending power than at any other time in modern history. In advanced markets, these on-the-go consumers show a penchant for sophisticated, easy-to-use goods and services that simplify lifestyles and address personal needs. Meanwhile, middle-income spending shifts to emerging markets such as China, India, Mexico, and Brazil. Collectively, roughly two billion people (29 percent of the world population) form the basis of this growing middle class. They purchase a lot of clothing and consumer durables (especially consumers who are younger than 25 years old, the age group that dominates many emerging markets). However, purchases of cars and first homes are sluggish, owing to economic growth rates that are lower than expected, and despite this broad convergence in purchasing power, a truly global "middle class" consciousness fails to take hold. Consumer preferences vary significantly from country to country— and frequently within countries.

Multinational corporations emerge as the most powerful players in international markets. Most maintain an extensive network of subsidiaries and affiliates, both in the advanced economies and the key emerging markets. This global network not only allows corporations to tap into overseas markets, but it also makes it easier for them to strategically allocate financial resources in ways that reduce taxes and circumvent national and regional regulations. National governments find it increasingly difficult to regulate corporations, largely due to the mass exodus of talented senior policy makers seeking more lucrative careers in the private sector.

Confronted with tight budgets and growing obligations to care for their aging populations, governments turn to corporations to handle a number of formerly public sector services, including technical training programs, law enforcement, and healthcare. As corporations assume a more visible role in the public sphere, they become increasingly sensitive about how they are perceived by the general public. They join a growing number of industry-wide taskforces and community groups designed to tackle problems ranging from water quality to illiteracy.

As government oversight declines, a broad coalition of activist groups steps into the breach to enforce certain standards of corporate behavior. These grassroots networks consistently challenge corporations to live up to their own rhetoric on corporate social responsibility, and take violations directly to consumers through boycotts and public awareness campaigns. For the most part, companies recognize that a commitment to social responsibility can reduce long-term costs and differentiate their brands among consumers. But public perceptions of what constitutes socially responsible corporate behavior vary from region to region. Different countries and cultures have divergent views on the benefits of genetically modified foods, the ethics of human cloning and stem cell research, and what constitutes appropriate standards of privacy protection in the use of information technology. Faced with these divergent viewpoints and consumption patterns, corporate expansion from one market into another proves especially challenging.

Scenario Two: Castles and Moats

This is not where the international community expected to end up. Security and survival preoccupy not only the world's poor, but also advanced countries, which have taken every possible means to insulate themselves from a world largely embroiled in vicious cycles of war, crime, terrorism, resource competition, and disease (*see Figure 6.4*). In fact, citizens in affluent countries have willingly given up certain civil liberties and privacy in favor of broad and technically sophisticated defensive measures. This is a time of splitting the existing economic "pie" rather than expanding it, and companies operate as creatively as they can given the constrained access to markets, the risks that abound, and a general mood of pessimism that prevails even among those still enjoying a good standard of living.

The world in 2015 is plagued with instability. Terrorist groups have continued their campaign of well-coordinated attacks against the United States and its institutions abroad, eroding global confidence in what was once seen as the world's preeminent political and economic superpower. Although most of al Qaeda's leaders have been caught and killed, the still-unresolved question of Palestinian statehood, ongoing conflicts in Central Asia and the Caucasus region, and worsening standards of living

Figure 6.4 Scenario Two: Castles and Moats

Dimension	Full-spectrum scenarios		
	Long winter	Bipolar world	Long boom restored
Globalization	• Rise of localization	• Bilateral half-measures	• *Homo economicus*
Demographics	• Restless masses	• Immigration queue	• Global talent flow
Consumption patterns	• Rice and beans	• World bazaar	• Hey, big spenders
Natural resources and environment	• Constrained energy	• Necessary innovation	• Fuel for growth
Activism and regulation	• Big Brother is watching	• Partial restraint	• Chicago boys II

Source: A.T. Kearney

Indicates the combination of subscenarios that comprise the castles-and-moats scenario

in Middle Eastern countries have galvanized a new generation of Islamic militants and local freedom fighters.

Among Western nations, national security trumps all other concerns. Civil liberties have taken a backseat to security concerns, as governments subject their citizens to constant surveillance. With xenophobia on the rise, immigrants, foreign workers, and even ethnic minorities are viewed with suspicion. Fewer and fewer people are willing to travel, work, or live abroad, knowing that they will be subjected to intense scrutiny.

As a siege mentality sets in, rising nationalist and populist sentiment is the catalyst for heightened levels of economic protectionism. Countries no longer believe in the efficacy of multilateral arrangements and prefer alliances with small groups of like-minded countries they feel they can trust. As advanced countries become preoccupied with their own problems, extremist groups see an opportunity to pursue their own causes more aggressively. Latin American guerillas wage a violent campaign throughout the Andean region and in southern Mexico. Armed separatists provoke a civil war in Indonesia, while fighting renews in the disputed territory of Kashmir, potentially drawing Pakistan and India into a nuclear conflict.

Although some regions, notably Europe, expand their use of renewable energy, the lack of technological development in this field renders it a cost-ineffective source of power. Instead, the world continues its dependence on fossil fuels. The intensive use of coal and oil worsens air quality in certain countries, such as China and India, while concerns over pollution and climate change remain largely localized, absent a multilateral framework to address the problem.

Economic malaise in Japan and the United States undercuts the global demand for goods and services. Several economies have plummeted from recession into outright depression. New security regulations to protect critical infrastructure and restrict the cross-border movements of potentially harmful cargo, people, and money have put the brakes on international trade and investment. The European Union and the North American Free Trade Agreement still function, although national governments have grown somewhat more assertive within each organization, and in Asia, Japan and China forge a loose regional network that provides cheap raw materials and markets for high-end services and final manufactured goods. Spiraling security costs and high insurance premiums make overseas expansion increasingly expensive. Multinational companies scale back operations, generally limiting their scope to specific regions or small groups of affiliated countries, where perceived risks are low or where local trade agreements have minimized regional tariffs and taxes.

As consumers are swept up in rising nationalism, they increasingly prefer goods and services made at home. Marketers and retailers pitch their merchandise with appeals to patriotism. Corporations find competitive advantage in assembling products—especially at the lower end of the cost spectrum—within their domestic markets and branding them with national symbols. Upscale consumers are more accepting of foreign brands, since there are not many local alternatives to these expensive niche products. Due to higher tariffs on imported goods and higher domestic production costs, rising prices have a dampening effect on consumption among almost all consumer categories. The keys to consumer loyalty are affordable prices and high quality.

> *As consumers are swept up in rising nationalism, they increasingly prefer goods and services made at home.*

Anemic growth in equity markets chips away at many pension and retirement funds. Confronted with diminished savings and high prices, senior citizens have surprisingly little impact on most consumer markets. Instead, they behave more like cost-conscious middle-class consumers.

Companies seek to gain competitive advantage by demonstrating how they can serve national interests. Some businesses gain protection from foreign competitors in exchange for safeguarding strategic assets and keeping large numbers of people gainfully employed. To some extent, this new environment suits those who had vigorously opposed globalization just a decade earlier. Governments now consider it a high priority to protect jobs and prevent them from going overseas. And barriers to foreign investment and cross-border travel ensure that countries can safeguard their own unique ways of life. However, protectionism has also raised the cost of goods and services and undermined living standards in both advanced countries and the developing world. Amid worsening socioeconomic conditions, activist groups press for policies to help those who need it most. But the dwindling power of corporations means they are no longer considered the source of all social ills. Instead, activists direct their protests almost exclusively against governments and a select group of "national champions."

Scenario Three: Open Borders, Lingering Fears

The United States and China are the dominant economic, political, and demographic players on the world scene—with large, robust markets that are highly intertwined, as well as muscular roles in the world that sometimes collide. Policymaking often moves in a different direction than it did in the late twentieth century and is not always in synch with business interests. Governments are less concerned about directly supporting corporations and opening new markets than they are about ensuring security, responding to populist impulses, and providing a stronger regulatory counterweight to unfettered market forces. Nevertheless, this is a time of intense business activity and technological innovation, and the rising tide of affluence continues to lift living standards in countries open to the global economy, even as further trade liberalization remains gradual. In the richest markets, companies tap into new consumption patterns emphasizing high-end, lifestyle-enhancing products and services (*see Figure 6.5*).

Figure 6.5 Scenario Three: Open Borders, Lingering Fears

Dimension	Full-spectrum scenarios		
	Long winter	Bipolar world	Long boom restored
Globalization	• Rise of localization	• Bilateral half-measures	• *Homo economicus*
Demographics	• Restless masses	• Immigration queue	• Global talent flow
Consumption patterns	• Rice and beans	• World bazaar	• Hey, big spenders
Natural resources and environment	• Constrained energy	• Necessary innovation	• Fuel for growth
Activism and regulation	• Big Brother is watching	• Partial restraint	• Chicago boys II

Source: A.T. Kearney   *Indicates the combination of subscenarios that comprise the open-borders, lingering-fears scenario*

By 2015, lowered barriers to trade and investment have boosted international commercial activity, with per capita income levels rising throughout the industrialized and developing world. The United States and China emerge as the world's chief beneficiaries, dominating global markets with their unprecedented economic clout. Although the two countries disagree on a number of issues, this competitive relationship does not morph into a Cold War–style rivalry. Instead, the two nations manage to carve out economic and geopolitical spheres of influence that counterbalance one another and maintain a stable world order. The European Union remains important but often plays a balancing role, as it finds consensus among its expanded membership elusive.

Trade in services is booming, and secure digital connections allow far-flung, truly global production and distribution networks to emerge. Countries with advanced economies have relocated the bulk of their manufacturing capacity to emerging markets. Responding to the public outcry over lost blue-collar jobs, governments divert more federal spending toward social safety nets and retraining programs, which helps mollify opposition to free trade. Still, free trade negotiations have reached an impasse, as governments find it difficult to reach consensus on several thorny issues such as governing the services trade and regulating biotech exports. Countries have also imposed some controls on international capital flows under the auspices of the newly created World Investment Organization. As a result, the total volume of cross-border capital flows has declined, but they are significantly less volatile than they were in the days of the financial crises that struck emerging markets in Asia and Latin America.

As the ratio of workers to retirees continues to shrink, industrialized countries have no choice but to open their doors to substantial numbers of immigrants from all regions of the world. Immigration programs expand for all categories of labor, placing special emphasis on recruiting workers with advanced degrees and rare skills. Despite tighter border controls and contentious public debates about immigration, authorities do not seriously crack down on the problem, since industrialized countries view immigration as a force for moderating wage pressures at the lower end of the income scale.

Sustained economic growth in emerging markets such as China, India, Mexico, and Brazil gives rise to a vast middle class of consumers. These consumers, many of them young, place a high premium on products that allow them to show off their newfound affluence and enhance their individual control. In advanced economies, many consumers are graduating into the upper class. On the one hand, their newfound affluence translates into more choices than ever before; on the other hand, these busy, on-the-go consumers have shorter attention spans and little patience for mastering new technologies. As such, they prefer sophisticated, yet easy-to-use, services that facilitate transactions, save time, and address their individual needs. They look to technology to simplify as many of their routine activities as possible (paying the bills, renting movies, refilling prescriptions, buying groceries, and so on). For such purchases, consumers are looking for brands that promise and deliver consistent quality, but for less routine purchases, consumers favor brands that tap into their desire for exploration, self-discovery, and entertainment. Rising expectations, coupled with a demand for constant innovation, makes consumers less and less tolerant of products and services that are cumbersome to use and do not deliver on their promises.

Acting on the belief that social responsibility can help differentiate their brands from those of their competitors, companies increasingly rely on self-regulation to guarantee the highest labor and environmental standards throughout their supply chains. Corporations seek out respected international nongovernmental organizations (NGOs) to earn their seal of approval by working together to develop codes of conduct. The NGOs appoint third-party companies to monitor corporations and ensure they are complying with these standards. This proactive approach toward corporate social responsibility reduces public pressure for the government to intervene. As such, most regulation of corporate behavior remains self-imposed. Governments do, however, remain entrenched within the economy. Tax rates in most countries grow higher and higher as governments scramble for funds to provide medical coverage and pension benefits for their aging populations, and to increase education, job training, and social safety nets to aid blue-collar workers affected by structural adjustment.

Parsing Out the Implications

These three scenarios reflect measured judgments based on the best available insights at a given point in time. Circumstances and conditions undoubtedly will change, and with them the projected outcomes. For corporations operating in the real world, the process of discerning and calibrating these changes must be a continuous and dynamic one that allows corporate executives to seize the opportunities presented by change while understanding and managing the risks that accompany it.

Of course, the implications of change will vary considerably across industries and companies. Executives must think carefully through the range of possible future scenarios to improve their corporate judgment and make solid business plans. For example, an open global trading environment where multilateral liberalization proceeds without significant protectionism (as in the "open borders" scenario) might allow a corporation to pursue an expansionist operational strategy, because constraints to market access would be limited. Conversely, the "castles and moats" scenario, where the trading environment is characterized by a proliferation of bilateral or regional agreements, rather than broader global trade liberalization, might require business decisions focused

> *The process of discerning and calibrating these changes must be a continuous and dynamic one.*

more on geopolitics and the macroeconomic potential of target markets. Under this scenario, a corporation might choose to concentrate its efforts within open trade areas, where returns are likely to be higher, instead of areas where mercantilist policies might dominate. Alternatively, a corporation alert to trade restrictions might seize opportunities to negotiate preferential market access or create strategic alliances with domestic producers. In that case, a regulated commercial environment would argue in favor of greater attention to maintaining good relations with the local government, thereby enabling the company to seek special market advantage.

Similarly, different trajectories in the global business environment may have implications for the way that people and employees are managed. The "open borders" scenario anticipates relatively free movement of workers across borders and could enable truly "global" talent pools to emerge. Then again, under the restrictive immigration policies described in the "castles and moats" scenario, global corporations might find themselves disaggregating the availability and cost of critical human resource capabilities by geography. Corporations might require creative ways to rationalize their core competencies and "wire around" their human resource bottlenecks. Executives who anticipate those needs might have an important lead on their competitors by inventorying, developing, and managing their complex global human resources supply chain.

Likewise, anticipating the kind of vibrant economic growth among the large emerging economies that the "open borders" scenario describes might lead executives to position their corporations to take advantage of the explosive growth in demand for "stuff" in places like China and India, while understanding the need for life-enhancing experiences among the industrialized world's richer but older consumers. A "patchwork world" or more dramatically "castles and moats" would require executives to differentiate much more finely between individual markets and the kinds of products their corporations offered in each. At the same time, executives might choose to dedicate more modest investment streams to markets constrained by mounting demographic pressures, where economic growth may slow.

Some scenarios envision a world characterized by environmental degradation and shortages of natural resources, which would also have an enormous impact on long-term global business forecasts. Just as oil shocks in the 1970s conditioned energy-intensive companies to hedge future energy price volatility, today's corporations might also benefit from better planning for possible water scarcity and other environmental constraints. Other scenarios envision a world in which governments respond to apprehensive constituencies with increasingly activist and interventionist policies. Under such scenarios corporations might invest more heavily in public affairs and liaison functions designed to communicate with employees, investors, communities, consumers, civic groups, media, and governments. In a scenario with largely deregulated markets and more comfortable relationships between corporations, governments and the public would require far less stakeholder management by corporate executives.

These are among the most obvious, high-level potential effects that scenarios might have on executive planning and decision making. Possible scenarios will change and evolve as each of the five drivers moves forward, but the process of monitoring global business environment change and developing scenarios gives corporations a distinct advantage. Scenarios allow well-tuned corporations to glean the kind of specific market and customer intelligence that ultimately constitutes competitive advantage in the emerging business landscape. As management guru Peter Drucker suggests, corporations must constantly reassess their core competencies and their specific mission as assumptions about society, the market, the customer, and technology change.

Things That Go Bump in the Night: The Wild Cards

While the preceding scenarios might well follow logically from an assessment of the five drivers, exogenous forces can and do alter what might seem like "logical" outcomes. Our introductory chapter addressed global volatility in the context of Newton's Third Law of Motion, which states that for every action there is an opposite and equal reaction. Newton's First Law—that an object moving in a straight line will continue moving in a straight line unless acted on by an outside force—also applies. The trajectory of each of our drivers—globalization, demographics, consumer preferences, natural resources and the environment, and regulation and activism—are not predetermined to move forward along a designated straight line. Rather, their trajectories may constantly change (and, in some cases, slow to a near-complete stop) as they are subjected to multiple outside forces. We call these outside forces *wild cards*, defined as low-probability, extremely high-impact events that are potentially disruptive (negatively or positively), rapidly moving, global in scope, and intrinsically beyond the control of any institution, group, or individual.[1]

Global Epidemic

Global integration not only facilitates the movement of goods, services, money, and ideas across international borders, it also accelerates the spread of microbes. From the Black Death of the Middle Ages to the influenza outbreak in the early twentieth century, humanity has been plagued with infectious diseases. But whereas it took slow-moving ocean liners months to spread influenza around the world after World War I, the 2003 SARS epidemic traveled with airline passengers from China to the West in a matter of weeks. Pandemics threaten to undermine economic growth in emerging markets by devastating their workforces and scaring off foreign investors. In our interconnected world, even small-scale outbreaks can have a widespread impact on trade, travel, and economic growth. A cholera outbreak in Peru in 1991 cost the country an estimated $770 million in lost tourism and trade due to a temporary ban on seafood exports.[2] In 1994, an outbreak of the plague in Surat, India, sparked the panicked exodus of several hundred thousand people and led to abrupt shutdowns of entire industries.[3] The World Health Organization (WHO) estimated the outbreak cost India some $2 billion.[4] The recent outbreak of SARS not only affected travel, tourism, and retail industries of the affected regions—particularly southern China—it affected the operations of multinational firms in those areas as well. The WHO issued its first ever travel alert for Hong Kong and the Guangdong Province, prompting most companies to cease all business travel to and from those areas. In response, HSBC, the largest financial institution in Hong Kong, began using backup trading floors originally designed for situations such as fires or earthquakes. Technology companies built up inventories in preparation for a possible disruption to the airfreight business. Ports in Europe delayed shipments from Asia for health reasons. A Motorola cell-phone factory in Singapore closed after an employee came down with SARS, and Flextronics instituted strict health security policies at its flagship plant in southern China.

Major Wars

Deep-rooted animosities or geopolitical rivalries can erupt at any time into full-fledged wars with regional, or even global, implications. Possible powder kegs include the ongoing Arab-Israeli dispute in the Middle East and a troublesome "Arc of Instability" defined by radical Islam and stretching from the Balkans through Central Asia and Kashmir on toward Indonesia. Aspiring powers such as China, India, and Pakistan could ignite simmering tensions with rivals including the United States, Japan, and Taiwan—or more ominously, with one another. Acute shortages of water could spur conflicts in some of the world's least stable regions, including the Middle East, Central Asia, Southeast Asia, and sub-Saharan Africa. Within the next 20 years, climate change could disrupt crops and cause famine worldwide, prompting nations to fight wars to safeguard their dwindling supplies of food. These scenarios are all the more frightening, given the ongoing proliferation of weapons of mass destruction. At present, four countries that possess (or are suspected to possess) nuclear weapons have refused to sign the international Nuclear Non-Proliferation Treaty (Israel, North Korea, Pakistan, and India), while nine countries (including Egypt, Iran, Russia, and China) are suspected of developing illegal chemical and biological weapons.

Country Disintegration

Catastrophic failures in key markets could plunge the global business environment into a new round of chaos and financial contagion. Sharply diverging growth rates among China's provinces could undermine the country's central control, while rising political expectations in the country might ignite social unrest, rendering its authoritarian regime irrelevant. The Arab countries in the Middle East, which sit atop the world's largest supplies of oil and natural gas reserves, could explode into violent unrest owing to poor economic conditions and lack of civil liberties. The threat is particularly acute in Saudi Arabia, which controls one-fourth of the world's proven oil reserves. The country's unemployment is over 20 percent and there is no clear line of succession for a king who is over 80 years old. In Russia, ultra-nationalist parties could come to power that would shut off foreign investment in the country's oil and natural gas sector, or exact high fees and taxes from overseas companies. Restless, unemployed populations in Africa, Central Asia, and Central America could erupt into mass migration flows, and poor countries, where economic development cannot keep pace with swelling population growth, might collapse into failed states, which would become havens for arms dealers, narcotics traffickers, and terrorists.

Terrorist Resurgence

Groups with violent agendas could attack the global economic infrastructure, igniting fears and financial panic. Although much of al-Qaeda's leadership has been captured and arrested, the organization's anti-Western ideology is still finding recruits among disaffected youth in the Middle East, Pakistan, Central Asia, and Southeast Asia. There are also myriad other groups with their own diverse agendas, including the Revolutionary Armed Forces of Colombia (FARC), which the U.S. State Department identifies as Latin America's "largest, most capable, and best-equipped insurgency of Marxist origin"[5] and the Islamic militant group Hezbollah (Party of God), which has established cells throughout Europe, Africa, South America, North America, and Asia.[6] Even well-funded individuals with ideological agendas or personal grudges pose a possible threat, since relatively inexpensive chemical and biological weapons empower them with a lethal capacity once limited to nation-states. Terrorist groups might attack stock exchanges, banks, or corporations, seeking to cripple business confidence and bring economic activity to a halt, or they might try to frighten away tourists and business travelers by attacking popular vacation resorts. Alternatively, they might seek to disrupt the world energy supply by using weapons of mass destruction against oil fields and pipelines in Saudi Arabia, Central Asia, or Texas in the United States.

Hacker Hell

As corporations and governments increasingly rely on networked systems to manage information, the intentional and unintentional spread of computer viruses can infect and damage those systems. In 2004, the Sasser computer worm struck more than one million PCs worldwide during just one weekend, shutting down computer systems at banks, transport reservation systems, and even the offices at the European Commission.[7] Branches of Westpac Bank in Australia had to rely on pen and paper to keep trading.[8] Also, increasingly sophisticated individuals and groups can hack into private systems, thereby endangering the security of governments and corporations alike. Making the problem even worse, the availability of free, easy-to-use, and increasingly powerful online search engines allows even amateur hackers to exploit poorly secured computer systems. Hackers are notoriously difficult to track down and governments cannot implement new national laws fast enough to contain and punish them—guaranteeing that hacking will remain a popular tool for disrupting the world order.

Quantum Leap

Critical technological breakthroughs might radically boost economic performance and improve the quality of human life. History is littered with failed predictions of the future that did not take into account the power of technology to transform. In 1899, U.S. Patent Commissioner Charles Duell declared that "everything which can be invented has been invented." IBM Chairman Thomas J. Watson, Sr., estimated in 1943 that the worldwide market for computers would be "about five or six." And, in the 1970s, the Club of Rome issued a report, *The Limits to Growth*, predicting that overpopulation would soon lead to a global energy crisis and mass starvation. As it turns out, inventions didn't end in 1900. (General Electric alone filed more than 50,000 patents in the twentieth century.)[9] The human race didn't run out of food, thanks to the "Green Revolution" that introduced more productive agricultural techniques to the developing world. Tom Watson Sr.'s prediction was off by an order of several million. Today, there are some 350 million computers in the world.[10] We drive cars and use appliances enabled by more computing power than what was used in the early Apollo space program. The first modern computer, named ENIAC, which was built in 1944, took up more space than an 18-wheel tractor trailer truck, weighed more than 17 mid-sized cars, and could execute up to 5000 basic arithmetic operations per second. One of today's most popular microprocessors, the Intel® Pentium® 4, is built on a tiny piece of silicon the size of a postage stamp, weighs less than a sugar packet, and can execute two billion instructions per second.

As the saying goes, you ain't seen nothing yet. In 1965, Gordon Moore postulated that the power of computing would double every 18 months while cost is halved. That prediction, known as Moore's Law, is still valid. Indeed, within the next couple of decades, we might see the emergence of quantum computers that will make today's most powerful supercomputers look like an abacus. Quantum computers make use of the superpositions and entanglements of quantum states. *Superposition* means that a particle can exist in two places simultaneously, which allows a quantum computer to examine all possible solutions to a problem at the same time. *Entanglement* describes a condition in which two or more particles become bound together, so that a change in one particle affects a change in another, even if the particles are trillions of miles apart. If you think that sounds weird, you're not alone. Albert Einstein described it as downright "spooky."[11] So, whereas contemporary computers are limited by the speed of electrons moving through silicon wires, a quantum computer would not even be confined by the speed of light. In practical

> By 2060, a $1000 computer might be equal to all human brains combined.

terms, that means a supercomputer would require 10 billion years to factor a 400-digit number, but a quantum computer could get the job done in 30 seconds.[12] Today $1000 buys a computer with the speed and capacity of an insect brain. By 2030, $1000 might buy a computer that's the equivalent of a human brain. By 2060, a $1000 computer might be equal to all human brains combined.[13]

The biotech revolution also portends dramatic changes. Genetic engineering can reduce the need for pesticides through the creation of plants that produce their own insect-killing toxins, or by genetically altering crop pests so they produce sterile offspring. By slowing the ripening process of fruit and vegetables, genetic engineers can ensure that more produce reaches markets without rotting, thereby allowing developing world farmers to generate more income. Biotech researchers have already created so-called golden rice enriched with vitamin A, offering a solution to a nutritional deficiency that causes blindness among some two million children per year. Similarly, researchers in India are now developing a protein-rich potato that can help combat malnutrition.[14] All told, biotech breakthroughs might improve food production as dramatically in this century as the Green Revolution did in the previous one. Genetic engineering also has the potential to yield breakthrough treatments for such diseases as cancer, Alzheimer's, and Parkinson's. Researchers are also looking at methods to alter the bacteria in women's bodies to produce proteins that protect against HIV[15]—thereby providing countries with a safe, cost-effective means of confronting one of the worst pandemics in history.

Then there's nanotechnology, which describes a body of technology in which products and other objects are created through the manipulation of atoms and molecules. A nano is a billionth of a meter, which is the width of five carbon atoms. The promise of nanotechnology is the creation of micromachines that can do work that humans cannot do, such as repairing human organs without surgery or handling dangerous industrial materials. These nanobots might be able to repair and perform routine maintenance inside human cells, offering a treatment for cancer or obesity. Magnetic nanoparticles injected into the bloodstream could help pinpoint the exact location of deadly viruses.[16] There are multiple applications for manufacturing new materials. Threads made from carbon nanotube fibers could be used to create bullet-proof vests as light as t-shirts, or to conduct electricity for microsensors embedded in clothing that could monitor everything from body temperature to heart rates.[17] Nanomaterials might also be used to create inexpensive solar energy cells that could be painted on any flat surface, or to create more efficient hydrogen fuel cells that would provide a clean, inexpensive form of energy that would put an end to the conflicts arising from access to oil and natural gas.[18]

The Wild Card Impact?

Each of these wild cards, occurring individually or in tandem, could influence the trajectory of the drivers of the global business environment. For instance, a rash of renewed terrorist attacks, sluggish economic growth, and a devastating pandemic could put the brakes on globalization. Perceived external threats to national security and economic well-being would lead to a revival of protectionism and nationalism. Wealthy countries would become gated communities, shutting their doors to young, unemployed people in the developing world in search of a higher standard of living. Or, to consider another possibility, political unrest and financial collapse in key emerging markets such as China could trigger a global recession and reshape consumption patterns. The middle class in emerging countries would not grow as fast as previously anticipated, middle-class consumers in advanced markets would have less disposable income and would delay large-scale purchases such as cars and homes until they could find the best deals possible, and the poor performance of equity markets and pension funds would chip away at the purchasing power of the elderly. The overthrow of the monarchy in Saudi Arabia by extremist elements could significantly reduce the global output of oil, leading to higher energy costs for consumers and industries alike, putting a damper on economic growth.

Value-building companies confront these risks with a distinct sense of how to minimize their capacity to thwart global expansion. Some exogenous shocks offer companies few alternatives, but there is no excuse for ignoring the potential impact of civil unrest or inter-state conflicts in countries or regions that are increasingly prone to instability and where the company may depend on a critical supplier. Put another way, if the drivers of the global business environment are your coordinates, then our guide to risk management allows you to plug those coordinates into your very own personalized Global Positioning System. Once these are understood, CEOs and their teams are in a position to create mitigation and contingency plans accordingly. The goal is not to eliminate risk altogether (an impossible proposition) but to develop operational resilience, foster the ability to recover quickly, and plot alternative courses to work around the disruption.

Navigating Risks in Turbulent Times

> *If the primary aim of a captain were to preserve his ship, he would keep it in port forever.*
>
> — Thomas Aquinas

THE TRAGIC EVENTS of September 11, 2001, served as a wake-up call to many senior executives. The staggering loss of life and infrastructure invoked an unprecedented sense of risk and vulnerability. But, in reality, the days following September 11th were no riskier than the days leading up to it. The difference was a newfound—and acute—*awareness* of the potential risks posed by today's increasingly dangerous world. In the three years since the attacks, many companies have made great progress in identifying threats and improving security. These improvements have been costly (*see Figure 7.1*), but companies have been slow to make fundamental changes on the ground to reduce risks and enhance the resilience of their operations. Indeed, few have taken a truly strategic look at the range of operational risks they face on a global scale.

This process is proving even more difficult in light of emerging business strategies. To reduce costs and serve high-growth developing markets, for example, companies have been rapidly extending their

Figure 7.1 Estimated Additional Annual Security Costs after September 11th Attacks

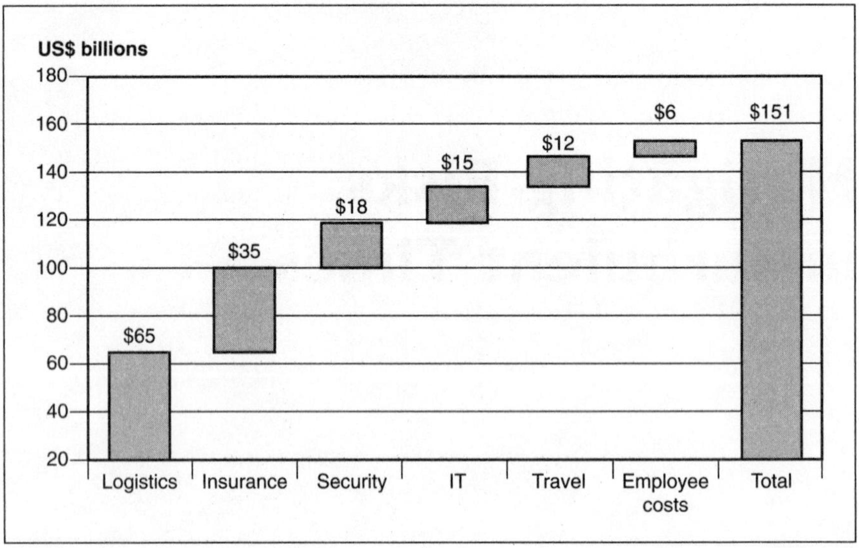

US$ billions

	Logistics	Insurance	Security	IT	Travel	Employee costs	Total
	$65	$35	$18	$15	$12	$6	$151

Source: Fortune, *February 13, 2002.*

international operations through global sourcing, offshore operations, and foreign subsidiaries. For all of the benefits such strategies offer, they also open up companies to an increasing range of both known and unknown risks. The Gartner Group predicts that one in five businesses will experience a crisis over the next five years—anything from a fire to a major IT failure—and that 60 percent of those companies will be forced to shut down within two years.

Clearly, the concern has registered. How can executives anticipate and then protect their companies against the virtually limitless array of possible disruptions? Returning to the days of domestic operations and large buffer inventories is not the answer. Smart, value-building companies realize that every opportunity requires some risk. Understanding vulnerabilities, surveying global risks, and implementing safeguards and contingency plans are not just about avoiding the costs of disaster. By integrating risk management into strategic planning, companies can turn smart risk taking into a competitive advantage.

Hope for the Best; Expect the Worst

Driven by an intensely competitive business environment, corporations have become increasingly dependent on global markets. Whether the drivers are revenue growth, cost reduction, or access to new knowledge, many of the most successful corporations already operate on a global basis. Even domestically focused companies are finding that competitive pressures are increasingly forcing them to expand beyond their borders. As already discussed, the cost advantages of production in key developing markets combined with higher growth rates and demographic shifts moving greater consumer power to developing nations will compel corporations to move more and more of their value chain offshore. While offering new opportunities, such shifts will also present a new set of challenges.

As increasingly frequent, disruptive events have made painfully clear, companies are more vulnerable than ever to economic crises, security threats, supply chain disruption, and consumer backlash. The major strategies businesses have implemented with such success in recent years—global sourcing, lean manufacturing, outsourcing, offshoring, and extended information technology networks—are increasing efficiencies enormously. But they have also created extremely fragile networks built on the false assumption that the world is a predictable and stable place. In fact, the very innovations that have helped improve business efficiency and profitability increasingly are based on an integrated global business environment that also brings with it a series of interdependent risks. Consider the following examples:

> *Companies are more vulnerable than ever to economic crises, security threats, supply chain disruption, and consumer backlash.*

Just in time. Some manufacturers have reduced inventory almost to zero. Chrysler, for example, keeps just two hours of inventory on hand at its plants near Detroit. Estimates suggest that the shift to just-in-time scheduling in the U.S. automotive industry alone has saved companies more than $1 billion a year in inventory carrying costs. The problem, however, is that while costs have come down, risks have increased. If deliveries of critical components are delayed, the entire factory must shut down. Similarly, retailers have become increasingly reliant on automatic replenishment and vendor managed inventory. Even brief delays can lead to empty shelves and lost sales.

Extended enterprise. Increasingly, firms depend on a complicated network of customers, suppliers, and partners that must all work together, and often no one person has oversight of the entire supply chain. In addition to day-to-day problems with forecasting, security, and information exchange, there is the increased risk of system failure if a key member of the network shuts down, even temporarily. In some cases, the supply chain is so complex that it is impossible to understand fully the true risk involved at any single point of failure.

Outsourcing. While companies once outsourced manufacturing or bill processing, they are now outsourcing IT support, customer call centers, benefits administration, human resources, and other increasingly sophisticated corporate functions. Although outsourcing can greatly reduce costs and often improve service levels, it can also compound risk as critical operations are managed outside the company, and increasingly outside of the country.

Global sourcing. Procurement policies that rely on foreign markets involve longer lead times, increased uncertainty, and heightened security concerns. Although suppliers in developing economies are often the lowest-cost producers, logistics and tariff costs can add up to 40 percent to the landed cost of a product. Goods can pass through as many as 11 middlemen in transit, greatly increasing the risk of disruption.

Supplier consolidation. Just as companies are outsourcing and adding complexity, they are also increasingly dependent on single suppliers. Single sourcing and industry consolidation mean companies must rely on one or a few suppliers for key components. Also, the trend toward design collaboration and information sharing multiplies the time and expense required to switch suppliers.

Information revolution. The rise of e-commerce (whether through intranets, extranets, or the Internet) means that more companies depend on information transfer to manage their operations. These systems are both increasingly critical to daily operations and vulnerable to attack as the number of access points rises. As noted previously in this book, verifiable digital attacks are estimated to have cost more than $16 billion in 2003 alone. Attacks can come from inside the company, from hackers targeting a specific company, or viruses that infect the entire network. The speed at which such viruses can spread across the network has increased from three years in 1990 to 10 minutes in 2003.

Increased competition. Tighter margins mean that even a small disruption to operations can show up on the bottom line; shortened product life cycles can make even small delays very costly. Companies have improved their operations to meet the needs and expectations of increasingly demanding customers. But most operational improvements have been designed for a stable environment in which risks are fairly well known. In reducing their everyday risks, companies have inadvertently increased the potential impact of exceptional events.

None of these aforementioned factors would be a concern if the world were a stable, predictable place. Unfortunately, it isn't, nor is it likely to become more stable or predictable anytime soon. No business is entirely immune to the impact of global economic and political trends. As we have discussed throughout this book, global integration has increased the volatility of the global business environment in a number of ways.

Mapping Your Risk Profile

Conducting business has always been a risky proposition, and all businesses have some tools in place to manage risk. Companies insure against losses, institute safety, health, and environmental procedures, lobby governments, hedge currencies, trade commodity futures, and protect their IT systems with firewalls and other measures. But generally these decisions are silo-based: managed by plant managers, country managers, finance departments, and IT administrators. While these may have sufficed in the past, they are inadequate in the era of interdependent risk. No one department or business unit (or even one company) has the peripheral vision needed to manage these risks.

What's more, the trend in corporate governance reform over the past few years means that more corporate boards have new legal responsibilities for enterprise-wide risk management. Since the mid-1990s and particularly after the accounting scandals at Enron, WorldCom, and others, standards bodies in Australia, New Zealand, Canada, Germany, the United Kingdom, and the United States have all emphasized the board's responsibility in identifying and managing business risks.

Facing greater risks, many businesses are at a loss, and ask questions such as: "What can we do about acts of God or terrorists?" or "Aren't my competitors just as vulnerable as I am?" They may believe that they cannot afford to take risks, or, having taken risks already, they cannot afford to invest in risk mitigation, believing that it will increase their costs, slow them down, and make them less competitive. Managing risk, however, is about becoming more flexible and competitive, not less. Risk must be examined in the overall context of corporate strategy and market opportunity, but the old adage still applies, "There is no reward without risk."

As a result, companies are turning to strategic risk management to improve outcomes while continuing to actively engage a volatile global business environment. More than just a checklist of safety measures, a strategic risk management approach identifies the core processes that drive a company's earnings and monitors both internal processes and external events to ensure that risk and reward are continually reevaluated and rebalanced. It is a dynamic approach demanded by a dynamically changing global business environment. The ultimate goal is, through an iterative process, to help companies evaluate their risk management process in the context of a structured "stages of excellence" approach (*see Figure 7.2*).

Rather than cataloguing all the possible risks a company might face, the first stage in strategic risk management is to understand the company's internal processes in order to isolate the most relevant and critical risks. Once a company understands its own internal vulnerabilities, it can monitor the external environment for danger signs and then begin to create mitigation and contingency plans accordingly. While companies may not be able to prevent disasters, they can reduce the impact by understanding how their operations may be affected.

> *While global corporations are vulnerable to many of the same risks, each company has a unique risk profile.*

Figure 7.2 Stages of Excellence in Risk Management

Dimension	Stage 1	Stage 2	Stage 3	Stage 4
Responsibility level	• Business unit	• Business unit	• Corporate (chief risk officer)	• Board level
Scope of risk	• Market risks (foreign exchange, credit, commodity) • Property or safety risks • IT security	• Market risks • Property or safety risks • Operational risks • IT disruption • Easily quantified risks	• All enterprise risks • Business continuity • Country risks • Key business processes • Day-to-day risks	• Strategic risks • Operational resilience • Global business environment • Organizational or cultural components of risk management
Risk-mitigation tools	• Financial derivatives, property insurance	• Incident data and trend analysis • Supplier contract reviews • Self-assessment	• Contingency planning • Scenario analysis • New business and new venture reviews • Independent audits • Risk adjusted performance measures	• Advance warning systems • Back-up processes as well as data • Quarterly drills that include key partners
Motivation	• Follow regulations, reduce financial exposure	• Avoid operational disruptions, costs or accidents	• Protect brand image, maintain earnings stability	• Create competitive advantage, generate shareholder value
Updates to risk plan	• Never	• After major incidents	• Annually	• Quarterly
Supply chain	• Buffer inventories based on static forecasts	• Alternate suppliers	• Coordinate forecasts throughout supply chain • Create strategic reserves of emergency stock	• Supply chain transparency • Dynamic reserves of critical components • Ability to change transportation modes in transit
Collaboration	• Focus internally	• Communicate policies to suppliers	• Collaborate with suppliers, industry associations	• Lead industry initiatives, collaborate with government

Source: A.T. Kearney

The goal is not to eliminate risk altogether (an impossible proposition) but to develop operational resilience, foster the ability to recover quickly, and plot alternative courses to work around the disruption.

While global corporations are vulnerable to many of the same risks, each company has a unique risk profile. There are five key steps in the development of this profile:

Prioritize earnings drivers. The first step is to identify and then map a company's earnings drivers, which provide operational support for the overall business strategy (*see Figure 7.3*). These are the factors that would have the biggest impact on earnings if disrupted, and a shock to any one could endanger the business. For example, a financial services firm might depend on information technology to the extent that even 10 minutes of downtime could have a major impact on earnings. A consumer products company depends on its brand reputation.

Identify critical infrastructure. The next step is to identify the infrastructure—including processes, relationships, people, regulations, plant, and equipment—that supports the firm's ability to generate earnings. Brand reputation, for example, might depend on product quality control processes, supplier labor practices, and key spokespeople within the firm. Research and development might depend on specific laboratory loca-

Figure 7.3 Top Earnings Drivers by Industry

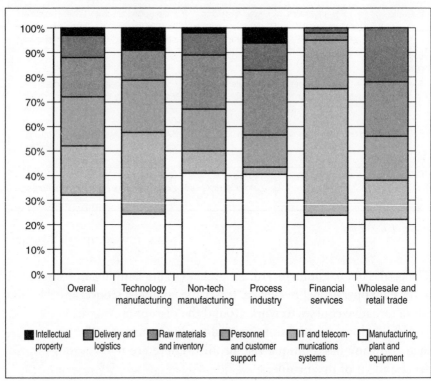

Sources: National Association of Corporate Treasurers and FM Global Survey of 200 CFOs, treasurers, and risk-management professionals

tions, critical personnel, and patent protection. Again, every company is unique, and even companies in the same industry will prioritize their drivers differently. The goal is to identify the essential components required for the earnings driver. One way to do this is by asking, "What are the processes which, if they failed, would seriously affect my earnings?"

Locate vulnerabilities. Having mapped the critical operational infrastructure, the next step is to identify the main vulnerabilities. What are the weakest links, the elements on which all of the others depend? It could be a single supplier for a critical component, a border that 80 percent of your products must cross to get to your key markets, a single employee who knows how to restore data if the IT system fails, or a regulation that makes it possible for you to stay in business. Vulnerabilities are characterized by:

- An element on which many others depend; a bottleneck
- Processes with no alternatives
- Association with high-risk geographic areas, industries, and products (war or flood zones, or economically troubled industries, such as airlines)
- Insecure access points to important infrastructure

Notice that the focus is still on the internal processes rather than potential external events. In many ways, the impact of a disruption does not depend on the precise manner in which these elements fail. Whether your key supplier fails because of a fire in a plant, an earthquake, a terrorist attack, or an economic crisis, you may have the same response plan.

Develop responses. After mapping its risk profile, a company will have detailed knowledge of its operational vulnerabilities and how these relate to its strategic goals and earnings. Simply understanding these vulnerabilities at the enterprise level will clarify critical decisions. The decision to move production from South America to China, for example, will have a clear impact on the company's risk profile, as will a decision to adopt new corporate social responsibility standards.

But completing a risk profile will also bring to light opportunities to reduce risk while at the same time indicating the value to be gained. Risk mitigation plans can be put into two broad categories: flexibility and redundancy. Flexible responses generally require advanced planning but little or no upfront investment and include:

- Identifying alternate suppliers
- Identifying alternate modes of transportation
- Using products designed for rapid switching of components
- Adopting manufacturing designs for rapid switching of products
- Having multiple (flexible) locations for various tasks
- Identifying additional production capacity
- Cross-training employees

Redundant solutions, on the other hand, generally require an investment in capacity that may not be needed and include:

- Increasing inventory
- Developing a cadre of alternate suppliers
- Preparing back-up IT and telecom systems
- Holding unused capacity
- Fostering long-term supplier contracts

Monitor the risk environment. For each vulnerability, there will be a number of potential responses. In order to evaluate which responses are most appropriate, it is necessary to look at the external environment. To be sure, some risks—notably, the wild cards outlined in the previous chapter, such as a worldwide pandemic or a simultaneous resurgence of terrorism in several countries—defy easy countermeasures. But most other risks—those that affect a specific country, region, or industrial sector—are manageable. By gauging the likelihood of various events, the company can evaluate how much to invest for each vulnerability. A company's risk profile is constantly changing—economic and market conditions change, consumer tastes change, the regulatory environment changes, as will products and processes. It is essential that the company's risk map change in tandem, implementing an early warning system so contingency plans can be activated as soon as possible. Although a detailed development of a company's risk management profile is a fairly elaborate process, a simple self-assessment can quickly identify the largest gaps (*see Figure 7.4*).

Figure 7.4 Risk Self-assessment

Key characteristics of a risk-management strategy	Not yet being considered	On the "to-do" list	Imple-mentation underway	Getting results
Transparent				
Board-level responsibility for enterprise-wide risk management				
Third-party audit of risk management practices				
Strategic				
Risk assessment focused on key earnings drivers				
Risk management clearly tied to creation of competitive advantage				
Collaborative				
Collaboration with industry associations and government (local, state, or national) for contingency planning				
Key suppliers or partners included in contingency planning				
Regular evaluations of risk for key suppliers/customers				
Flexible				
Succession plans for critical personnel				
Inventory levels adjusted continuously in response to risk analysis				
Ability to change modes of transport while in transit				
Redundant				
Alternate suppliers for key components				
Critical processes backed up offsite (both IT and non-IT)				
Up-to-date				
Risk plan updated at least annually				
Country risk and potential implications for operations tracked				
Regular drills for critical contingency plans				

Number of "getting results" and "underway" replies	Risk-management competency
12 or more	On track
6 to 11	Questionable
0 to 5	At risk

Sources: A.T. Kearney

Clearly, being able to reduce the costs of a disaster is a major benefit of risk management. But risk management is much more than an insurance policy that kicks in after disaster strikes. By understanding the relationship between corporate strategy and risk profile, corporations can ensure that they are not taking unnecessary risks, while at the same time reducing the potential impact of essential risks. Through flexibility and redundancy, companies can react quickly to changes in the marketplace, whether those changes are as common as varying consumer demand or as rare as political revolutions. The agility that results will ultimately allow corporations to maintain their equilibrium and come out on top, even in a world perpetually out of balance.

Riding the Whirlwind

No amount of nostalgia for the halcyon days of relative global stability will return us to a time when business-planning assumptions changed more slowly or predictably. It may well be that those times never were at all. As Will Rogers once reminisced, "Things ain't what they used to be—and probably never was!" Business conditions prior to the onset of globalization generally did, in fact, evolve more gradually than today. In a world connected by fewer threads, occurrences far from home had less direct, immediate impact on companies.

Today's business leaders seek to hide from the world at their own peril, because one way or another the world will eventually find them. As we have demonstrated in these pages, the dynamic drivers of twenty-first century business conditions—imbued and turbo-charged by extraordinary, ever-expansive technological innovation—underlie a world of continuous change and volatility. Those who fail to rigorously plan for and seize this future are abdicating their responsibility to their shareholders and stakeholders.

Stewards of the successful global corporation will not keep their corporate vessel docked at their home port waiting for calmer seas. Rather, with a constant eye on the telltale signs of changing conditions, and with all the expert input possible from a good crew and instrumentation alike, today's successful executive will ride the winds of change, meet the challenges they present, and realize the potential of these new global realities.

Endnotes

Introduction

1. James Woolsey, Remarks at the Foreign Press Center, Washington, DC, March 7, 2000, http://www.politrix.org/foia/echelon/echelon-cia.htm (accessed on May 4, 2004).
2. Fritz Kroeger, James McGrath, Michael Traem, and Jorg Rockenhaeuser, *The Value Growers* (New York: McGraw-Hill: 2000), 15, 22-23.
3. Fritz Kroeger, et al.
4. Graeme K. Deans and Fritz Kroeger, *Stretch! How Great Companies Grow in Good Times and Bad* (New Jersey: John Wiley & Sons, 2004).
5. Kroeger, et al., 16.
6. Leonard Fuld, "Be Prepared," *Harvard Business Review*, November 1, 2003.
7. Fuld.
8. Bill Clinton, "American Security in a Changing World," Dispatch Magazine August 5, 1996. http://www.law.uh.edu/cdrom/USFAC/DISPTCH7/DISV7 N32.PDF.
9. Roger N. Anderson, "Oil Production in the 21st Century," *Scientific American*, March 1998.
10. *Arab Human Development Report 2003*, United Nations Development Programme.
11. The Black Death is estimated to have killed from 7.5 million and 20 million people between 1347 and 1350, representing between 30 and 50 percent of the region's population. The so-called Spanish influenza of 1918 was smaller in relative terms, killing perhaps 50 million people worldwide. Current estimates from the United Nations suggest that the population of the European Union member countries will decline by 7.5 million over the coming 45 years, while its economically active population may decline by 88 million, while the populations of most other regions continue to grow. As a result, Europe's relative share of the world population will decline from 6 to less than 4 percent, making this an absolute and relative decline more substantial than any other period except the Black Death. Niall Ferguson, "Eurabia?" *New York Times Magazine*, April 4, 2004, 13. See also, Philippe Colombani, ed, "World Trade in the 21st Century," Institute Francaise des Relations Internationales, January 1, 2002.

12. CIA, "Long-Term Global Demographic Trends: Reshaping the Geopolitical Landscape," July 2001, http://www.cia.gov/cia/reports/Demo_Trends_For_Web.pdf.
13. United Nations Department of Economic and Social Affairs, "World Urbanization Prospects" (2001 revision), March 20, 2002, 3. http://www.un.org/esa/population/publications/wup2001/wup2001dh.pdf.
14. A.T. Kearney analysis of data from the United Nations Population Information Network and United Nations Food and Agriculture Organization (FAO).
15. John Quelch, presentation to the Global Business Policy Council CEO Retreat, June 5, 2002, Berlin, Germany, and "New Market for Ageing Populations, World Economic Forum," January 22, 2004.
16. Energy Information Administration, *International Energy Annual 2001*, Department of Energy, 11-13. China announced plans for one hundred major new plants by 2020, but placed orders for a total of 144 new generators in 2003 alone. *Power Engineering International Magazine*, March 2004.
17. CIA, "Global Trends 2015: A Dialogue about the Future with Non Government Experts," December 2000. http://www.cia.gov/cia/reports/globaltrends2015/index.html.
18. *Climate Change and the Financial Services Industry: Threats and Opportunities*, "Climate Change Working Group, United Nations Environment Programme Finance Initiatives," U20, 6-8.02.
19. "Value Opportunity Three: Improving the Ability to Fulfill Demand," PLM Article Series, The Product Development Company, 2002. http://www.ptc.com/company/tl/.

Chapter 1

1. Emma Rothschild, "Who Is Europe? Globalization and the Return of History," *Foreign Policy*, Summer 1999.
2. Emma Rothschild.
3. Nicholas Kristoff, "A Better System in the 19th Century," *The New York Times*, May 23, 1999.
4. "Singer Corporation Chronological History," http://www.singer.com/corp_history_chronological.html (accessed 5/11/04).
5. "From Trees to Trousers: A Century of Man-made Cellulosic Fibres," *Nonwoven*, http://www.nonwoven.co.uk/reports/Kewtalk92.htm (accessed 5/11/04).
6. General Motors corporate history, http://www.gm.com/company/corp_info/history/gmhis1920.html (accessed May 13, 2004).
7. Medard Gabel & Henry Bruner, "Globalinc. An Atlas of the Multinational Corporation," (New York: The New Press, 2003).
8. Halvor Moorshead, "The Transatlantic Cable," http://www.history-magazine.com/cable.html (accessed 5/7/04).
9. "Human Development Report 2001," UND, (New York: Oxford University Press, 2001), 30.
10. Ben Charny, "Study: Global Mobile Phone Use to Double," *ZDNet News*, August 7, 2003. http://www.bigpicturesmallworld.com/Global%20Inc%202/pgs/repcorp/com.html.

11. "The Hitchhiker's Guide to Cybernomics," *The Economist*, September 28, 1996, p. 1.
12. "Foreign Shareholders' Stake in Nokia Exceeds 90%," *Helsingin Sanomat*, August 27, 2001.
13. Mark Landler, "As Exchange Rates Swing, Carmakers Try to Duck," *The New York Times*, January 17, 2004.
14. United Nations Conference on Trade and Development, *World Investment Report 2003*.
15. "International Trade Statistics, 2003" World Trade Organization.
16. Kishore Mahbubani, "If the U.N. Were Being Created Today . . .," *The New York Times*, March 15, 2003.
17. "Compendium of Tourism Statistics 2003," *World Tourism Organization*.
18. Devesh Kapur and John McHale, "Migration's New Payoff," *Foreign Policy*, Nov/Dec 2003.
19. "Remittances Senders and Receivers: Tracking the Transnational Channels," *Pew Hispanic Center and Inter-American Development Bank*, Washington D.C., November 24, 2003.
20. Laura Wides, "Mexican Immigrant Group Looking Toward Politics," *Associated Press*, 1/20/04.
21. "Outsourcing: Make the Best of It," *Business Times*, 2/3/04.
22. "U.S. Outsourcing Backlash Growing," *Australian IT*, 2/3/04.
23. "Job Exports: Europe's Turn," *BusinessWeek Online*, April 19, 2004.
24. Kalpana Srinivasan, "Foreign Telecom Takeover Faces Hurdles," *Associated Press*, September 7, 2000.
25. Lee Chi-dong, "Is Korea Becoming a Hermit Kingdom Again?" *Korea Times*, 1/2/04.
26. "Ostalgie," *The Economist*, September 11, 2003.
27. Stephen Morse, "Microbial Threats to Health: Emergence, Detection, and Response: Regulating Viral Traffic," NAP, 2003.
28. "Spectre of SARS Reemerges," *BBC News*, 1/22/04.
29. Sandra G. Boodman, "Running Out of Wonder Drugs," *Washington Post*, March 16, 1993.
30. "Economic Costs of Malaria Are Many Times Higher Than Previously Estimated," Press Release WHO/28, *World Health Organization*, 25 April 2000.
31. Isabel Teotonio, "Alberta, Ontario Take New Measures to Help Beef Industry," *Globe and Mail*, July 25, 2003.
32. Thomas Friedman, *The Lexus and the Olive Tree: Understanding Globalization*, Farrar Strauss & Giroux, 1999, 421.
33. Bart Hobijn, "What Will Homeland Security Cost?" *Federal Reserve Bank of New York Economic Policy Review*, November 2002.

Chapter 2

1. This quote is also attributed to Richard Easterlin, Professor of Economics at The University of Southern California.
2. Paul Ehrlich, *The Population Bomb* (New York: Ballantine Books, 1968).
3. Limits to Growth: A Report for the Club of Rome's Project on the Predicament of Mankind (Sydney: Pan, 1972).
4. Ronald Bailey, *Eco-Scam* (New York: St. Martin's Press, 1993).

5. Michael Holtzman, "A Graying World Population Calls for Global Pension Reform," *Christian Science Monitor*, 7/29/97.
6. Peter G. Peterson, "Gray Dawn: The Global Aging Crisis," *Foreign Affairs* (January/February 1999): 42.
7. Nicholas Eberstadt, "Power and Population in Asia," *Policy Review*, no. 123 (February/March 2004). See also: United Nations Population Division: World Population Prospects: The 2002 Revision Population Database, http://esa.un.org/unpp (accessed 5/4/04).
8. Long-Term Global Demographic Trends: Reshaping the Geopolitical Landscape," CIA, July 2001, 21.
9. "World Population Prospects 1950-2050: The 2002 Revision," United Nations Department of Economic and Social Affairs, Population Division, New York, 2003.
10. Ronald Inglehart "The Population Implosion," *Foreign Policy Magazine*, March/April 2001.
11. "The World at Six Billion," United Nations Population Division, October 12, 1999.
12. Ayako Doi "Japan's Hybrid Women," *Foreign Policy Magazine*, November/December 2003. "Japan's Hybrid Women," Ayako Doi, *Foreign Policy Magazine*. Nov/Dec 2003.
13. "World Population in 2300," *United Nations Department of Economic and Social Affairs: Population Division*, 12/9/03 Draft.
14. Nicholas Eberstadt, "The Future of AIDS: Grim Toll in Russia, China, and India," *Foreign Affairs*, Vol. 81, No. 6 (November/December 2002).
15. Edward E. Gordon, "Bridging the Gap," *Training*, Vol. 40, Issue 81 (September 2003).
16. "Living Happily Ever After: The Economic Implications of Aging Societies," World Economic Forum, developed in partnership with Watson Wyatt Worldwide, 2004.
17. Patricia Van Arnum and Pamela Sauer, "The Changing Workforce of the Chemical Industry," *Chemical Market Reporter*, June 3, 2002.
18. David W. De Long, "Chemicals Industry Leaders: Are You Ready for the Workforce of the Future?" *Changing Workforce Demographics*, No. 2 (November 25, 2001).
19. "Bank on Workforce for Growth—Panel," *The Times of India*, April 18, 2003.
20. Ken Dychtwald, Tamara Erickson, and Bob Morison, "It's Time to Retire Retirement," *Harvard Business Review*, March 1, 2004.
21. "Long-Term Global Demographic Trends: Reshaping the Geopolitical Landscape," CIA, July 2001, 25.1.
22. "Long-Term Global Demographic Trends: Reshaping the Geopolitical Landscape," CIA, July 2001, 25.
23. Richard Jackson, "The Global Retirement Crisis," Center for Strategic and International Studies, April 2002, 21.
24. Peter G. Peterson, "The Shape of Things to Come: Global Aging in the Twenty-First Century," *Journal of International Affairs*, Fall 2002.
25. Peter G. Peterson.
26. "Relegation Ahead." *The Economist*, April 3, 2004: 78.
27. "Rick Wagoner: 'We Needed a Spark'," *Businessweek Online*, February 10, 2003.
28. Kathryn Tully, "GM Tests the Limits of Financial Engineering," *Euromoney Institutional Investor plc*, February 1, 2004.

29. "Retirement Blues," *The Economist*, July 30, 2003.
30. Stephen Lynch, "Pension Peril Looming," *New York Post*, 1/11/04.
31. "Siemens Revamps Its Pension Fund," *Financial News*, October 26, 2003.
32. "G8 Report 2001: Towards Shared Responsibility and Global Leadership," *Institute for International Economics*, 9.
33. "Defusing Europe's Pensions Time Bomb," Speech by Frits Bolkestein, Member of the European Commission in charge of the Internal Market and Taxation. Given on February 6, 2001, Brussels. http://europa.eu.int/rapid/start/cgi/guesten.ksh?p_action.gettxt=gt&doc=SPEECH/01/52I0IAGED&lg=EN (accessed 5/4/04).
34. Richard Jackson, "The Global Retirement Crisis," Center for Strategic and International Studies, April 2002, 28.
35. "Retirement Blues," *The Economist*, July 30, 2003.
36. Linday Whipp, "Japan to Raise Mandatory Pension Payments," *International Herald Tribune*, December 17, 2003.
37. Jacqueline Thorpe, "The Generation Bomb: The United States, Europe and Japan Are Facing a Severe Pension Crunch as Baby Boomers Begin to Retire," *Financial Post*, March 3, 2004.
38. *BBC News*, "Clashes Mar French Pension Debate," 6/10/03.
39. *BBC News*, "Strikes Weaken French Economy," 7/11/03.
40. "100 Most Powerful," *Modern Healthcare*, http://www.modernhealthcare.com/page.cms?pageId=419 (accessed 5/5/04).
41. "The Russian Party of Pensioners," *Global Action on Aging*, http://www.globalaging.org/pension/world/rpp.htm (accessed 5/5/04).
42. Association of American Medical College, "Facts—Applicants, Matriculants, and Graduates," http://www.aamc.org/data/facts/2003/2003slr.htm (accessed 5/5/04).
43. Immigration Policy Center, Immigration Policy in Focus: Health Worker Shortages and the Potential of Immigration Policy," Vol. 3, Issue 1 (February 2004).
44. Mariko Thompson, "Is There a Surgeon in the House?" *Los Angeles Daily News*, 2/2/04.
45. Sandy Gamliel, Robert M. Politzer, Marc L. Rivo, and Fitzhugh Mullan, "Managed Care on the March: Will Physicians Meet the Challenge?" *Health Affairs*, Summer 1995.
46. Tina Melan, "Luring Japanese Retirees," *The New Straits Times*, October 17, 2001.
47. Christina Valhouli, "Sun, Fun, & Plastic Surgery?" *Forbes*, 10/17/02.
48. Shyam Bhatia, "India Can Earn $ 1 Billion from Medical Tourism," *Rediff.com*, 12/6/03, http://www.rediff.com/money/2003/dec/06health.htm (accessed 5/5/04).
49. Peter G. Peterson, "The Shape of Things to Come: Global Aging in the Twenty-First Century," *Journal of International Affairs*, Fall 2002.
50. James Coomarasamy, "France's New Baby Boom," *BBC News*, January 16, 2003.
51. Nancy R. Lockwood, "The Aging Workforce," *HRMagazine*, Vol. 48, Issue 12 (December 2003).
52. Richard Jackson, "The Global Retirement Crisis," Center for Strategic and International Studies, April 2002, 32.
53. Steven Spiegel, "Privatization of Pensions: The Final Frontier," *MMC Views*, Winter 1997 http://www.mmc.com/views/97winter.spiegel.shtml (accessed 5/5/04).

54. Kim Sung-mi, "Elderly Want to Work until 68 but 54% Jobless," *The Korea Herald*, 2/4/04.
55. Moon-gap Sik, "Retirement Age to Be Raised to 60," *The Chosun Ilbo*, 1/19/04.
56. "Long-Term Global Demographic Trends: Reshaping the Geopolitical Landscape," CIA, July 2001, 33.
57. "Long-Term Global Demographic Trends: Reshaping the Geopolitical Landscape," CIA, July 2001, 45.
58. "Italian Police Swoop on People Traffickers," *Agence France-Presse*, December 12, 2001.
59. Peter G. Peterson, *Gray Dawn: How the Coming Age Will Transform America— and the World*, (New York: Random House, 1999), 55.
60. Ronald Inglehart "The Population Implosion," *Foreign Policy Magazine*, March/April 2001.
61. Sasha Polakow-Suransky & Giuliana Chamedes, "Europe's New Crusade," *The American Prospect*, 8/26/02.
62. "Long-Term Global Demographic Trends: Reshaping the Geopolitical Landscape," CIA, July 2001, 39.
63. "Tehran University Official Describes Iran Health Care System to HSPH," *Harvard Public Health Now*, 1/24/03, http://www.hsph.harvard.edu/ now/jan24/iran.html (accessed 5/5/04).
64. United Nations Department of Economic and Social Affairs, "World Urbanization Prospects" (2001 revision), March 20, 2002, 5. http://www.un.org/ esa/population/publications/wup2001/wup2001dh.pdf (accessed 5/6/04).
65. United Nations Department of Economic and Social Affairs, "World Urbanization Prospects (2001 revision), March 20, 2002, 4. http:// www.un.org/esa/population/publications/wup2001/wup2001dh.pdf (accessed 5/6/04).
66. "Asia's Megacity Problems Can Be Averted, Says ADB," *Asian Development Bank*, News Release No. 026/97, April 21, 1997, http://www.adb.org/ Documents/News/1997/nr1997026.asp (accessed 5/5/04).
67. "Asia's Best Cities," *Asiaweek*, Vol. 26, No. 32 (August 28, 2000).
68. Sudibyo M. Wiradji, "Indonesia: Ignoring Water Concerns Will Lead to Disaster," *The Jakarta Post*, March 23, 2004, http://www.waterconserve. info/articles/reader.asp?linkid=30361.
69. "Long-Term Global Demographic Trends: Reshaping the Geopolitical Landscape," CIA, July 2001, 65.
70. "OECD Science, Technology, and Industry Scoreboard 2003—Towards a Knowledge-based Economy," http://www1.oecd.org/publications/e-book/ 92-2003-04-1-7294/PDF%5CA123.pdf (accessed 5/5/04).
71. Andy Mukherjee, "India's Software Advantage Isn't Just in Wages," *International Herald Tribune*, 12/23/03.
72. Mario Cervantes, "Scientists and Engineers: Crisis, What Crisis?" *OECD Observer*, 1/16/04.
73. "OECD Science, Technology and Industry Scoreboard 2003—Towards a Knowledge-based Economy."
74. Chikako Usui, "Japan's Aging Dilemma?", *The Demographic Dilemma: Japan's Aging Society, Asian Program Special Report* (January 2003): 18.
75. "For Shinsei Employees, Free Childcare," *Japan Times*, 1/7/04.
76. Stephen Baker, "The Coming Battle for Immigrants," *BusinessWeek Online*, 8/26/02.

77. Deloitte Research, "The Cusp of a Revolution: How Offshoring Will Transform the Financial Services Industry," 2003, www.deloitte.com.
78. "Roadmap for Kerala as Healthcare BPO Provider," *The Hindu Business Line*, 5/16/03.
79. John Shinal, "No Smooth Sailing for Offshoring / Moving IT Work Overseas Can Have Unexpected Costs," *The San Francisco Chronicle*, November 16, 2003.
80. Barbara McIntosh, "An Employer's Guide to Older Workers: How to Win Them Back and Convince Them to Stay," *U.S. Department of Labor, Employment, and Training Administration*, http://www.doleta.gov/Seniors/other_docs/EmplGuide.pdf (accessed 5/5/04).
81. Daniel Yankelovich, "A Fourteen Year Gift of Life," Address to the symposium on aging, Tokyo, Japan, 1999, http://www.danyankelovich.com/a14year.pdf (accessed 5/5/04).
82. Joy Davia, "Xerox Tries New Health Plan," *Democrat & Chronicle* (Rochester, NY), July 5, 2003.
83. National Center for Policy Analysis, "Consumer Health Care," *Daily Policy Digest*, August 1, 2002, http://www.ncpa.org/iss/hea/2002/pd080102e.html.
84. Misbah Tahir, "GM Executive Tackles Rampant Healthcare Costs," *The Monroe Street Journal*, 4/7/03.
85. Darryl L. Landis, Patrick Cua, and David R. Walker, "Disease Management: A Tool for Employers to Manage Healthcare Outcomes," *Health & Productivity Management*, Vol. 2, No. 1, 2003.

Chapter 3

1. Calculations are based upon contemporary population and per capita consumption estimates. Countries are drawn to scale based on the size of the world's three main consumer groups: middle consumers (spending $10,000 to $25,000 per year), upper middle consumers (spending $25,001 to $40,000 per year), and upper consumers (spending $40,001 and up per year).
2. Douglas Fraser, "India's Elephant Economy Is Anything But a White One," *Sunday Herald*, October 14, 2003.
3. John A. Quelch, "The New Market for Ageing Populations," World Economic Forum Annual Meeting 2004, January 22, 2004, http://www.weforum.org/site/knowledgenavigator.nsf, (accessed May 4, 2004).
4. Teenage Research Unlimited Study press release, "Teens Spent $175 Billion in 2003," *Teenage Research Unlimited*, January 9, 2004, http://www.teenresearch.com/home.cfm (accessed April 27, 2004); gross domestic product statistics from "Gross Domestic Product, current U.S. $" series, World Development Indicators Online, The World Bank Group, 2004.
5. David E. Kennedy, "Coming of Age in Consumerdom," American Demographics, April 1, 2004.
6. Sheridan Prasso and Diane Brady, "Can the High End Hold Its Own?" *BusinessWeek*, June 30, 2003.
7. Ellen Yau, Kurt Gurka, and Peter Sailer, "Comparing Salaries and Wages of Women Shown on Forms W-2 to Those of Men, 1969-1999," Internal Revenue Service, U.S. Department of the Treasury, http://www.irs.gov/pub/irs-soi/99inw2wm.pdf (accessed April 19, 2004).

8. "Italian Mothers," OECD Observer, November 10, 2003, http://www.oec-dobserver.org/news/fullstory.php/aid/1035/Italian_mothers.html (accessed May 4, 2004).

9. "Stocks of Foreign and Foreign-born Populations in Selected OECD Countries, 1995 and 2002," OECD Trends in International Migration, January 21, 2004, http://www.oecd.org/dataoecd/7/49/24994376.pdf (accessed May 4, 2004).

10. "Minority Population Growth: 1995-2050," U.S. Department of Commerce Minority Business Development Agency, September 1999.

11. Cliff Peale, "Gain Detergent an Ethnic Winner," *The Cincinnati Enquirer*, January 23, 2004.

12. Mindy Charski and Rebecca Flass, "Old Navy to Tailor Message to Hispanics," *AdWeek*, August 4, 2003.

13. Andrew Chang, "Money Changes Everything," ABC News, June 25, 2002.

14. Syed Saleem Shahzad, "U.S. Will Delay Attack on Iraq at Its Peril," *Asia Times*, August 23, 2002, http://www.atimes.com/atimes/Middle_East/DH23Ak01.html (accessed May 5, 2004).

15. Theodore Levitt, "The Globalization of Markets," *Harvard Business Review*, May–June 1983.

16. Tiffany Wu, "GM Offers Tailor-made Chinese Family Cars," *Japan Today*, June 22, 2001.

17. Laszlo Buhasz, "Marketing to the New Senior," *Globe and Mail*, October 11, 2003.

18. Emiko Terazono, "Diamonds Are an Old Girl's Best Friend," *Financial Times*, February 10, 2004; brackets in original quote.

19. Nat Ives, "A Jarring Message to Madison Avenue from Senior Citizens," *The New York Times*, January 12, 2004.

20. Nielsen//NetRatings, "Senior Citizens Lead Internet Growth," PR Newswire press release, November 20, 2003.

21. Simon Jeffrey, "Over 60s Reach for the Mouse," *The Guardian*, July 8, 2003.

22. SeniorNet survey, "Seniors Online Increase," *SeniorNet*, February 4, 2003, http://www.seniorjournal.com/NEWS/SeniorStats/3-02-04SnrsOnline.htm (accessed May 5, 2004).

23. Maria Ligerakis, "Nescafé Caffeinates the Next Generation," *B&T*, http://www.bandt.com.au/news/f3/0c003ef3.asp, June 18, 2001.

24. "Serving the Youth Market, Messaging for the Youth Market," *Mobile Messaging Analyst*, 6/1/03.

25. Sarah Westcott, "Upwardly Mobile," *The Express*, March 27, 2004.

26. Ellen Sheng, "Update: Wireless Cos Woo Young with Ring Tones, Games," Dow Jones Newswires, March 24, 2004.

27. "China SMS Revenue at $1.3 Bln Jan–Oct 2003," *China News Digest*, January 28, 2004.

28. Jenny Strasburg, "Housewares Retailer Beats Expectations," *The San Francisco Chronicle*, March 19, 2004.

29. David Brooks, *Bobos in Paradise: The New Upper Class and How they Got There*, (New York, Simon & Schuster, 2001).

30. C. K. Prahalad and Allen L. Hammond, "Serving the World's Poor, Profitably," *Harvard Business Review*, Vol. 80, No. 9, September 2002.

31. As estimated by the A.T. Kearney global consumer model, based on real GDP data from the Economist Intelligence Unit's Country Data service, Gini coefficient data from the World Bank, and population figures from the U.S. Census Bureau.
32. Prahalad and Hammond, "Serving the World's Poor, Profitably."
33. Prahalad and Hammond, "Serving the World's Poor, Profitably."
34. Maitreyee Handique, "Gizmo gaga," Business Standard, February 27, 2004.
35. "Hindustan Lever Launches One Rupee Ice Candy Max Uno Nationwide," IPAN press release, October 5, 1999,http://www.ipan.com/press/99oct/0510hl.htm (accessed May 6, 2004).
36. "Ethnic Markets Are Growing Up," *Brandmarketing*, July 2000.
37. Joel J. Smith, "Marketing to Hispanics Pays Off," *The Detroit News*, December 14, 2003.
38. Verity Murphy, "Mecca Cola Challenges U.S. Rival," *BBC News Online*, January 8, 2003, http://news.bbc.co.uk/2/hi/middle_east/2640259.stm (accessed May 7, 2004).
39. Chang, "Money Changes Everything."
40. Marketplace Morning Report, Minnesota Public Radio, 2/15/02.
41. Anita Chabria, "Companies Try Marketing to Muslims Amid Ramadan," *PR Week U.S.*, November 24, 2003.
42. "LG Unveils New Mobile Phone Targeted at Islamic World," *Agence France Presse* press release, September 8, 2003.
43. Jack Ewing, Gerry Khermouch, and Jennifer Picard, "Heineken," *BusinessWeek International*, September 8, 2003.
44. "Saudi Flags on Burger Bags," *Los Angeles Times*, June 8, 1994.
45. Jennifer Bain, "Food as the Foundation of a Distinct Society," *The Globe and Mail*, November 6, 1999.
46. Sonia Kolesnikov-Jessop, "BMW Finding Success in China," *United Press International*, February 10, 2004.
47. "The 100 Top Brands," *BusinessWeek*, August 6, 2001.
48. Clotaire Rapaille, "The PT Cruiser Example," *Archetype Discoveries Worldwide*, http://www.archetypediscoveriesworldwide.com/HTML/ptcruis-ersessions.htm (accessed May 7, 2004).
49. "Chrysler Group to Increase Production of Chrysler PT Cruiser to Help Meet Demand," Automotive Intelligence News, April 25, 2001, http://www.autointell-news.com/News-2001/April-2001/April 25-01-p2.htm (accessed May 7, 2004).
50. Sean Silverthorne, "Will American Brands Be a Casualty of War?" *HBS Working Knowledge*, April 21, 2003.
51. Steve Jurvetson, "What Is Viral Marketing?" CNET, http://news.com.com/2010-1071-281328.html, June 22, 2000 (accessed May 7, 2004).
52. "Evite," About Ticketmaster website, http://www.aboutticketmaster.com/advertise/adevite.html (accessed May 7, 2004).
53. Larry Armstrong, "Big Enough to Turn Heads," *BusinessWeek*, April 22, 2002.
54. Mini Cooper Web offer 2003 (no longer valid), www.miniitalianjob.com (accessed May 7, 2004).
55. "60 Minutes," CBS News, October 26, 2003.
56. "The Raging Cow Boycott," http://www.bloggerheads.com/raging_cow/ (accessed May 7, 2004).

Chapter 4

1. *Environmental Issues in International Relations*, "Task Force Report on Water Scarcity in River Basins as a Security Program," Georgetown University, 1997.
2. Population Action International, "Sustaining Water, Easing Security," December 15, 1997. http://www.populationaction.org/resources/publications/water/water97.pdf.
3. Central Intelligence Agency, *Global Trends 2015: A Dialogue about the Future with Nongovernment Experts*, December 2000. http://www.cia.gov/cia/reports/globaltrends2015/index.html.
4. Seth Hettena, "State's Rice Farmers Evolve from Friend to Foe." *Associated Press*, December 21, 2003.
5. Pimentel, D., C Wilson, C. McCullum, R. Huang, P. Dwen, J. Flack, Q. Tran, T. Saltman, and B. Cliff.. "Economic and Environmental Benefits of Biodiversity." *BioScience*, 47(11), 1997.
6. Bonn Freshwater Meeting, Johannesburg Summit 2002, December 3, 2001. http://www.johannesburgsummit.org/html/whats_new/feature_story2.html.
7. Carmen Revenga, "Will There Be Enough Water?" *Pilot Analysis of Global Ecosystems Freshwater Systems*, October 2000.
8. "It Isn't Agriculture," *Down to Earth Magazine* (Special Supplement), February 15, 2004.
9. Government of Canada, "Environment Canada: The Management of Water," http://www.ec.gc.ca/water/en/manage/use/e_manuf.htm (accessed March 2004).
10. "Guidebook to Global Water Issues," ITT Industries, http://www.itt.com/waterbook/ind_USA.asp (accessed May 2004).
11. "The Business Case for Pursuing Water Sustainability: Intel Corporation," The Global Environmental Management Initiative. http://www.gemi.org/water/intel2.htm (accessed May 2004).
12. "It Isn't Agriculture."
13. *The China Post*, "Drought Gives Scare to Stocks," May 7, 2002.
14. "Southern Africa—A New Growth Opportunity," National Treasury of South Africa, 1997. http://www.treasury.gov.za .
15. Danielle Knight, "Water Scarcity in China Threatens World Food Prices," *Asia Times*, May 13, 2000.
16. Knight, "Water Scarcity in China Threatens World Food Prices."
17. *All Africa*, "Water and Sanitation: Dire Food Shortages Predicted for Sub Saharan Africa," November 2, 2003.
18. "Water and Sanitation: Dire Food Shortages Predicted for Sub Saharan Africa."
19. Lester Brown, *Plan B: Rescuing a Planet Under Stress and a Civilization in Trouble* (New York: W.W. Norton Company, 2003), 15.
20. *PR Newswire Europe*. "Promising New Technology from Procter & Gamble Proven Effective in Purifying Water for the Developing World," June 19, 2003.
21. Vanessa Houlder, "Water Lobbyists Pressure Pepsi," *Financial Times*, May 7, 2003.
22. Saritha Rai, "Indians Fault Coke and Pepsi Anew," *The New York Times*, May 22, 2003.
23. Government of Canada, "Environment Canada: Quickfacts." http://www.ec.gc.ca/water/en/e_quickfacts.htm (accessed March 2004).

24. Nick Coleman, "UN Forum Exposes Rifts Over Central Asian Water Crisis," *Agence-France Presse*, August AFP, Nick Coleman, 8/31, 2003.
25. Faustine Rwambali, "Tanzania Ignore Nile Treaty, Starts Victoria Water Project," *The East African*, February 11, 2004.
26. Jonathan Treat, "Mexico and U.S. Cut Rio Grande Deal, but Tensions Run High as Border Waters Run Low," *Borderlines*, June 2001.
27. Sandra L. Postel and Aaron Wolf, "Dehydrating Conflict," *Foreign Policy*, September/October 2001.
28. Richard Ingham, "Water Wars Risk Not So Bad as Feared Says UN Report," *Agence-France Presse*, March 3, 2004.
29. Sandra L. Postel and Aaron Wolf.
30. Robert Stavins, "Most Precious Resource Is Underpriced," *The New York Times*, August 14, 1999.
31. Robert Stavins.
32. *The UN World Water Development Report*, "Valuing Water." http://www.unesco.org/water/wwap/facts_figures/valuing_water.shtml (accessed May 2004).
33. *XINHUA Online*, "Beijing to Set New Water Prices," February 25, 2002. http://news.xinhuanet.com/english/2004-02/25/content_1330639.html.
34. "The Business Case for Pursuing Water Sustainability: New Opportunities, New Risks," The Global Environmental Management Initiative. http://www.gemi.org/water (accessed May 2004).
35. "The Coca-Cola Company," The Global Environmental Management Initiative, http://www.gemi.org/water/coca-cola.htm (accessed May 2004).
36. "Abbott Laboratories," The Global Environmental Management Initiative, http://www.gemi.org/water/abbott2.htm (accessed May 2004).
37. *Federal Document Clearinghouse*, "Is Water the Oil of the 21st Century?" Congressional Testimony of Paul E. Dean, May 22, 2003.
38. Claudia H. Deutsch, "Companies Hope Profits Run from Clean Water," *The New York Times*, February 15, 2004.
39. Claudia H. Deutsch.
40. James Kloeppel and Sara Chilton, "NSF $20 Million Water Purification Center Takes New Materials Approach to Age-old Problem," College of Engineering University of Illinois at Urbana-Champaign Press Release, September 30, 2002. http://www.engr.uiuc.edu/news/index.php?xId=06760896.
41. Margot Roosevelt, "The Winds of Change," *Time*, August 26, 2002.
42. Jeremy Rifkin, "The Forever Fuel," *The Boston Globe*, February 23, 2003.
43. *All Africa*, "BP Promotes Energy Use in Tanzania," November 14, 2003.
44. Terry Macalister, "World Needs $16 Trillion Energy Boost," *The Guardian*, November 5, 2003.
45. Stephanie Anderson, "ExxonMobil's Boss on Energy Security," *Businessweek Online*, February 13, 2003. http://www.businessweek.com/bwdaily/dnflash/feb2003/nf20030213_3403_db053.html.
46. Chen Aizhu, "China's Top Oil Firms to Copy CNOOC in Gas Race," *Forbes.com*, February 26, 2004. http://www.forbes.com/home_asia/newswire/2004/02/26/rtr1278409.html.
47. Keith Bradsher, "China's Boom Adds to Global Warming Problem," *The New York Times*, October 22, 2003.
48. Marvin J. Cetron and Owen Davies, "Trends Shaping the Future," *The Futurist*, January 1, 2003.

49. Roger N. Anderson, "Oil Production in the 21st Century," *Scientific American*, March 1998.
50. Alfred Cavallo, "Oil: The Illusion of Plenty," *Bulletin of Atomic Scientists*, January 1, 2004.
51. Marvin J. Cetron and Owen Davies.
52 . C. H. Peterson, S. D. Rice, J. W. Short, D. Esler, J. L. Bodkin, B. E. Ballachey, D. B. Irons, "'Long-term Ecosystem Response to the Exxon Valdez Oil Spill," *Science Magazine*, December 19, 2003.
53. *Greenwire*, "Energy Markets," November 5, 2003.
54. *The Economist*, "Still Holding Consumers Over a Barrel," October 25, 2003.
55. Jon. D. Markman, "Sauds' Royal House of Cards," *The Street.com*, February 5, 2004. http://www.thestreet.com/pf/funds/supermodels/10141852.html.
56. Dmitry Zhdannikov, "Russia Says Oil Output Much Above 9 mbpd Unlikely," *Reuters*, October 15, 2003.
57. Stanley Reed, "The Oil Lord," *BusinessWeek*, October 27, 2003.
58. Catherine Belton, "BP Strikes Record $6.75 Bln TNK Deal," *St. Petersburg Times*, February 14, 2003.
59. Stanley Reed.
60. Bright Okogu, "Middle East to Dominate World Oil for Many Years," *Finance & Development*, , March 1, 2003. http://www.imf.org/external/pubs/ft/fandd/2003/03/okog.htm.
61. Chip Cummins, "Companies: Shell to Expand Gas Operations— Commodity May Outstrip Oil as a Fuel in 20 Years; U.S., Asian Demand Rises," *The Wall Street Journal Europe*, June 3, 2003.
62. *Bloomberg*, "China's Shenhua Plans R24bn Project with Sasol," March 23, 2004.
63. Luke Hunt, "Global Energy Supplies Abundant, but Access is Critical," *Agence-France Presse*, September 21, 2002.
64. *World Markets Research Centre*, "Brazil—Petrobras Makes Large Natural Gas Discovery in Brazil," April 30, 2003.
65. Will Smale, "Growing Concern Over Gas Imports," *BBC News*, January 20, 2004. http://newsvote.bbc.co.uk/mpapps/pagetools/print/news.bbc.co.uk/1/hi/business/3401083.stm.
66. Jack Z. Smith.
67. Carl Mortished, "Deep-frozen Gas Is the Hot New Global Energy," *The Times*, May 17, 2003.
68. Carl Mortished.
69. Stephanie Anderson Forest, "The Quest for a New Energy Prize," *BusinessWeek Online*, March 1, 2004. http://yahoo.businessweek.com/magazine/content/04_09/b3872106_mz009.html.
70. U.S. Department of Energy *International Energy Outlook 2003* Press Release, "Emerging Asia Drives World Energy Use," May 1, 2003. http://www.eia.doe.gov/neic/press/press214.html.
71. *Advanced Materials & Composites News*," GE Energy Announces Strong Growth for Its Wind Energy Sector," March 15, 2004.
72. Peter Heing, "Bright Idea: Mainstream VCs Are Betting Big on Clean Energy Deals. Will They Get a Jolt or End Up in the Dark?" *Venture Capital Journal*, November 1, 2003.
73. Jennifer Graham, "GCEP Researchers Divided on Viability of Renewables," *Stanford Daily*, August 7, 2003. http://daily.stanford.edu/tempo?page=content&id=11647&repository=0001_article.

74. Robert L. Olson, "The Promise and Pitfalls of Hydrogen Energy," *The Futurist*, July 1, 2003.
75. *DaimlerChrysler Top Stories*, "NECAR 5 Completes First Ever Fuel-Cell Cross Country Trip through the USA," June 5, 2002. http://www.daimler chrysler.com/dccom.
76. Miguel Bustillo and Gary Polakovic, "Hydrogen Fuels Schwarzenegger Vision for Future," *Los Angeles Times*, January 25, 2004.
77. Robert L. Olson.
78. Robert L. Olson.
79. Virginia L. Woodwell, "Toyota Prius in High Demand," *The York Weekly*, April 14, 2004.
80. Robert L. Olson.
81. www.iea.org.
82. Robert L. Olson.
83. *New Scientist News Service*, "First Power States to Harness Moon Opens," September 22, 2003. http://www.newscientist.com/news/news.jsp?id=ns9999 4188.
84. Susanne Quick, "Mining the Moon for Energy on Earth," *Milwaukee Journal-Sentinel*, January 19, 2003.
85. National Oceanic and Atmospheric Administration, "Global Warming." http://lwf.ncdc.noaa.gov/oa/climate/globalwarming.html (accessed May 2004).
86. National Oceanic and Atmospheric Administration.
87. National Oceanic and Atmospheric Administration.
88. BBC News, "Global Warming 'Detected' in the U.S.," November 15, 2003. http://news.bbc.co.uk/1/hi/sci/tech/3267775.stm.
89. Paul Recer, "Study Finds Europe's Summer of 2003 Likely Was Hottest in 500 Years," *Associated Press*, March 5, 2004.
90. Lisa Schmidt, "Developing Nations Will Bear Brunt of Global Warming," *Canadian Press*, February 18, 2001.
91. *American Geophysical Union News*, "AGU Adopts Position on Climate Change and Greenhouse Gases," January 28, 1999. http://www.agu.org/sci_soc/ prrl/prrl9903.html.
92. Mark Townsend and Paul Harris, "Now the Pentagon Tells Bush: Climate Change Will Destroy Us," *The Guardian*, February 22, 2004.
93. *Environmental News Network*, "Many Ski Resorts Heading Downhill as a Result of Global Warming," December 2, 2003.
94. "Costs of Global Warming and Climate Change," Transcript: NPR/Talk of the Nation/Science Friday, June 7, 2002.
95. "Global Warming Accelerates China's Sea Level Rise," *People's Daily Online*, April 13, 2002. http://english.peopledaily.com.cn/200204/13/eng20020413_ 93966.html.
96. "Global Warming to Cost $300 Billion a Year—UN Report," *Reuters*, February 4, 2001.
97. Richard Ingham, "Climate Change Boosting Flood, Disaster Peril for Billions," *Agence-France Presse*, February 27, 2003.
98. Clare Nullis, "Red Cross Warns of 'Super Disasters'," *Associated Press*, June 24, 1999.
99. Richard Ingham.
100. Rebecca Allison, "Heatwave: Records Sound Red Alert Over Climate," *The Guardian*, October 11, 2003.

101. Richard Ingham.
102. Vanessa Houlder, "Climate Change 'Increasing Financial Risks," *The Financial Times,* October 9, 2002.
103. Stephen Leahy, "Environment: "Oceans Now Facing Threat from Global Warming," *Inter Press Service,* August 22, 2002.
104. L. Carr and R. Mendelsohn, "Valuing Coral Reefs: A Travel Cost Analysis of the Great Barrier Reef," *Ambio,* Vol. 32, No. 5 (August 2003).
105. *Nature,* "Extinction Risk from Climate Change," January 8, 2004.
106. *XINHUA Online,* "Johannesburg Summit Delegates Call for Immediate Action on Biodiversity," August 27, 2002. http://news.xinhuanet.com/english/2002-08/27/content_540234.html.
107. The Intergovernmental Panel on Climate Change, "Climate Change 2001: Impacts, Adaptation and Vulnerability—Contribution of Working Group II to the Third Assessment Report of IPCC," 2001. http://www.grida.no/climate/ipcc_tar/wg2/index.html.
108. Christopher Hopson, "ExxonMobil," *Upstream: The International Oil and Gas Newspaper,* October 25, 2002.
109. Dave Ebner, "Is Exxon Getting Kyoto-Friendly?" *Globe and Mail,* October 14, 2003.
110. Lester Brown.
111. Lester Brown.
112. *Plan B,* Lester Brown, Norton, 2003.
113. United Nations Environment Programme, *Climate Change and the Financial Services Industry,* 2002. http://unepfi.net.
114. Darcy Frey, "How Green Is BP?" *The New York Times,* December 8, 2002.
115. Tracey Ober, "Brazil: CVRD Sees Amazon-Friendly Mining as Industry Trend," *Amazonia,* September 13.1999. www.amazonia.net/Articles/349.html.
116. International Finance Corporation, *Developing Value: The Business Case for Sustainability in Emerging Markets,* 2003. http://www.sustainability.com/developing-value/contents.asp (accessed May 2004).
117. Darcy Frey.

Chapter 5

1. Brian Friel, "Faith Healers," GovExec.com, April 1, 1998, http://www.govexec.com/features/0498s5s2.htm (accessed May 2004).
2. "The NES Guide to Public Opinion and Electoral Behavior," *The National Election Studies,* http://www.umich.edu/~nes/nesguide/toptable/tab5a_1.htm (accessed May 2004).
3. Francis Fukuyama, "The End of American Exceptionalism," *New Perspectives Quarterly,* Vol. 18, No. 4, Fall 2001, http://www.digitalnpq.org/archive/2001_fall/exceptionalism.html (accessed May 4, 2004).
4. Infobase Europe Database Record, "Eurobarometer Suvey Shows Fall in Support for EU," Record No. 7390, December 10, 2003, http://www.ibeurope.com/Records/7300/7390.htm (accessed May 4, 2004).
5. U.S. Department of Homeland Security Press Office. "Department of Homeland Security Announces FY 2005 Budget in Brief," U.S. Dep't of Homeland Security, February 2, 2004, http://www.dhs.gov/dhspublic/display?content=3133 (accessed May 4, 2004); U.S. Department of State Office of the Spokesman. "International Affairs-FY 2005 Budget," U.S. Dep't of State, February 2, 2003, http://www.state.gov/r/pa/prs/ps/2004/28709pf.htm (accessed May 4, 2004).

6. Chris Strohm, "Homeland Security Critical Infrastructure Effort Proceeds Unevenly," GovExec.com, February 9, 2004, http://www.govexec.com/dailyfed/0204/020904c1.htm (accessed May 4, 2004).

7. "Internet Worm Taking Its Toll on Global Firms," *Independent Online*, January 31, 2004, http://www.iol.co.za/index.php?click_id=115&art_id=qw1075536182256B253&set_id=1 (accessed May 4 2004).

8. Dan Verton, "Feds Say IT Security Lacking," *Computerworld*, December 8, 2003, http://www.computerworld.com/securitytopics/security/story/0,10801,87924,00.html (accessed May 4, 2004).

9. Bob Keefe, "Cybercops Demand More Secure Net," Atlanta Journal-Constitution, December 4, 2003, http://www.ajc.com/business/content/business/1203/04secure.html (accessed May 4, 2004); brackets in original quote.

10. "Junk E-mails Costing Billions of Dollars: UNCTAD Report," AFP, November 20, 2003, http://www.keepmedia.com/ShowItemDetails.do?item_id=354188&extID=10026 (accessed May 4, 2004).

11. OECD, "Opening Remarks at the OECD Workshop on Spam," February 2, 2004, http://www.oecd.org/dataoecd/4/43/28766599.pdf (accessed May 4, 2004).

12. Ed Foster, "Friends Should Never Ask Friends to Spam—Even if Big Blue Says to Do So," InfoWorld.com, September 18, 2000, http://archive.infoworld.com/articles/op/xml/00/09/18/000918opfoster.xml (accessed May 4, 2004).

13. Amy Worlton, "Governments Worldwide Move to Curb Spam," *Privacy in Focus* (newsletter), Wiley Rein & Fielding, December 2003, http://www.wrf.com/publications/publication.asp?id=12484512192003 (accessed May 4, 2004); exchange rate of USD1.233 per euro as of March 24, 2004.

14. Brian Krebs, "EU Stirs Up Internet Sales Tax Debate," BizReport reported by *Washington Post*, June 10, 2003, http://www.bizreport.com/article.php?art_id=4481 (accessed May 4, 2004).

15. Scarlet Pruitt, "Europe's Net Sales Tax Takes Effect," IDG News Service July 1, 2003, via PCWorld.com, http://www.pcworld.com/news/article/0,aid,111422,00.asp (accessed May 4, 2004).

16. Brian Krebs.

17. Emad Mekay, "U.S. WTO Dispute Could Bend Poor Nations to GMOs—Groups," *Inter Press Service*, May 14, 2004, http://www.ipsnews.net/print.asp?idnews=18192 (accessed May 14, 2004).

18. Paul Magnusson, "A Grand Deal for the Trade Dispute," *BusinessWeek Online*, May 16, 2003, http://www.businessweek.com/bwdaily/dnflash/may2003/nf20030516_3683_db046.htm (accessed May 4, 2004).

19. "GM Ruling Hits Exporters," March 1, 2004, FoodQualityNews.com, http://www.foodqualitynews.com/news/news-NG.asp?id=50255# (accessed May 10, 2004).

20. "Taco Bell Taco Shells Sold in Grocery Stores Contain Banned Corn—Report," *Reuters*, September 18, 2000, http://www.cnn.com/2000/FOOD/news/09/18/food.comrn.reut/ (accessed April 27, 2004).

21. John Vidal, "Firm Drops Plan to Grow GM Maize," *The Guardian*, April 1, 2004.

22. Inae Riveras, "Monsanto Brazil Seeks Royalties for Illegal Roundup Ready Soy," *Reuters*, May 5, 2003.

23. "The GMO Debate," *Global Policy Forum*, September 16, 2002, http://www.globalpolicy.org/ngos/role/globdem/globgov/2002/0916gmo. htm (accessed May 10, 2004).
24. Joan Olson, "Tracking Seed to Shelf," *Farm Industry News*, November 1, 2000.
25. "Harvard Plans Stem Cell Research Center," *Associated Press*, March 1, 2004, via CNN.com, http://www.cnn.com/2004/HEALTH/03/01/harvard.stemcell. ap/ (accessed April 22, 2004).
26. Francis Fukuyama, "Gene Regime," *Foreign Policy*, March/April 2002.
27. Sang-Hun Choe, "Stem Cell Research Exhilarates S. Koreans," *The Kansas City Star*, February 13, 2004, http://www.kansascity.com/mld/kansascity/ news/local/7948824.htm?1c (accessed May 6, 2004).
28. "Attracting and Keeping the Best and the Brightest," The Council for Excellence in Government, July 2002.
29. "The Federal Workforce for the 21st Century," U.S. Merit Systems Protection Board, September 2003, p. viii, http://www.mspb.gov/studies/ mps_2000/merit_principles.pdf (accessed May 6, 2004).
30. "Calling Young People to Government Service," A Peter A. Hart Research Study for the Council for Excellence in Government, http://www. excelgov.org/usermedia/images/uploads/PDFs/FINAL_Richardson_Poll_ Report.pdf (accessed May 10, 2004).
31. Kirsi Äijälä, "Public Sector—An Employer of Choice? Report on the Competitive Public Sector Project," *OECD*, 2002, pp. 6-7, http://www.oecd. org/dataoecd/37/29/1937556.pdf (accessed May 6, 2004).
32. *The Economist*, "We're (Still) in the Money," April 17, 2003.
33. "We're (Still) in the Money."
34. John A. Byrne, "The Economic Drag of CEO Funk," *BusinessWeek Online*, February 27, 2003. http://www.businessweek.com/bwdaily/dnflash/feb2003/ nf20030227_8494_db042.htm (accessed May 2004).
35. John A. Byrne.
36. Luigi Zingales, "Want to Stop Corporate Fraud? Pay Off Those Whistle Blowers," *Washington Post*, January 18, 2004.
37. Luigi Zingales.
38. Dale Buss, "Executives Need to Fix Image to Regain Trust," *Detroit News*, August 25, 2002.
39. Bruce Horovitz, "Scandals Grow Out of CEOs' Warped Mind-Set," *USA Today*, October 10, 2002.
40. Bill Marsden, "Cholera and the Age of the Water Barons," The Center for Public Integrity, February 3, 2003. http://www.icij.org/water/report.aspx? sID=ch&rID=44&aID=44 (accessed May 2004).
41. Bill Marsden.
42. Jim Geraghty, "FCC's Powell Warns 'Regulatory Ethos' Growing in Washington," *States News Service*, August 18, 2003.
43. Mike Taugher, "Davis Disappointed after Feds Fail to Curb Skyrocketing Power Prices," *Contra Costa Times*, December 16, 2000. http://www.con-sumerwatchdog.org/utilities/nw/nw000906.php3 (accessed May 2004).
44. Claudia Kolker and Tom Fowler, "The Fall of Enron," *The Houston Chronicle*, August 4, 2002.
45. CNN/USA Today/Gallup Poll, July 26-28, 2002. http://www.pollingreport. com/business.htm (accessed May 2004).

46. "Do You Trust Corporate America?" *BusinessWeek Online*, June 21, 2002. http://www.businessweek.com/bwdaily/dnflash/jun2002/nf20020621_8356. htm (accessed May 2004).
47. *EU Business On-Line*, "EU Tells Company Bosses to Shape Up After Parmalat Affair," February 11, 2004. http://www.eubusiness.com/afp/040211170334.ync1x698 (accessed May 2004).
48. "EU Tells Company Bosses to Shape Up After Parmalat Affair."
49. Peter J. Wallison, "Blame Sarbanes-Oxley," *On the Issues: AEI Online*, September 1, 2003. http://www.aei.org/publications/pubID.19123/pub_detail.asp (accessed May 2004).
50. U.S. Securities and Exchange Commission, "Final Rule: Management's Reports on Internal Control Over Financial Reporting and Certification of Disclosure in Exchange Act Periodic Reports," SEC, 17 CFR Parts 210, 228, 229, 240, 249, 270 and 274. http://www.sec.gov/rules/final/33-8238.htm (accessed May 2004).
51. David Henry and Amy Borrus, "Honesty Is a Pricey Policy," *BusinessWeek Online*, October 27, 2003. http://www.businessweek.com/magazine/content/03_43/b3855136_mz020.htm (accessed May 2004).
52. David Henry and Amy Borrus.
53. Dan Roberts, "GE Reveals $30 Million Compliance Cost," *Financial Times*, April 28, 2004.
54. David Henry and Amy Borrus.
55. U.S. Securities and Exchange Commission.
56. Robert O. Keohane and Joseph S. Nye Jr., "Globalization: What's New? What's Not? (And So What?)," *Foreign Policy*, Spring 2000.
57. Curtis Sittenfeld, "No-Brands-Land," *Fast Company*, Issue 38, September 2000. http://www.fastcompany.com/magazine/38/nklein.html (accessed May 2004).
58. David P. Baron, "Facing-Off in Public," *Stanford Business Magazine*, August 2003. http://www.gsb.stanford.edu/news/bmag/sbsm0308/feature_face_off. shtml (accessed May 2004).
59. As cited in "Facing-Off in Public."
60. Dale Buss, "Executives Need to Fix Image to Regain Trust," *Detroit News*, August 25, 2002. http://www.detnews.com/2002/editorial/0208/25/a17-570385.htm (accessed May 2004).
61. Gary Gereffi, Ronie Garcia-Johnson and Erika Sasser, "The NGO-Industrial Complex," *Foreign Policy*, July/August 2001.
62. Peter Ford, "NGOs: More Than Flower Power," *Christian Science Monitor*, July 11, 2003. http://www.csmonitor.com/2003/0711/p06s01-wogi.htm (accessed May 2004).
63. Jeff Shaw, "From Worst to First: Under Pressure, Boise Cascade Agrees to Stop Logging Old-growth Forests," *Multinational Monitor*, November 2003.
64. "British Cyber-Detectives Keep an Eye Out on Blue-Chip Clients," *The Wall Street Journal*, January 31, 2001.
65. http://www.ngowatch.org/info.htm (accessed May 2004).
66. www.eWatch.com.
67. CEO Forum: Australia's leading website for CEOs, "The Evolving Global Company: Threats and Challenges," http://www.ceoforum.com.au/200202_reflections.cfm (accessed May 2004).

68. Social Funds, "Resolution on Arctic Wildlife Refuge Planned for BP Amoco," January 16, 2001. http://www.socialfunds.com/news/article. cgi/article473.html (accessed May 2004).

69. Vanessa Houlder, "Companies Pressed to Adopt Higher Standards," *Financial Times*, October 16, 2003.

70. Alison Maitland, "Corporate Care in the Global Community," *Financial Times*, January 8, 2004.

71. William Baue, "The Sun is Rising on SRI in Japan," *ASRIA*, June 19, 2003. http://www.asria.org/news/press/1056511976 (accessed May 2004).

72. "One Mantra Growing in Popularity among Japanese Business Leaders is Corporate Social Responsibility," *South China Morning Post*, February 21, 2004.

73. George White, "Mattel Will Unveil Plan to Detect Abuses Labor: Community Groups Are to Monitor Production Sites, with Their Results to be Made Public by an Independent Panel," *Los Angeles Times*, May 6, 1998.

74. "Arco Withdraws from Burma," *Shareholder Victories!*, *Shareholder Investment Forum*. http://www.shareholderaction.org/victories_95-99.cfm (accessed May 2004).

75. Amalgamated Bank Press Room, "Unocal Corporation Responds to LongView Fund Proposal on Fundamental Labor Rights," March 14, 2003. http://www.amalgamatedbank.com/site/press_aflcio_icem.html (accessed May 2004).

76. Thomas d'Aquino, "You Can Run but You Cannot Hide," *Perspectives*, Spring 2003. http://www.ceocouncil.ca/publications/pdf/18c6b623706457f0519ad13a8a628 3b1/perspectives_2003_06_01.pdf (accessed May 2004).

77. Gary Gereffi.

78. "Fair Labor Association: About Us," http://www.fairlabor.org/all/about/ index.html (accessed May 2004).

79. *International Herald Tribune*, "A Growing Emphasis on Corporate Social Responsibility," January 6, 2004.

80. Business for Social Responsibility, "Rights of Indigenous People: Leadership Example," December 2003. http://www.bsr.org/CSRResources/ IssueBriefDetail.cfm?DocumentID=49771 (accessed May 2004).

81. John Donnelly, "Deal Paves Way for Generic HIV Drugs. Drug Companies to Allow Sales in Sub-Saharan Africa," *The Boston Globe*, December 11, 2003.

82. Jean Pierre Garnier, "Head of Glaxo—He Will Drop the Prices of His Drugs to the Poorest Countries," *The Guardian*, February 23, 2003.

83. *The Indian Express*, "Capitalism with a Human Face," November 25, 2003.

84. Jennifer Comiteau, "Do Do-Gooders Do Better?" *Adweek*, November 29, 2003.

85. Jennifer Comiteau.

86. Jennifer Comiteau.

87. "Capitalism with a Human Face."

88. John Quelch and V. Kasturi Rangan, "Profit Globally, Give Globally," *Harvard Business Review*, December 2003.

89. "Facing-Off in Public."

90. "The Banana Giant That Found Its Gentler Side," *Financial Times*, Sara Silver, December 2002.

91. "The Banana Giant That Found Its Gentler Side."

92. "The Banana Giant That Found Its Gentler Side."

93. Shawn Zeller, "Profiting from Homeland Security," *The Chief Executive*, December 2002.
94. Shawn Zeller.
95. Murray Weidenbaum, "The Role of Business in Fighting Terrorism," *Business Horizons*, May/June 2003.
96. Murray Weidenbaum.
97. David Rothkopf, "Business Versus Terror," *Foreign Policy*, May/June 2002.

Chapter 6

1. Adapted from definition by John L. Peterson, "Wild Cards: The Nature of Big Future Surprises," *The Arglington Institute Future edition newsletter*, http://www.arlingtoninstitute.org/focus_topics/wild_cards.html (accessed May 17, 2004).
2. Impact of Cholera, World Health Organization Website, http://www.who.int/csr/disease/cholera/impactofcholera/en/.
3. *The Global Infectious Disease Threat and Its Implications for the United States*, U.S. National Intelligence Council, 1999, http://www.cia.gov/cia/reports/nie/report/nie99-17d.html.
4. *The Global Infectious Disease Threat and Its Implications for the United States*.
5. Patterns of Global Terrorist 2003, State Department, http://www.state.gov/s/ct/rls/pgtrpt/2003/31711.html.
6. Patterns of Global Terrorist 2003.
7. "Sasser Worm Rips Through Internet: Banks, EU Hit," *Reuters*, by Bernhard Warner, 5/4/04, http://www.reuters.com/newsArticle.jhtml?type=internetNews&storyID=5027435&section=news.
8. "Sasser Worm Strikes Hundreds of Thousands of PCs," *Reuters*, by Brett Young, 5/3/04, http://www.washingtonpost.com/wp-dyn/articles/A62063-2004May3.html.
9. "Top Ten Tips for Business," *Sunday Business Post*, by Elaine O'Regan, 3/17/02 http://archives.tcm.ie/businesspost/2002/03/17/story316383.asp.
10. "Rage Against the Machine," BBC 4 Radio, by Dominic Arkwright, 5/8/04 http://www.bbc.co.uk/radio4/today/reports/archive/science_nature/computers.html.
11. David Whitehouse, "Quantum Computer Draws Closer," BBC, 5/21/03, http://news.bbc.co.uk/2/hi/science/nature/3043731.stm.
12. "NSF Funds New Institute for Quantum Information at Caltech," Caltech Press Release, 9/13/00, http://pr.caltech.edu/media/Press_Releases/PR12075.html.
13. Ray Kurzweil, *The Age of Spiritual Machines: When Computers Exceed Human Intelligence* (Penguin Books, 2000), 103-105.
14. "Genetically Modified 'Protato' to Feed India's Poor," *New Scientist*, by Andy Coghlan, 1/2/03, http://www.newscientist.com/news/news.jsp?id=ns99993219.
15. "'Living Condom' Could Block HIV," *New Scientist*, by Philip Cohen, 9/9/03, http://www.newscientist.com/news/news.jsp?id=ns99994141.
16. "Nanoparticles to Pinpoint Viruses in Body Scans," *New Scientist*, by Andy Coghlan, 8/22/03, http://www.newscientist.com/news/news.jsp?id=ns99994076.
17. "Super-Tough Nanotube Threads Created," *New Scientist*, by David Cohen, 6/12/03, http://www.newscientist.com/news/news.jsp?id=ns99993823.
18. Robert L. Olson.

Index

About the Author

PAUL A. LAUDICINA is vice president and managing director of A.T. Kearney's Global Business Policy Council, a strategic service helping chief executives and government leaders monitor and capitalize on macroeconomic, geopolitical, socio-demographic, and technological change worldwide. Before joining A.T. Kearney and founding the Council nearly 15 years ago, Paul spent 20 years working on global strategic issues in various positions with industry, government, and research institutions worldwide.